ETHNOPORNOGRAPHY

ETHNO—
PORNOGRAPHY

Sexuality, Colonialism, and Archival Knowledge

EDITED BY PETE SIGAL, ZEB TORTORICI,
AND NEIL L. WHITEHEAD

DUKE UNIVERSITY PRESS *Durham and London* 2020

Designed by Matthew Tauch
Typeset in Minion Pro by Westchester Publishing Services

Cataloging-in-Publication Data is available from the Library
of Congress.
ISBN 978-1-4780-0315-1 (hardcover)
ISBN 978-1-4780-0384-7 (pbk.)
ISBN 978-1-4780-0442-4 (ebook)

Cover art: Details from Plate 24 in Walter Roth's *Ethnological
Studies among the North-West-Central Queensland Aborigines*
(Brisbane, Aus.: Edmund Gregory, Government Printer, 1897).

WE DEDICATE THIS BOOK TO NEIL L. WHITEHEAD,

a radical thinker and wonderful friend with whom

we began this project so many years ago.

Contents

Acknowledgments

Pete and Zeb would like to thank the original participants of the "Ethno-pornography" conference held at Duke University in 2006, and sponsored by the office of the Dean of Trinity College, the Franklin Humanities Institute, the Departments of Cultural Anthropology and History, and the Sexuality Studies Program at Duke University. Many of those participants—including Francisco-J. Hernández Adrián, Rebecca Parker Brienen, Martha Chaiklin, Martha Few, Maria Lepowsky, Harriet Lyons, Andrew P. Lyons, Negar Mottahedeh, Irene Silverblatt, Rachel O'Toole, Helen Pringle, Carina Ray, Olga Romantsova, Marc Schachter, Mary Weismantel, Robyn Wiegman, and Ara Wilson—were instrumental in helping us think through the issues at stake in this volume. The same goes for those—including Kata Beilin, Christopher Butler, Glenn Close, Pernille Ipsen, Tomislav Longinović, Carol Siegel, and Helene Sinnreich—who participated in the "Sexuality, Violence, & Cultural Imagination" conference, organized by Neil at the University of Wisconsin–Madison in 2007. Gisela Fosado and Sara Leone at Duke University Press have, as always, been fabulous editors with whom to work. We are especially grateful to Erika Robb Larkins, whose friendship and support throughout the years has been crucial in enabling us to complete this project. We also greatly thank Theresa Whitehead, who was crucial in letting us pursue this project after Neil's untimely death in 2012. Finally, our own ethnopornographic endeavors have been thoughtfully provoked, in theory and practice, by Brooke Buchanan and Su Anne Takeda, who have our deepest gratitude.

INTRODUCTION | PETE SIGAL, ZEB TORTORICI,
AND NEIL L. WHITEHEAD

Ethnopornography as Methodology and Critique

Merging the Ethno-, the Porno-, and the -Graphos

We began this intellectual journey over a decade ago with a deceptively simple question proposed by Neil: are ethnography and pornography really different forms of knowledge production? When he brought this question to the table, Pete thought the answer obvious: yes, they are different. While some similarities exist in method (both seek to understand embodied "truths" and delve into desire), differences abound in goals: one seeks to inform while the other seeks to titillate, one seeks knowledge, while the other seeks a good performance. But could prurient interests be at the core of ethnography—responsible ethnography—the type used by professional anthropologists?

Neil quickly convinced Pete and, later, Zeb (and most of the other participants in the "Ethnopornography" conference at Duke University in 2006 and at the "Sexuality, Violence, & Cultural Imagination" conference at the University of Wisconsin–Madison in 2007) of the productivity of relating pornography to ethnography as a particularly pointed critique of the formation of objective knowledge in the "modern West."[1] Further, perhaps the differences that Pete had presumed to exist were not so pertinent at all. In his comments, Neil argued for the importance of understanding ethnography as a *form* of pornography invested with institutional power:

> The positionality and cultural gaze of Western academics may not be unique but it is historically privileged and heavily inflected with a form of epistemological rectitude, an intellectual BDSM, through which the pleasures of classification and analysis become akin to the corporeal binding of the ethnological subject. As a result, this philosophical trajectory displaces "desire" into the space of the "unclassified" or ethnologically pristine. The sensual intellectual thrill of penetrating the unknown to encounter the virgin and pristine native still often drives the self-imagining of the ethnographer, a pleasure which in turn has been culturally generalized through the ethnopornography of such representational media as *National Geographic Magazine* or the *Discovery Channel.*[2]

Particularly with the types of popular ethnography Neil describes, individuals go into the field to uncover the truth of the "untouched" and thus uncategorized people. They are exotic beings, destined for penetration through categorization awaiting them upon the dissemination of the ethnographer's work. The reader of the ethnography experiences great pleasure in uncovering Napoleon Chagnon's Yanomamö, William and Jean Crocker's Canela, and Gilbert Herdt's Sambia, envisioning them as great examples of primitivity and perversion.[3] In this very act of categorization, we, the readers, formulate desires similar to those we experience when we watch or read pornography. We become excited as we readily discover new, exotic beings in the pages or on the screen. In ethnography, we find individuals who unselfconsciously go about their daily routines without much provocation from the outside observer, and we get to peer into the seemingly most intimate moments of their lives. In pornography, we find individuals who, in theory, unselfconsciously engage in sexual activity with others without much provocation from the outside observer, and we get to peer into (visual constructions of) the most intimate moments of their sex lives. In both cases, we witness arcane setups, magical spells, and deep desires.[4] In both cases, the setup either hides the position of the observer or alternatively places great emphasis on the ritual of self-reflection.

The domination that Neil describes, what he elsewhere discusses as a "will to know," presents us with the disturbing theory that all ethnography relates to a deep-seated desire to penetrate the other.[5] This is what we call ethnopornography. We have formulated this volume around the term because we believe that ethnopornography is an important method of hiding the eroticized power of the ethnographer, anthropologist, historian, colonizer, and cleric: that is, the power of any observer of the "other." Similarly, an analysis of ethnopornography can bring these power dynamics to the surface and provide a method for proceeding with ethnographic studies that does not destroy ethnopornography but instead frames the concept as both *method* and *object* of analysis.

Ethnopornography: A Genealogy

> With regard to the chapter on Ethno-pornography, I am well aware that it is far from suitable for the general lay reader; the subject matter, however, being essential to a scientific account of these aboriginals, I have decided upon its publication, at the same time placing it at the very last, in the hope that those who do not wish to peruse its pages need not unwittingly find themselves doing so.
> —WALTER E. ROTH, *Ethnological Studies among the North-West-Central Queensland Aborigines*, v

With the twentieth century about to dawn, the term "ethnopornography" came into existence as a neologism coined by Walter Roth, an English anthropologist and physician appointed the first Northern Protector of Aborigines in Queensland, Australia, in 1898. The term has distinctly colonial and anthropological origins, linked to Roth's efforts to record and document the cultural and religious practices of Queensland's aboriginal peoples for audiences back home and in the British overseas colonies. His "Ethno-Pornography" chapter treats a variety of subjects and initiation rites and "first ceremonials" among aboriginal men and women, penile introcision and vaginal laceration, puberty, marriage, betrothal, love-charms, consanguinity, venery (i.e., sexual pleasure or indulgence), pregnancy, labor, abortion, infancy, menstruation, "micturition and defæcation," and foul words.[6] Practically assuring that most readers will turn straightaway to this chapter, Roth begins with the caveat: "AUTHOR'S NOTE—*The following chapter is not suitable for perusal by the general lay reader*" (figure I.1). The slippages and contradictions inherent in this first iteration of ethnopornography are instructive: the production of explicit knowledge about the bodies, desires, and sexual rites of the aborigines, even when geared in theory toward scientific and intellectual pursuits, harbored the potential to be misread, misused, and misappropriated by the "general lay reader."

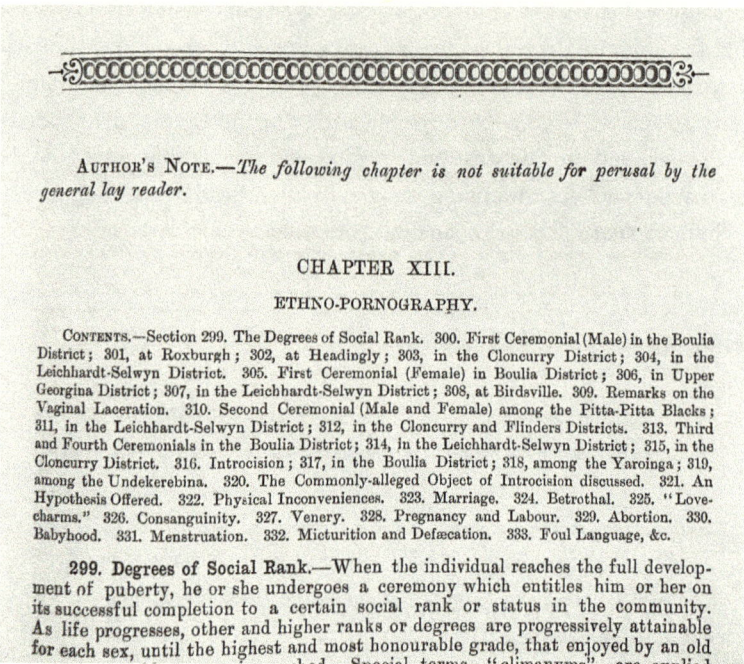

FIGURE I.1 Title page to chapter 13 of Walter Roth's *Ethnological Studies among the North-West-Central Queensland Aborigines* (Brisbane, Aus.: Edmund Gregory, Government Printer, 1897), 169. Zeb Tortorici's personal copy.

Looking at Roth's chapter today, few readers would find it pornographic. At the time of its publication, though, Roth, concerned about his professional reputation, did not want his book associated with Victorian era pornography. Despite his hesitation Roth published the chapter because he believed it "essential to a scientific account of these aboriginals."[7] Roth provided this material for those whose ends were scientific (and anthropological), not for vulgar readers without training or credentials. The ethnopornographic appeal here lies in the very promise or potential of ethnography's distortion or misuse—a slippage from "science" to "pornography." This slippage, or the failure of the gaze to signify a scientific pursuit, is endemic to ethnopornography.

Being simultaneously inspired by and critical of Roth, we define "ethnopornography" as the production of eroticized material regarding people deemed different from the people expected to digest (read/watch/listen to) any particular piece of research. The contributors to this anthology frame the concept, and methodology, of ethnopornography through the following: historical and ethnographic accounts of human exhibitions and ethnographic displays of "exotic" peoples; freak shows; scientific displays and medical reports; museum exhibits; personal letters and other intimate archival records; religious accounts of colonial encounter and spiritual conversion; travel narratives and Orientalist discourse; colonial art; (interracial) pornography; photographic and film archives; and rumors that circulate often uncontrollably around specific ethnographic events. The idea of ethnopornography indicates a cluster of concerns about the meanings of pornographic representation, the plurality of sexualities, the legacies of colonial representation, and so forth rather than a neatly formulated definition of an already analytically distinct phenomenon. According to Andrew P. Lyons, in a recent essay on the historiography and circulated imagery of Sara Baartman, ethnopornography "implies the description and construction in the folk and scientific discourses of dominant cultures— by travel writers, colonial officials, anthropologists, human biologists, and ethnohistorians—of dehumanising representations and images concerning the sexuality/sexual practices and discourses of 'others.'"[8] Ethnopornography, though not always necessarily coupled with dehumanization, shifts radically and along several axes with the particular speaker and depicted actors, the historical context, and the medium of transmission. All of our contributors criticize ethnopornography to an extent, but some also envision it as a methodology to be productively retheorized and critically embraced.

The etymological root of both "ethnography" and "ethnology" lies in *ethnos*, the Greek word used to refer to a group, people, or nation. By the 1840s "ethnology" had emerged as a historical and scientific discipline in Europe that used cultural, physical, social, and linguistic traits to examine and better understand the relationship between different human groups.[9] Toward the end of the nineteenth century, the discipline of anthropology and its very methodology, "ethnography," studied humans in a broader sense, discovering populations described as "'natural' groupings of people with similar features (physical, mental, cultural, etc.) rooted in a common past; a collection of such groups could be considered to be of the same race."[10] Thus "ethnography" came to refer to the very science of describing and classifying the particular "races" of mankind, while "ethnology" came to mean the comparative science of the characteristics, customs, and history of those races.

"Pornography," too, has its etymological roots in Greek—the term *pornographos* originally referred to written material about prostitutes. Yet, as Lynn Hunt has found, "pornography did not constitute a wholly separate and distinct category of written or visual representation before the early nineteenth century," after which the term came to refer to sexually explicit depictions.[11] Hence, the term "ethnopornography" is a neologism that merges the *-ethno*, the *-porno*, and the *-graphos*, describing the depiction of sexually explicit classifications of groups of people based on some conception of difference, typically broached through some type of colonial encounter or exchange, and often conceived through categories of "race" and racial difference. Of course, we need to historically situate such a definition, which means that we must work to understand the cultural and intellectual traditions—the ethnopornographic rationale—of the individuals engaged in the study of another group.

In their article, "Skin Flicks: Pornography, Ethnography, and the Discourses of Power" (1989), Christian Hansen, Catherine Needham, and Bill Nichols call upon scholars to radically critique both pornography and ethnography.[12] They analyze both, calling into question the distinctions between the two—and in particular arguing that we need to develop alternatives to each. They criticize "the pornographic imagination (control, dominance, objectification, voyeurism . . .) and, more radically, the ethnographic imagination (empathy, participant-observation, a liberal ethic of tolerance, good will, and understanding)."[13] In developing a critique of the creation of liberal subjectivity, Hansen, Needham, and Nichols argue for an alternative form of knowledge production through erotics and dialogue. While we do not advocate the same type of alternative epistemology, we build on the arguments that these scholars developed in 1989 and ask why their article received such scant attention among cultural studies theorists, anthropologists, and ethnohistorians.[14]

If "ethnography is a kind of legitimate pornography, and pornography a kind of strange, 'unnatural' form of ethnography," then the researcher, writer, producer, reader, and viewer become complicit in constituting a form of ethnopornography (or something that has ethnopornographic potential) in each case.[15] Both ethnography and pornography are constituted by a particular individual or group's desire to authenticate and render legible and knowable the "true" bodies and desires of the Other. In each case, we, as consumers, privilege our own minds and desires over those of the others, whom we witness only at a distance. Giving the examples of Nuer chants and Debbie doing Dallas, Hansen, Needham, and Nichols note that "we experience concepts and images of knowledge and possession instead of direct face-to-face encounters that might place us at risk rather than securely hold us within an Imaginary opposition of Them/Us."[16]

In the typical ethnopornographic encounter, the reader/viewer can imagine direct contact with the Other but in fact maintains a safe distance. Roth largely erases his role by pretending that the reader has direct access to the erotics of the Other, as defined by colonial encounters and unequal relations of power and the technologies of documentation and observation. In this sense, we can say that Roth hides the potential voyeurism behind the veil of the "researcher" and seeker of "authenticity" and "truth"—connections explored at length in Pringle's contribution to this collection.

This is what we have termed the problem of (the lack of) researcher positioning. The researcher has left his position entirely out of the textual description. We imagine Roth's gaze—with the help of his own illustrations— as he peers upon a native man's lacerated penis, by itself, and when it enters the vagina. In one excerpt Roth tells his readers that "the female lies on her back on the ground, while the male with open thighs sits on his heels close in front: he now pulls her towards him, and raising her buttocks drags them into the inner aspects of his own thighs, her legs clutching him round the flanks (Fig. 433), while he arranges with his hands the toilette of her perineum and the insertion of his penis" (figure I.2).[17] The researcher's gaze continues long enough to witness the semen discharged into "its proper quarter" (or not). We cannot know enough about the researcher's position; instead Roth wants us—the scientific and the lay readers—to imagine and fantasize about aboriginal sex as if it takes place in front of *us*, without the presence of the researcher. And of course, in Roth's discourse, our—now the anthropologist's—sexual fantasies are qualitatively different from the pornographic fantasies of the lay readership because our fantasies are in the name of science. Pringle offers us the incisive observation that a scientific ethnopornography "is not merely a procedure for the collection of certain materials about the 'natives'; it is also a practice of representation through which to make a spectacle of them."

Art historian Kelly Dennis questions the extent to which "'pure ethnography' exists independent of erotic motivation and colonial determination," pointing to the dialectics of imperial rule and pornographic representation.[18] We thus use the concept of ethnopornography as a theoretical, disciplinary, and methodological provocation to consider the role and power of observation in the construction of an observed sexual subject and the subsequent commodification of the resultant study. We also focus a critical

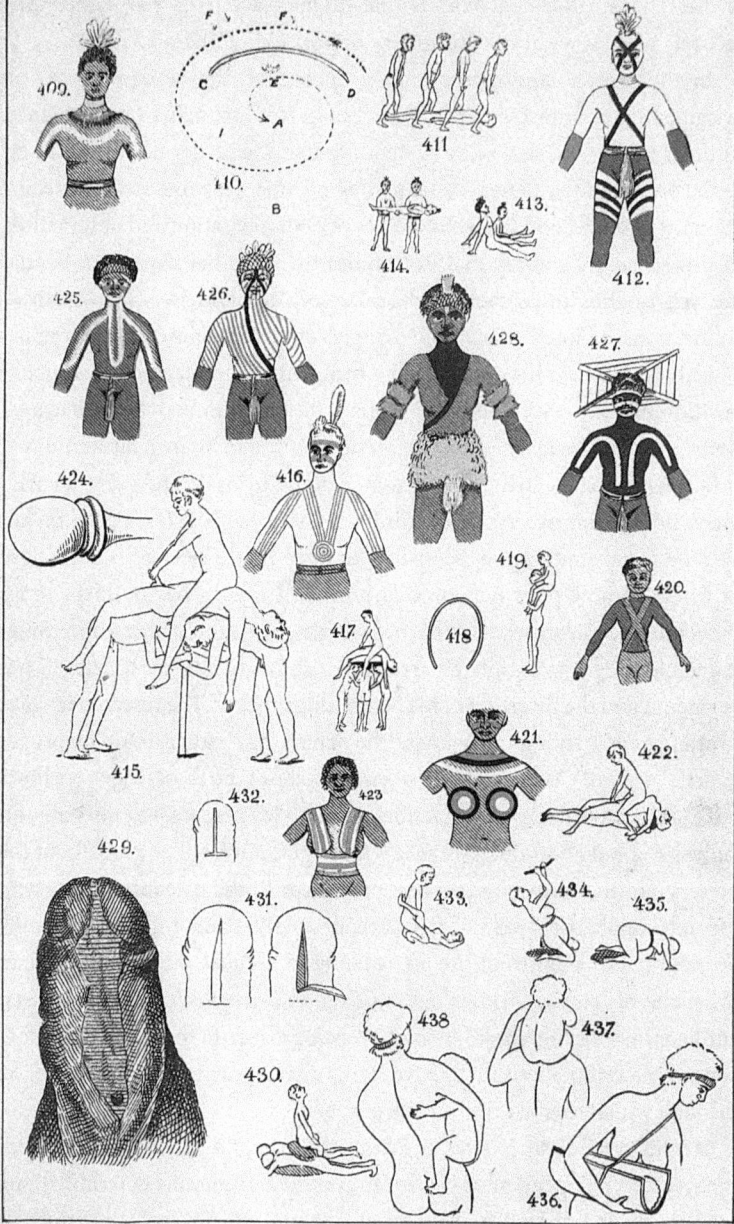

FIGURE I.2 Plate 24 in Walter Roth's *Ethnological Studies among the North-West-Central Queensland Aborigines* (Brisbane, Aus.: Edmund Gregory, Government Printer, 1897). Zeb Tortorici's personal copy.

gaze on the practices of anthropology, ethnography, ethnohistory, and cultural studies. Most importantly, we use the concept of ethnopornography to analyze the production, circulation, and corresponding consumption of "facts," studies, observations, images, and documentary texts that seek to represent the body, desires, and rituals of another individual (or a particular group, in the vein of ethnology and ethnography) in a way that has the *potential* to be read as "erotic" and "pornographic." We seek to study the circulation of erotic concepts of those deemed "other" to the broader public that Roth terms the "lay reader." The ways in which ethnography forms this lay reader's notion of having penetrated the *true* world of bodies and selves deemed "other" most concerns us here. For, if, as pornography studies scholars have shown, pornographic consumption relates to the fantasy of penetrating not just the bodies but also the "true" desires of the pornographic subjects, then we maintain that ethnographic and ethnohistorical consumption relate to the fantasy of penetrating both the bodies and desires of the human subjects studied by anthropologists, ethnographers, historians, and other observers.[19]

Visualizing Race

> When we see, for example, a pinkish penis and balls slapping up against a dark pubis, or creamy white ejaculate on black female skin, it is no longer just sexual difference that we see, but a racial one.
> —LINDA WILLIAMS, "Skin Flicks on the Racial Border," *Porn Studies*, 274

We begin our discussion of the first section of *Ethnopornography*, "Visualizing Race," with a quote from film scholar Linda Williams, analyzing interracial heterosexual pornography. Her groundbreaking declaration that pornography related to the "frenzy of the visible" allowed pornography studies to flourish as a field.[20] Here she relates the visual to race, asking what it means when hard-core pornographic film broaches a topic (interracial desire) rarely discussed in mainstream US cinema. In pornography studies, the recent spate of work on race and pornography has emphasized the ways in which the visual interacts with skin color and ultimately with race.[21]

In Williams's classic article on the topic, "Skin Flicks on the Racial Border: Pornography, Exploitation, and Interracial Lust," she critiques the theoretical exploration of Abdul JanMohamed, who argues that racialized sexuality has been characterized by a peculiar silence, resistant to the deployment of sexuality proffered by Foucault.[22] Williams shows, in contrast to JanMohamed's argument, that, in golden age pornographic film, racialized sexuality became a key concept to excite viewers. The films discussed, particularly *Mandingo* and *Behind the Green Door*, mobilized interracial lust and racial stereotypes in order to carry forward a narrative that turned fear (of the black phallus) into desire. Building on the works of Jane Gaines and Celine Parreñas Shimizu, Williams shows that this mobilization of racial stereotypes goes beyond the charge of racism but never erases racial violence.[23]

Two recent books on race and heterosexual pornography, Mirielle Miller-Young's *A Taste for Brown Sugar* and Jennifer Nash's *The Black Body in Ecstasy*, build upon Williams's arguments while criticizing her for ignoring the material positions of the pornographic actresses and insufficiently reading for the multitude of ways in which race interacts with the visual in the pornographic archive. Miller-Young notes that black women who are engaged in pornography as actresses and directors have struggled to develop significant power over their work environments. In some cases, they have mitigated the levels of violence and degradation, while in other cases, they had less power over their professional lives. In fact, she notes that the emergence of black women as directors of pornographic film has led to more chances for these women to engage in pleasurable sexual acts and have more control over their labor. These participants in the hardcore pornography industry have consistently faced the double bind of racial fetishism that encompasses "a voyeurism that looks but also does not look, that obsessively enjoys, lingers over, and takes pleasure in the black female body even while it declares that body as strange, Other, and abject."[24] Analyzing the same theme, Jennifer Nash shows that the black feminist archive has emphasized only the second part of this equation, the abject black female body, at the expense of understanding moments of pleasure and ecstasy in the archive. She notes, "It is in this surprising location—the pornographic archive—that I find black pleasures articulated, amplified, and practiced."[25] This focus on the interaction between the visualization of interracial pleasure and the occlusion of violence in studies of racialized pornography has important implications for any analysis of ethnopornography.

Juana María Rodríguez's article on the classic pornography star Vanessa del Rio shows us that Latinidad, like blackness, became used in golden age pornography in a particularly racialized manner. Rodríguez notes that producers used del Rio for her willingness to engage in sexual acts that other (white) actresses would not perform. Yet del Rio herself notes that she

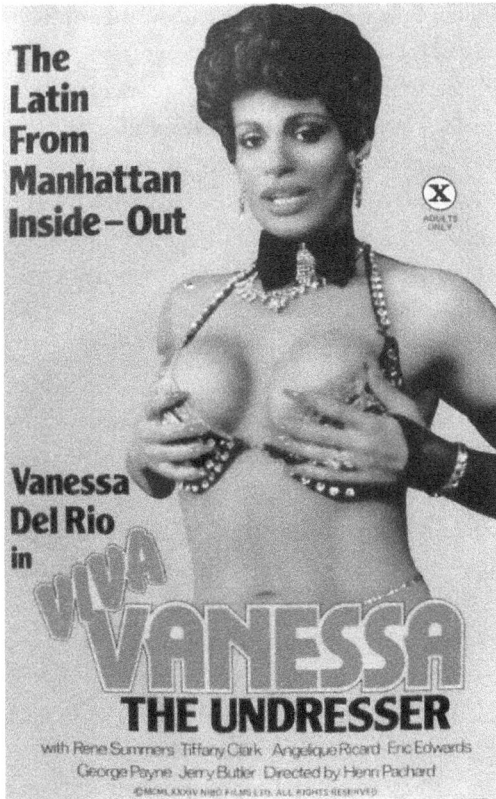

The
Latin
From
Manhattan
Inside–Out

Ⓧ ADULTS ONLY

Vanessa
Del Rio
in

VIVA
VANESSA
THE UNDRESSER

with Rene Summers Tiffany Clark Angelique Ricard Eric Edwards
George Payne Jerry Butler Directed by Henri Pachard
© MCMLXXXIV NIBO FILMS LTD. ALL RIGHTS RESERVED

FIGURE I.3 Vanessa Del Rio, "The Latin from Manhattan," 1980s.

would get bored with the standard pornographic scene and wanted more. Instead, she critiques the producers for failing to put her picture on the posters for the films. By the 1980s, even this had changed, and the poster for the film *Vanessa the Undresser* (1984) calls del Rio the "Latin from Manhattan" (figure I.3). After retiring from films, del Rio started her own porn empire, telling her story while selling her movies and memorabilia. In 2010, she cowrote her autobiography, *Fifty Years of Slightly Slutty Behavior*. Del Rio uses the hypersexuality associated with Latinidad to own her narrative and develop her career.[26] For Rodríguez, the story of del Rio becomes an example of resistance to the politics of respectability: "In a world where so many of us are defined as always already irrational and outside of structures of sexual and social legibility, those deeply painful and powerful moments of carnal pleasure, liberated from the constraints of language, image, and reason, might burst open to create possibilities for something akin to freedom."[27]

Other recent works have discussed this notion of the relationship between interracial pleasure and pornography as reconceptualizations of trauma and the history of abjection in order to create a productive politics of perversion. In particular, Darieck Scott's *Extravagant Abjection* and Nguyen Tan Hoang's *A View from the Bottom* have argued that the abject position of African American and Asian American men, respectively, in pornography and other mediums allows for a reenvisioning of the politics of masculinity.[28] Both argue not for a reparative and heteronormative reinscription of masculinity for African American and Asian American men but rather for the possibly perverse politics of embracing abject masculinities. In a related but perhaps even more controversial vein, Ariane Cruz, in *The Color of Kink*, argues that race play within BDSM and pornography can bring to the surface the position of chattel slavery in our attempts at deriving sexual pleasure from race.[29]

Building on these works and others that discuss the relationship between race and pornography, the chapters in this section ask how race becomes visualized within the ethnopornographic archive. This section on visualizing race focuses primarily on blackness, while the chapters in the following section ("Ethnopornography as Colonial History") speak to similar concerns in locales and time periods as diverse as early colonial Mexico, the Ottoman Empire, colonized West Africa, and British colonial Australia. In this sense, the anthology as a whole analyzes and engages several historical formations of "race" and "ethnicity," though for reasons of clarity and coherence, we gather most of our chapters on blackness in this first section.[30]

Mireille Miller-Young works to tell racial stories through visualization and occlusion. As the camera shows slave men and women, Miller-Young seeks to analyze the ethnopornographic violence incorporated in the scene that we see, the knowledge that we seek, and the silences in the image. The photographic archive of seven nineteenth-century slave men and women from South Carolina provides the impetus for Miller-Young to envision a spectacle of racial othering and violence based on the imagining of slave bodies for the ostensible purpose of promoting science. The early photographs that she examines, Miller-Young points out, represented an empiricist notion that the photograph could present the reality of the African American body. The never-pictured slave owner (present in the studio when the photograph is taken), the photographer, and the scientist consume the body of the other. The black women (and perhaps the men as well), photographed partially naked—the black men are fully nude—

appear to Miller-Young to hide their emotional states, while the power relationship involved in the creation of this gaze is designed to suggest that the individuals watching are interested only in "science." The ethnopornographic here emanates from the gaze mixed with technology, masquerading as scientific progress at the service of humanity.

Imagining these individuals within the photographer's studio and relating the theories and histories of racial formation to ethnohistory, one needs to ask whether the ethnographic impulse lies at the heart of interracial desire.[31] Interracial relationships form within imaginations and symbolic universes embedded with history. Literary scholar Werner Sollors, exploring interracial literature, shows that such relationships become embedded with anxieties produced in the social realm. Interracial desires interact with such anxieties. At times, these desires disrupt the social, developing particularly violent responses, including rape and murder. More often, they evince the pleasure of engaging in exploration of the individual deemed "Other."[32] Novelist Samuel Delany, in *Mad Man*, iterates the violence of interracialism but also notes that this violence leads to extreme forms of pleasure. In the novel, a white man who grew up as a southern "hillbilly" regularly urinates on (and in) the protagonist of the novel, a black philosophy graduate student. The "hillbilly" also loans out the graduate student to other homeless men for their own oral gratification—leading to a plethora of semen, urine, and feces in the protagonist's home. Through the intermediating figure of a dead Korean American male philosopher, the black protagonist and a series of homeless men from a variety of different racial and ethnic backgrounds develop deeply intimate excremental relationships, showing the possibility of a utopian queer sociality that does not ignore race but rather uses it to enhance the pleasurable experience within the utopia. The effects of racialization lead to extreme violence and deeply intimate, kind, and loving relationships. For Delany, the ethnopornographic (and excremental) imagination forms a key building block for interracial relationships.[33]

While we are unwilling to venture an answer to the question of whether *all* interracial desire stems from the ethnopornographic impulse, we note that all individuals bring historical structures and imaginations into all of their relationships with others. This means that, in effect, when we have sexual relationships, we engage in a necrophilic threesome, with history—and in the case of interracial sexual relationships, historical ethnography—forming the third partner. This structural relationship, in both Delany's view and ours, enacts violence at the same time as it promotes pleasure.

In the second chapter of *Ethnopornography*, Bryan Pitts shows that the interaction between pleasure and violence in gay pornography in Brazil allows us to analyze the ways in which publishers work to manipulate racialized desire. This study of gay pornography, and particularly of *G Magazine*, provides a reading of sexualized and racialized imagery. Pitts looks at both the conscious and subconscious decisions made by the editors to focus on particular desires of *G*'s readers. *G* focuses on racialized readings of the male body such that men identified as coming from an Afro-Brazilian background would fall into two recognizable categories: either highly masculine urban "pimps" or sports stars. At the same time, the editorials and other writings in *G* always express support for racial equality. The editors of *G* respond to the racial and sexual issues that dominated the Brazilian public sector during a particular historical moment, and they represent this moment by expressing antiracist views. Addressing the contradiction endemic in the racial discourse promoted by the editors, Pitts provides a historically nuanced reading of race, sexuality, and desire in late twentieth-century Brazil.

In emphasizing the contradictions between the racial visualization of desire and the antiracist politics of discourse, Pitts shows us that we must acknowledge ourselves as desiring subjects. Building on this theme, we call for a newly revitalized ethnographic and ethnohistorical practice that challenges the ethnopornographic relationship by committing to methods that use ethnopornography in a way that does not engage in colonial/imperial exploitation, and instead incorporates our many public audiences through different types of engagement with sexuality and violence. We must work to disrupt ethnopornography by developing an alternative practice of visualization, one that, following Rey Chow, takes seriously the task of reading the materiality of the image.[34] Chow's take, particularly when combined with the arguments put forward by José Muñoz, fundamentally disrupts traditional ethnography and archival engagement.[35] In our call for the study of ethnopornography, we listen to Muñoz as he tells us that both ethnographic and pornographic discourses are "teleologically cognate insofar as they both strive for the achievement of epistemological utopias where the 'Other' and knowledge of the 'Other' can be mastered and contained. Ethnotopia can be characterized as a world of limitless observation where 'we know them,' whereas pornotopia is a world where 'we have them,' 'a world of lust unlimited.'"[36]

Of course, past generations of anthropologists, ethnographers, and ethnohistorians have recognized significant problems with knowledge formation, understanding that we can always only have partial knowledge of our subjects of study. Some pornographers similarly have moved beyond the traditional portrayal of a world of lust unlimited where only the viewer's fantasy counts for anything. This shift is evidenced in North America, among other things, by the Feminist Porn Archive and Research Project headed by Billy Noble and Lisa Sloniowski at York University, the publication in 2013 of *The Feminist Porn Book*, and the Feminist Porn Conferences of 2013 and 2014—organized by Tristan Taormino and held at the University of Toronto with the support of the Mark S. Bonham Centre for Sexual Diversity Studies.[37] Still, Muñoz's critique remains prescient as he calls upon us to challenge "the formal protocols of such genres through the repetition and radical reinterpretation of such stock characters as the 'native informant' and the racialized body in porn."[38]

Muñoz proposes that we disarticulate the search for truth about the native and about pleasure from the ethnographic and the pornographic enterprises, respectively. He also argues that we must engage in a "radical reinterpretation" of the identities developed within, and the connections between, these projects. This combination of disarticulation and reinterpretation coincides with our project here: we wish to disarticulate ethnography from the fantasy of knowing the other, and to reinterpret ethnographic eroticism to both *recognize* traditional ethnopornography and *create* an alternative ethnopornography that approximates the interstices between the ethnographer's (or historian's) desires and the ethnographic (or historical) subject's discourses and performances.

But what happens if, instead of building an alternative ethnopornography, we promote a multicultural agenda through the *silencing* of racial animosity and even of race itself? What happens when pornography's (racialized) frenzy of the visible becomes not just invisible, but also absent? In chapter 3, Beatrix McBride points out that the controversial gay pornography film, *Gaytanamo*, enacts this peculiar silence. Taking the Guantanamo Bay prison complex as its site of enunciation, the reason for the prison's existence—as a place that the US government claims is to hide and imprison the worst Islamic terrorists—is completely absent from the film.

Torture, a common form of investigation at Guantanamo, becomes instigation and titillation at "Gaytanamo." And the use of forced homosexual degradation to torture Islamic men is placed in the film only by a suggestion that arouses the (presumably white) prisoner. Arguing that the lack of presence of Arab and Muslim men signifies an ethnopornographic haunting, McBride focuses attention on the repressed visibility of violence committed toward the other; perhaps these individuals maintain a presence in the repressed fantasy (we, the viewers, know Guantanamo Bay holds

Arab and Muslim men), but they fail to materialize on the screen. And, even if they were to, would that be any less problematic? McBride notes that the fantasy of the film would not have allowed for the presence of Arab and Muslim men. If they had been present, the real world of Guantanamo, torture, and the war on terror would have disrupted the escapist fantasy. Indeed, the fantasy of Gaytanamo is specifically a multicultural fantasy in which black, white, and Latino men have sex with each other: their presence signifies the multicultural West (in which Muslims are violently erased). McBride's chapter reminds us that the visibility of race in pornography may signify both a phantasm (promoting the myth of the melting pot) and an occlusion (the ghostly presence of Muslim men). This attention to absence and haunting forms a key component of any analysis of ethnopornographic content. The absence of Muslim men in a gay pornographic film based on a key symbol of the war on terror reminds us of the political valence of ethnopornography.

In chapter 4, Sidra Lawrence presents us with the most personalized ethnographic narrative in *Ethnopornography*—thereby taking us full circle in terms of her bold willingness to examine the social meanings of rumors of her own body, desires, and engagements that circulated in and around her anthropological field site. She situates her own ethnographic experience in West Africa in relationship to her sexual encounter with a West African man, discussing both the ethical quandaries of interracial sexual relationships "in the field" and the power relations involved in ethnographic research. By looking at such quandaries, Lawrence presents us with a reconceptualization of the relationship between desire, pleasure, and power. Through an exploration of her own fantasies and those of others—both white and black men—Lawrence provides a deeply personal ethnopornographic account that critiques and undermines the ethical dilemma involved in the making of ethnography and pornography. In this sense, Lawrence pushes the boundaries of ethnopornography in ways not unlike we, the editors of *Ethnopornography*, have sought to do in our own research and writing.

Ethnopornography as Colonial History

As we move on to the next section, "Ethnopornography as Colonial History," we note the ubiquitous presence of colonial violence in the ethnopornographic encounter.[39] Literary scholar Anne McClintock, in *Imperial*

Leather, proposes that one might deal with such legacies through a distinction between textual and material violence, with the idea that material violence was used to resolve the indecisiveness of colonial texts and representation.[40] However, violence, like, sex, is a way of knowing, and ultimately a social relationship.[41] For this reason, *Ethnopornography* focuses on the synergy of sexuality and violence in colonial (and postcolonial) processes, and on how that history becomes a legacy in the historical and ethnographic gaze as traditionally practiced by cultural commentators of various kinds.

When historians discover sexually explicit texts in the archives, they may reproduce those texts with little commentary, effacing the role of the archivist and researcher, suggesting that the documents provide access to the erotic past of some exotic (or temporally distanced) group, mediated only by social actors *in the past*. Social and cultural historians, in particular, can suggest some sort of knowledge production in which a notarial document reproduces the reality of a past society, as mediated by those in both the past and the present. In presenting the source in such a manner, the reader may think that she or he understands indigenous sexual practices, but those practices often came to the attention of the historian only through a series of violent encounters that progressively effaced the meaning of the (perhaps sexual) encounters to the people involved. A conqueror, a priest, or a bureaucrat engaged in acts of violence to stop a sexual practice that he considered sinful. These violent acts came to the attention of other colonial authorities, who supported or condemned the conqueror/priest/bureaucrat. The record of these encounters then went to an archivist, who appraised and decided how to categorize the events in a particular manner, hiding or describing the sexual act in question—if the archivist could decipher something meaningful about that activity. This categorization then attracts the attention of the historian, often hundreds of years later, who recategorizes the events according to her or his own interests. In each case, colonized bodies become distorted—misinscribed within the historical record. The historian attempts to produce knowledge of the other, but, in doing so, potentially distorts the relationship between sex and power.

Both anthropology and history, since their disciplinary founding, have gone through extensive self-critiques. Yet despite such developments, both disciplines, as presented in the broader popular and political arenas, are laden with ethnopornographic content. One has only to look at the recent controversy of Kim Kardashian on a 2014 cover of *Paper*, photographed by the famed photographer Jean-Paul Goude. Consciously mimicking the image of the so-called Hottentot Venus, Goude lets us know that he plans to "break the internet" with his provocation.[42] One can also note that the US military has used ethnographer Raphael Patai's *The Arab Mind*, a salacious account of the deviancy of Islamic men, in its attempt to build more Westernized communities in Afghanistan after 2001.[43] Any such representation, as the chapters in this collection show, have long genealogies that often go unrecognized, or simply ignored, in popular culture and in academia.

Zine Magubane's treatment of modern social science's memory of the Hottentot Venus is instructive in this regard. Magubane notes, for example, that early nineteenth-century understandings of Sara Baartman, the first woman named the "Hottentot Venus," did not mark her racially in the way that Sander Gilman did in his article in 1985. More recently, African American feminists have used the Hottentot Venus as the original representation of the ways in which Europeans treat black female sexuality. By analyzing the genealogy of the Hottentot Venus, we begin to understand the role of professional anthropology: early nineteenth-century cultural commentators see her as a sexual curiosity with a strange body that becomes all the rage in London and Paris but has little to do with a dividing line between iconic European and Black races; late twentieth-century anthropologists and feminist scholars instantiate race.[44]

Two elements are key to ethnopornography: circulation and consent. First, the manner of circulation of such materials, the contemporary ideas of "intention" and "reception," and how usage and commodification, interrelated in their circulation, determine the relationship between ethnopornography and the public. Second, the relation between observer and observed, and the degree of consent present in such a relationship, define the ethical dimension of ethnopornography. The implication here is that all codes of bodily presentation are distorted in the process of external representation to produce sexualized meanings that make such bodies desirable to colonial consumers. The key point is not the distortion of the sexualized bodies per se, but rather the ways in which ethnopornography, as historically constituted, hides power. When Jacobus X argues that both African men and women have large genitalia, he does so not simply to make an argument about the nature of African bodies, but more importantly to make a statement about his own expertise in relation to observation and domination, and the radical difference of Africans when compared with Europeans.[45] Whether the bodies of the colonized were desirable as objects of sexual contempt (as in the case of the Hottentot Venus) or sexual longing (in a variety of ethnographic and archival contexts), the lack of consent on the part of those observed is what signifies such materials as parts of a project of domination and control.[46]

Stabilized structures of colonial power and hierarchy become the means through which this potential excess of native and colonial lust and violent desire is domesticated.[47] In these ways the functional identity of epistemic and corporeal violence is masked through the presentation of the "sexual native" (as in the case of Roth's copulating Australian "aborigines") as pliant, obedient, and desirable. The failure of the indigenes to "live up" to this imagining is thus always met with a colonial response that is not just instrumentally violent in terms of economic and political repression but also sexually inflected and patterned by the categories of ethnographic representation.

Such legacies therefore reveal important histories to the contemporary erotics of cultural difference. The sexual and violent legacy of the colonial moment is reproduced in the globalized circulation of pornographic images whose erotics are firmly linked to the idea of cultural difference that emerged in part from the ethnographies of colonialism.[48] Is there, then, a redemptive analytical position from which Western intellectuals might contribute to the rehabilitation of intercultural knowledge? How can we account for the fact that ethnographers, anthropologists, and historians are people, in a particular cultural context, who arrive at their "field sites" and archives as fully equipped sexual—perhaps even violent—beings?

The chapters that make up this second section of *Ethnopornography* focus on the interaction between sex, violence, and pornography on the part of both colonizers and colonized. Pete Sigal's chapter discusses sixteenth-century Mexico, where Franciscan friars engaged in an extensive colonial project in which they delved into the language and culture of the indigenous populations under their purview. In order to Christianize these populations, the friars believed that they needed to engage in extensive studies of native peoples, with a particular focus on activities that would be deemed "idolatrous" and "sinful." Some Franciscans created extensive ethnographies of the people, and Sigal focuses on two of them: Diego de Landa's *Relación de las cosas de Yucatán* and Bernardino de Sahagún's *Historia general de las cosas de Nueva España*. In both cases, the ethnographies pay particular attention to ceremonies and daily activity that the friars determined particularly problematic, and they develop extensive ethnopornographic accounts of these activities, particularly focusing on phallic portrayals of the male body. Sigal argues that the ethnopornographic approach was central to the goals of the two Franciscans, albeit for different reasons. Landa wanted to defend himself against charges that he had punished the Maya population too harshly. Thus, he portrayed the Maya as exceptionally violent. Sahagún wanted to promote his ethnographic and pedagogical enterprise. To this end, he showed both the violent and sexual nature of the Nahua population, and ways in which one could link evangelism to the development of a proper colonized individual. In both cases, Sigal shows that a particularly violent strain of ethnopornography led to a misreading of indigenous rites and the creation of a new sexual subject.

Joseph Allen Boone brings us to the Ottoman Empire as he analyzes the historical linking of notions of excess sex—in particular, sodomy and "pederasty"—to Islamic culture. By studying European travelogues over three centuries, and pairing these with Turkish sources, Boone analyzes the interactions between ethnopornographers and the complex interchanges regarding "homosexual" acts that took place within the Ottoman Empire. Engaging in such work allows Boone, a literary scholar, to focus on intricate textual analysis to show us the specific ways in which different discourses come together to undermine binary differentiation between east and west, homo and hetero. Further, he complicates the views of gay ethnopornographic consumers, many of whom seem to believe in an Ottoman sexual freedom that did not exist except in the minds of the pornographers. As Boone shows, representations of (homoerotic and homophobic) Orientalist ethnopornography both rely on and subvert the sexual scripts of both Europe and the Ottoman world.

Pernille Ipsen's chapter shows us that seventeenth- and eighteenth-century European men traveled to West Africa expecting easy sexual access to African women. Using Dutch, British, German, and French travel narratives, Ipsen relates this history to modern interracial pornography. She argues that the narratives of European sexual power over West African women circulated in Europe to become examples of classical eighteenth-century pornography. Using Linda Williams's observation that interracial pornography is based on a history of racial subjugation and power relations, Ipsen argues that modern interracial pornography, while based on the earlier sexual relationships, differs in key ways from its eighteenth-century counterpart because of the development, in the nineteenth century, of scientific racism. Thus, by the nineteenth century, the development of a racial taxonomy promoted an essentialized race in which color could not disappear through erotic encounters. Linking early modern pornography to European male anxiety and danger related to the unknown African world, Ipsen shows that fantastical conceptions of African women became central to the development of ethnopornography.

We close this section with the very origin of the term "ethnopornography." Helen Pringle's chapter on Walter Roth shows that his invention of "ethnopornography" relates to his conception of (anthropological) science, which incorporates a voyeuristic interest in "exotic" sexual practices and bodies in the colonial Australian context. The scientific gaze, to Roth, is a form of knowing that shadows the shattering sexual violence of British colonialism. Roth's "Ethno-pornography" chapter was, in his own words, meant to circulate only among "men like us"—those who had a professional and scientific interest in such explicit depictions of aboriginal initiation rites and sexual customs. Pringle demonstrates that anthropological reports (and their circulation) are complicit in the impact of colonialism in the Australian context. By looking at Roth as well as contemporary white settlers in Queensland, Pringle demonstrates that scientific ethnopornography is not merely a procedure for the collection of certain materials about the "savages." It is also a practice of representation that makes a spectacle of the people studied. Staged displays of the "massacre of a bushman" and similar performances acted out at the Brisbane Theater Royal in 1892, for example, accompanied anthropological lectures by Roth's contemporaries. Similarly, in what Pringle terms the "entertainment-ethnological complex," professional anthropologists assisted showmen such as P. T. Barnum in collecting human "specimens" from North Queensland in the 1880s to display in Barnum's "Greatest Show on Earth." The circulated reports of what the anthropological gaze saw are an exertion of mastery through which the naked (and stripped) "native" is subordinated, and it is on and through such reports that the character and solidarity of "men like us" is constituted. Overall, Pringle places the invention and genealogy of "ethnopornography" within its proper Australian historical context, where "Aborigines were known as (authentic) Aborigines in and by their nakedness."

As we analyze the links between colonial violence and ethnopornography, the differences among the many examples of Mesoamerica, the Ottoman Empire, colonized West Africa, and nineteenth-century Europe show us that we must avoid the tendency to assume any transhistorical, transcultural unity in pornographic formulations. While in a wide variety of times and places, colonizers, explorers, and ethnographers have sought to eroticize the populations with which they came into contact, each group did so in vitally different ways. Sigal shows us that, when the Mexica of Tenochtitlan portrayed Huastec priests as hypersexual beings, they pictured them threatening to penetrate Tlazolteotl, a goddess of Huastec origin.[49] Such an ethnopornographic representation is significantly different from the ways in which Franz Fanon's French colonial officials portrayed hypersexualized African men as threats to white womanhood.[50] Nonetheless, in each case, the portrayal engaged the imaginations of various intended audiences (whether commoners of Tenochtitlan or French intellectuals), who reacted with a combination of desire and fear. In order to combat the essentializing of this project, we must pay close attention to cultural context, never allowing ourselves to overgeneralize the imaginative framework of those who receive the pornographic images.

As so many ethnographers and ethnohistorians eroticize the other in a violent manner, we argue here for the need to distinguish between an ethnopornographic violence implicated in the colonial project and one that engages in an erotic disidentification and imaginative manipulation without subsuming the indigenous or racialized other under the identity politics of the observer. We argue that such an approach allows the ethnography to provide a glimpse of the interstice: the liminal space between ethnographer, ethnographic subject, and consumer of ethnography. In essence then the core research project works to uncover both the erotic production of the liberal subject and the maintenance of indigeneity.[51]

Ethnopornographic Method

> I now seek to retool the stranger's lens of perverse sexuality so that it can be more of a productive optic, acknowledging how Asian/American women are seen by others and allowing them to see themselves anew—especially when desiring sexual perversity and shamelessly owning the pleasure and pain that comes from sexual representations of race.
>
> Speaking in one's own terms as made by one's context of hypersexuality can better explain and celebrate Asian American women who embrace perversity as productive. In their works, a passionate engagement of perverse sexuality ultimately embraces self-acceptance.
>
> —CELINE PARREÑAS SHIMIZU, *Hypersexuality of Race*, 1, 267

These two quotes bookend Celine Parreñas Shimizu's provocative study of the hypersexuality of Asian/American women in film. She begins with a painful episode of misrecognition in which a man on a bus believes she is a Filipina sex worker. After examining significant examples of plays and films, including mainstream Hollywood productions, stag films, pornography, and feminist film, Parreñas Shimizu concludes by suggesting the production and dissemination of particular types of self-affirming perverse sexuality. In her formulation Parreñas Shimizu does not negate the violence present in the forced hypersexuality of Asian and Asian American women but instead advocates confronting that violence with what she terms "politically productive perversity," promoting a forthright sexuality that both acknowledges violence and advocates pleasure.[52] Like Parreñas Shimizu's concept of politically productive perversity, in this volume we grapple with the violence involved in producing further studies.

The volume ends with Neil Whitehead's "Ethnopornography Coda," some thoughts on the origins of this project, and the theoreticial and methodological impulses that form ethnopornography. In these concluding remarks, Whitehead notes that in this volume we have recast ethnography not as a pristine venture into the minds and bodies of some other, but rather as an encounter between desiring beings. As such, Whitehead argues that, when we make violent and erotic engagements explicit and visible, we uncover a way of moving forward with such encounters in a more ethical manner.

Examples of ethnopornography in the development of anthropology as a discipline abound. Bronislaw Malinowski's *The Sexual Life of Savages* (1929) serves as an example of some early anthropologists' desires to scandalize and exoticize. In a section titled "orgiastic festivals," we find not so much an "orgy," but rather what we may perhaps call a sadomasochistic seduction ritual. Malinowski states, "When a boy and girl are strongly attracted to each other, and especially before the passion is satisfied, the girl is allowed to inflict considerable bodily pain on her lover by scratching, beating, thrashing, or even wounding with a sharp instrument."[53] Such an attack, Malinowski is told, would result in the two engaging, if the boy wanted, in sexual intercourse (Malinowski, in typically ethnopornographic fashion, describes one case by saying that a boy he treated for wounds from such an attack *"reaped his reward* that same night").[54] Malinowski's ethnographic observations are most intriguing for a study of ethnopornography because he states that he never actually observed one of these ceremonies. Still, he does not hesitate to tell us that "sexual acts would be carried out in public on the central place; married people would participate in the orgy, man or wife behaving without restraint, even though within hail of each other."[55] Malinowski intends his description to suggest the openness of the Trobriand people to sexual experimentation that will have positive results: the selection of a more mature mate, or even marriage that extends beyond the usual choices embedded in courtship rituals.[56] The point here is not for us to question the accuracy of Malinowski's report of this ritual but rather to suggest the ubiquitous nature of the connections between sex and violence asserted in such ritual practices, and the ways that such accounts may have circulated among his intended audience as well as, to use Roth's term, "the general lay reader." Further, we can note that Malinowski uses such descriptions to influence the course of debates regarding sexuality in Western societies.[57] Here Malinowski uses the "sexual life of the savages" as ethnopornography, in an attempt to allow readers to visualize a sexual life different from and more satisfying than their own.

Malinowski's text also functions as pornography: Malinowski himself stated that *The Sexual Life of Savages* was being sold on the boulevards of Paris alongside a series of pornographic books.[58] The trade paperback of Margaret Mead's *Sex and Temperament in Three Primitive Societies* in 1950 featured an alluring cover illustration by Robert Jonas, a well-known pulp illustrator (figure I.4).[59] While the literary scholar Paula Rabinowitz, in a recent study on American pulp, has stated that Jonas's "cubist-inspired covers pared down the lurid expressionism of most paperbacks [between the late 1930s and the early 1960s] into clean lines and bold primary colors," this particular cover, with its eroticized and exoticized illustration of a presumably "primitive" woman and man from Papua New Guinea, was meant to popularize anthropology and attract lay readers to the book.[60]

All such representations are, of course, always up for contestation and appropriation, as we witness in figure I.4, a reproduction of an advertisement from the 2016 "London Fetish Map."[61] The owners of the Worlds End Bookshop ask viewers of the map if they have a "fetish for books." The two book covers displayed in the advertisement are Mead's *Sex and Temperament*, along with the cover of a pulp novel, Wade Miller's *Kitten with a Whip* (1959). In 2016, Mead's classic work and Jonas's pulp imagery are ethnopornographic reflections of ethnography, used to promote *and fetishize* reading (and consuming) "beautiful, historic, collectors [*sic*] books" and other forms of "kink" within the BDSM/fetish community.

The links between anthropology and pornography are made more explicit the further we dig. In 1983, for example, in a book titled *Freie Liebe*, which was published in a German *Playboy* paperback series, author Roger Baker depicts the Trobrianders as promiscuous exhibitionists who regularly exchanged sex partners between married couples. His fantasies were built on Malinowski's *The Sexual Life of Savages*, which he declared "the bible" of the free love movement.[62] In a recent documentary, appropriately titled, *Savage*

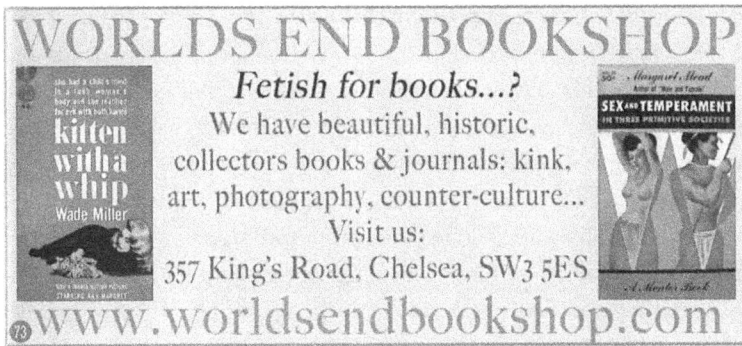

FIGURE I.4 Advertisement from "London Fetish Map," distributed in London, 2016. Pete Sigal personal collection.

Memory, we find that some Trobriand Islanders object to the sexual nature of Malinowski's book, while others embrace it.[63] The filmmakers even find some pictures of simulated sexual intercourse between two men, rhetorically asking how Malinowski convinced them to perform such acts.[64] Malinowski, a key figure in the genealogy of ethnopornography, is, of course, not alone in his discourse, and, while most modern ethnographers reject some of his more exploitative relationships with native populations, much of his ethnographic method remains a model for modern observers—particularly those engaged in more "popular" ethnographies.[65]

Malinowski, Mead, and the others aside, many anthropologists and ethnographers since the 1980s have engaged in research and writing practices that have altered the ethnographic gaze in such a way as to help us begin to develop a method for ethnopornographic critique. For example, Diane Nelson's work on the ways in which the Guatemalan state at the end of the twentieth century uses bodily metaphors to produce Maya individuals as coherent subjects with sexual desires points us toward a critical ethnopornography.[66] Elizabeth Povinelli's *Empire of Love* serves as a particularly strong model for an alternative ethnopornography. Povinelli, informed by queer theory, juxtaposes the radical faeries—a conscious critique of Western sexuality from within the West—and indigenous Australian groups. She uses ethnography to theorize about governance, intimacy, and sexuality. By doing so, Povinelli calls into question the concepts of authenticity, indigeneity, and liberal personhood. She shows the ways in which the related categories of love and emotion are used to effectively colonize indigenous peoples. In her theoretical reflection, she then critiques Western forms of knowledge and instead foregrounds a method for relating indigenous intimacy to alternative epistemologies.[67] This allows Povinelli to venture into alternative sexualities in an example of the critical ethnopornography we promote here.

We advocate the *creation* of ethnopornography in a critical mode. One way to do so is by participating in the groups we study, presenting particular kinds of public performances that suggest ways forward for scholarly activity. This does not mean that we engage only in "navel gazing" ethnographic and ethnohistorical approaches to scholarship. Rather, it means that we move into public discourse and performance as theoretically engaged and rigorous scholars, seeking to develop a different kind of knowledge-producing project. Thus, our ethnopornography becomes a productive form of disciplinary inquiry and methodological practice.

To this end, Neil pushed the very boundaries of his own subjectivity and his ethnographic forms of engagement. Best known for his work on cannibalism, shamanism, and the anthropology of violence in the Caribbean and South America, Neil was fascinated by an Amerindian "vision of a cosmos filled with predatory gods and spirits whose violent hungers are sated by humans."[68] This was a cosmos that Neil not only studied, but one that he incorporated himself into, whether he was conducting ethnographic fieldwork abroad, hunting in Wisconsin, or participating in posthumanist "performative ethnography." Most recently, prior to Neil's death, this took the form of participating in what he termed an "audio-visual project" through the goth-fetish band Blood Jewel that enabled him to explore the sexualized nature of violence, to challenge the boundaries of the "human," and to broach new possible domains for anthropological thinking.

In his earlier work, Neil had unwittingly become part of the ethnographic story that he wrote on the *kanaimà* in Guyana and Brazil. The gripping first chapter of his extraordinary ethnography *Dark Shamans* presents the background of a particular shaman's attacks on Neil's own body. This experience led Neil to reflect on the nature of ethnographic violence and on the scholar's will to know as a will to devour his or her subject. By the time he finished writing *Dark Shamans*, Neil had produced an ethnographic account heavily focused on the intimate details of bodily enactments of violence (so much so that one participant in the ethnopornography conference organized by Neil and Pete said that she could never teach *Dark Shamans* because it was "*too* pornographic"—this despite the fact that the book has no explicit sexual content).[69] Neil's analysis focused on the historical and social meanings of kanaimà—a form of dark shamanism practiced by certain Amerindian groups in the highlands of Guyana, Venezuela, and Brazil that, in Neil's words, "refers to the killing of an individual by violent mutilation of, in particular, the mouth and anus, into which are inserted various objects. The killers are then enjoined to return to the dead body of the victim in order to drink the juices of putrefaction."[70] For Neil, the pornographic did not necessarily have to do with sex, and his recounting of his own intimately personal interactions with kanaimà became a form of ethnopornographic engagement.

In his next project, Neil practiced a research method that he termed "performative engagement," instead of the method of "participant observation" proposed by many other ethnographers.[71] By participating in Blood Jewel, a production with Jeff Fields, Neil began to perform as a desiring subject. Neil produced music videos and promoted the band, which emphasized "structural violence and fetish sexuality." He argued that "artistically fetishized sexuality is represented as a medium for self-empowerment and an erotic response to the threatening and potentially toxic nature of off-line sexual encounter."[72] By becoming both subject and object of a sexualized and violent ethnography, Neil promoted what he terms a "post-human anthropology," becoming a theoretically engaged desiring machine. Reflecting on the imagery and music of Blood Jewel, much of which is still archived online, one cannot suggest that it is without problems.[73] It is an ethnopornography that promotes a vision of a violent, erotically charged world. As the images and music assault the senses, the purpose of the erotic violence is not always clear. Yet, one can certainly imagine that Neil promoted particular fantasies intended to evoke a world that brings colonial and postcolonial violence to the surface through a fetishized eroticism, both online and off.

Like Neil, Pete promotes a fetishistic erotic imaginary and practice in ways that both influence and inform (just as they are influenced and informed by) his scholarship. He participates in an extensive community of fetishists and sadomasochists and puts on events designed to envision a world that explores bodies beyond the limits of genital sexuality. In this world, Pete experiments with the boundaries of the human through a performative notion of pleasure in which the sadomasochistic scene moves beyond the narrative of sexual subjectivity, and in which skin itself becomes exoticized and eroticized through leather and latex. Unlike some of the writers in the 1980s who discussed the transcendental nature of sadomasochism, Pete does not argue for the politics of a "radical sexuality" based on a psychic or spiritual movement beyond sex.[74] Rather, he maintains that fetish and sadomasochism provide for a greater ability to reflect upon the historical contingencies of modern sexuality, particularly as the modern sexual regime focuses on genital sex and the movement toward respectability in the formation of sexual identity. Instead, fetish and sadomasochism *may* offer us an alternative history of queer debasement in which the mixture of pleasure and pain, along with the fetishized and embodied object, rather than the gender of the object choice, become key.[75] Of course fetish and sadomasochism do not signify utopia, and the community is replete with conspicuous consumption and various sexual phobias.

Still, in this scene, Pete imagines and seeks a collective community encounter through rituals that ensure pleasure and pain, a vision related to the type of history he writes: an encounter that is at once sexual and also moves beyond sexuality to bodily pleasures and extraordinary violence that may result in annihilation of the self. The concept of pleasure in sadomasochism becomes not the subsuming of another into the self but a knowledge that, by destroying the other, the self too comes to be destroyed. An amalgam of energy, an intense pleasure witnessed only through intense pain, turns feeling into a differential experience that can no longer be called experience because it no longer presumes a subject; it no longer has a self who *does* the experiencing. Through such a scene, Pete witnesses historical enactments that allow him to reimagine theories, histories, and ethnographies of sexuality. This has brought Pete to his next scholarly project, in which he works to provide a genealogy of the relationship between colonial violence and modern sexual pleasure.

In a similar vein, Zeb's scholarship on the history of sexuality in colonial contexts and the social meanings of (and autoethnographic engagements with) pornography have allowed him to push methodological boundaries in productive, though not necessarily unproblematic, ways. In his historical scholarship, Zeb has focused largely on archival narratives of the "sins against nature" of sodomy, bestiality, and masturbation—all acts that the Catholic Church deemed to be unnatural since they did not lead to procreation—in the context of Latin America between the early sixteenth and the early nineteenth century. His current research on "archiving the obscene" in Latin America analyzes censorship, erotica, and pornography, from the eighteenth to the mid-twentieth century. In dedicating himself to archival research to show how past bodies and desires come to be documented and archived, he gradually came to more explicitly interrogate the links between his own (archived) erotic subjectivity and the impulse to put the bodies of historical others on display in scholarship. As his archival research on colonial Latin American sexuality evolved, he found himself wanting to explore, in an increasingly public realm, the possibilities of putting his own body and desires on display alongside those of the historical subjects about whom he wrote academically.

Early in his research, in 2002, Zeb answered an advertisement in the UCLA school newspaper, where he was then working on his PhD in history, to do gay porn modeling, video, and photography work. Since then, he has written academically and autoethnographically about his experiences in mainstream and indie porn industries, webcam shows, and other forms of sex work.[76] His experiences navigating his status as a porn performer for a largely gay male audience when he was a graduate student, subsequently going on the academic job market (with porn in his past), and now teaching colonial history, gender/sexuality studies, queer studies, and archival theory as a university professor attend to the complicated ways that investments in the history of sexuality and in pornography can inform one another politically and methodologically. These auto/ethno/pornographic endeavors have led him to theorize the ways in which bodies (including his own) come to be archived, recorded, documented, and remembered in vastly different cultural and social media contexts, be they historical archives, videos and DVDS, or online repositories of images.[77] Such ethnopornographic engagements lay bare the ways in which Zeb himself can be caught up in the very cycles of historical voyeurism that he, at least initially, sought to engage in only as a spectator (and historian) in the archives.

These particular experiences promote a key change in the way we view knowledge production, a change experienced by some of the authors included in *Ethnopornography*. We no longer are ruled by a will to know, as Neil would never have told all about his experiences in Blood Jewel, Pete will never tell all about the erotic charge he receives in the BDSM community, and Zeb will never give away all of the records of his bodily desires. Rather we enter a world of a will to participate, to become an individual engaged in particular kinds of practices that challenge simplistic recreations of the history and ethnography of sexuality. Of course, such a method presents a set of ethical challenges. What are the limits of the observing participant? And how do the very acts of observing and participating radically shift the terrain of desire, the mode of archiving, and the disciplinary impulses of history and anthropology? As Neil put it: "*in order to understand desire we must become desiring subjects ourselves. In this way performative* engagement rather than observing participation changes the basis of ethnographic description from that of inferred and interpreted meanings and motivations to that of auto-ethnographic description and overtly positioned observation."[78] We need to develop some ethical regulations that go beyond the current set of guidelines developed by review boards. But this is not the purpose of our volume. Rather, we wish to show that this sort of productive engagement allows for ethnopornographies that provide different ways of envisioning the world around us and of encountering other groups, ethnographically and historically. Whether this method effectively and adequately analyzes colonial violence or not, it brings ethnopornography to the surface in a self-reflective manner, and it does so in ways that beg us to attend to the ethics and politics of representation.

Notes

Neil L. Whitehead and Pete Sigal cowrote the early drafts of this introduction before Neil's death in March 2012. Pete Sigal and Zeb Tortorici have subsequently revised and rewritten the introduction along the lines of notes and conversations that they shared with Neil between 2009 and 2011. Erika Robb Larkins, one of Neil's last students, has also participated in this project and provided extensive commentary on the introduction. We believe that the final version of the introduction conforms at least broadly to Neil's views of the ethnopornography project.

1   We note that the subtitle for this volume has gone through several iterations. Before Neil's death, the subtitle included the phrase, "Anthropological Knowledge" (and previously, "Anthropological Knowing"). Neil, as the reader will see in the "Ethnopornography Coda" to this volume, was deeply committed to engaging in a critique of the discipline of anthropology. While the volume and this introduction contain some of that critique, Pete and Zeb are both trained primarily in history, and thus do not have the requisite credentials to challenge anthropology as a discipline. In fact, even before Neil's death, the volume had moved significantly toward a critique of knowledge production in the humanities and the qualitative social sciences instead of a specific disciplinary engagement. While Pete and Zeb both believe that Neil and some other contributors to this volume have developed an incisive critique of anthropological methods, the contributors are much more engaged with a deep dive into cultural studies through an analysis of the roles of sexuality, colonialism, and the archive in the development of knowledge.

2   Neil Whitehead, "Comments," Ethnopornography Conference remarks, Durham, NC, 2006.

3 Napoleon Chagnon, *Yanomamö: The Fierce People* (New York: Holt McDougal, 1984); William H. Crocker and Jean G. Crocker, *The Canela: Kinship, Ritual, and Sex in an Amazonian Tribe*, 2nd ed. (Belmont, CA: Wadsworth, 2004); Gilbert Herdt, *Guardians of the Flutes: Idioms of Masculinity* (New York: McGraw Hill, 1981). These authors provide three very different genres of ethnography, and we do not mean to equate the three ethically. The first is by an ethnographer rejected by most anthropologists; the second is an example of "mainstream" ethnography that focuses on kinship and sex; and the third is an example of the critical ethnographies produced a generation ago that focused on sexualities that did not follow the standard heterosexual kinship model.

4 Linda Williams, in *Hard Core: Power, Pleasure, and the "Frenzy of the Visible"* (Berkeley: University of California Press, 1989), develops the different genres of golden age film pornography. *Deep Throat* has an arcane setup in which a woman requires medical intervention to understand why she fails to have an orgasm (her clitoris is in her throat, so she needs to give fellatio in order to have the orgasm). *Behind the Green Door* presents a woman in the act of self-discovery in which, through her kidnapping, as she is convinced to have sex with multiple women and men, she discovers her deepest desires. The use of magic is also central to many films. In a more recent example than the golden age films Williams discusses, the gay pornography film *Dig* (All Worlds Video, dir. Rafael, 2000) presents us with an example of archaeologists who go to Mexico and become seduced by the spell of an ancient Aztec warrior.

5 See Neil Whitehead, "Post-Human Anthropology," *Identities: Global Studies in Culture and Power* 16 (2009): 1–32.

6 Walter E. Roth, *Ethnological Studies among the North-West-Central Queensland Aborigines* (Brisbane, Aus.: Edmund Gregory, Government Printer, 1897), 176.

7 Roth, *Ethnological Studies*, vii.

8 Andrew P. Lyons, "The Two Lives of Sara Baartman: Gender, 'Race', Politics and the Historiography of Mis/Representation," *Anthropologica* 60 (2018), 328.

9 Sadiah Qureshi, *Peoples on Parade: Exhibitions, Empire, and Anthropology in Nineteenth-Century Britain* (Chicago, IL: University of Chicago Press, 2011), 6.

10 Andrée Tabouret-Keller, "Western Europe," in *Handbook of Language and Ethnic Identity*, ed. Joshua A. Fishman (New York: Oxford University Press, 1999), 335.

11 Lynn Hunt, ed., *The Invention of Pornography: Obscenity and the Origins of Modernity, 1500–1800* (New York: Zone Books, 1993), 9–10.

12 Christian Hansen, Catherine Needham, and Bill Nichols, "Skin Flicks: Pornography, Ethnography, and the Discourses of Power," *Discourse* 11, no. 2 (1989): 64–79.

13 Hansen, Needham, and Nichols, "Skin Flicks," 78.

14 In a different manner of thinking about the relationship between ethnography and sexuality, Don Kulick and Margaret Willson focus on the way in which the ethnographer's own sexual subjectivity enters into his or her fieldwork. See Don Kulick and Margaret Willson, eds., *Taboo: Sex, Identity and Erotic Subjectivity in Anthropological Fieldwork* (New York: Routledge, 1995). See also Fran Markowitz

and Michael Ashkenazi, eds., *Sex, Sexuality, and the Anthropologist* (Urbana: University of Illinois Press, 1999).

15 Hansen, Needham, and Nichols, "Skin Flicks," 67.

16 Hansen, Needham, and Nichols, "Skin Flicks," 68.

17 Roth, *Ethnological Studies*, 179.

18 Dennis, "Ethno-Pornography: Veiling the Dark Continent," *History of Photography* 18, no 1 (1994): 23.

19 For a historically oriented study that allows us to focus more attention on the political uses of pornography, see Hunt, ed., *The Invention of Pornography*.

20 Williams, *Hard Core*.

21 See, for example, Celine Parreñas Shimizu, *The Hypersexuality of Race: Performing Asian/American Women on Screen and Scene* (Durham, NC: Duke University Press, 2007); Darieck Scott, *Extravagant Abjection: Blackness, Power, and Sexuality in the African American Literary Imagination* (New York: New York University Press, 2010); Mireille Miller-Young, *A Taste for Brown Sugar: Black Women in Pornography* (Durham, NC: Duke University Press, 2014); Jennifer C. Nash, *The Black Body in Ecstasy: Reading Race, Reading Pornography* (Durham, NC: Duke University Press, 2014); Nguyen Tan Hoang, *A View from the Bottom: Asian American Masculinity and Sexual Representation* (Durham, NC: Duke University Press, 2014); Darieck Scott, "Big Black Beauty: Drawing and Naming the Black Male Figure in Superhero and Gay Porn Comics," in Tim Dean, Steven Ruszczycky, and David Squires, eds., *Porn Archives* (Durham, NC: Duke University Press, 2014); Ramón E. Soto-Crepo, "Porno Ricans at the Borders of Empire," in Dean, Ruszczycky, and Squires, *Porn Archives;* Juana María Rodríguez, "Pornographic Encounters and Interpretive Interventions: Vanessa del Rio: Fifty Years of Slightly Slutty Behavior," *Women and Performance: A Journal of Feminist Theory* 25, no. 3 (2015); Ariane Cruz, *The Color of Kink: Black Women, BDSM, and Pornography* (New York: New York University Press, 2017); and many of the articles in Tristan Taormino, Celine Parreñas Shimizu, Constance Penley, and Mireille Miller-Young, eds., *The Feminist Porn Book: The Politics of Producing Pleasure* (New York: Feminist Press at the City University of New York, 2013).

22 See Abdul JanMohamed, "Sexuality on/of the Racial Border: Foucault, Wright, and the Articulation of Racialized Sexuality," in *Discourses of Sexuality*, ed. Donna Stanton (Ann Arbor: University of Michigan Press, 1992).

23 See Celine Parreñas Shimizu, "Master-Slave Sex Acts: *Mandingo* and the Race/Sex Paradox," *Wide Angle* 21, no. 4 (1999): 42–61; Jane Gaines, *Fire and Desire: Mixed Race Movies in the Silent Era* (Chicago, IL: University of Chicago Press, 2001).

24 Miller-Young, *Taste for Brown Sugar*, 9.

25 Nash, *The Black Body in Ecstasy*, 147.

26 Vanessa del Rio and Dian Hanson, *Fifty Years of Slightly Slutty Behavior* (Cologne, Germany: Taschen, 2010)

27 Rodríguez, "Pornographic Encounters," 331.

28 Scott, *Extravagant Abjection*; Hoang, *View from the Bottom*.

29 Cruz, *Color of Kink*.

30 Of course this sense of clarity and coherence stems from a particular history that relates visual signs of blackness to race. See Nicole R. Fleetwood, *Troubling Vision: Performance, Visuality, and Blackness* (Chicago, IL: University of Chicago Press, 2011).

31 We wish to acknowledge one of our anonymous reviewers for bringing up this question.

32 See Werner Sollors, *Beyond Ethnicity: Consent and Descent in American Culture* (New York: Oxford University Press, 1986); Werner Sollors, *Neither Black Nor White Yet Both: Thematic Explorations of Interracial Literature* (New York: Oxford University Press, 1997).

33 Samuel R. Delany, *Mad Man* (New York: Masquerade Books, 1994).

34 Rey Chow, "Where Have All the Natives Gone?," in *Writing Diaspora: Tactics of Intervention in Contemporary Cultural Studies* (Bloomington: University of Indiana Press, 1993), 52–54. While we disagree with Chow's conclusion that the ethnopornographic image should not be reproduced, we believe that a responsible ethnography will necessarily read the image to understand its genealogy, material position, and cultural work.

35 We are not arguing that ethnographic practices must end. Nor are we saying, following James Clifford (*The Predicament of Culture: Twentieth Century Ethnography, Literature, and Art* [Cambridge, MA: Harvard University Press, 1988]), that ethnography must become more self-reflexive. This simply is not the debate with which we wish to engage. Rather, we argue here that both acknowledging the erotic relationship between the ethnographer and the subject *and* also taking the next step to promote an alternative erotic relationship are necessary for the movement of ethnography into a more adequately theorized encounter.

36 José Esteban Muñoz, *Disidentifications: Queers of Color and the Performance of Politics* (Minneapolis: University of Minnesota Press, 1999), 80.

37 The Feminist Porn Conference: http://fpcon.org/ (accessed May 10, 2019); York University Feminist Porn Archive: http://www.yorku.ca/bnoble/feminist_porn/ (accessed May 10, 2019); Taormino, Shimizu, Penley, and Miller-Young, eds., *Feminist Porn Book*.

38 Muñoz, *Disidentifications*, 80.

39 Anne McClintock, *Imperial Leather: Race, Gender and Sexuality in the Colonial Conquest* (New York: Routledge, 1995), 10–13.

40 McClintock, *Imperial Leather*, 16.

41 See Neil Whitehead and Sverker Finnstrom, eds., *Virtual War and Magical Death: Technologies and Imaginaries for Terror and Killing* (Durham, NC: Duke University Press, 2013); Bruce Kapferer, *Legends of People, Myths of State Violence, Intolerance, and Political Culture in Sri Lanka and Australia* (Washington, DC: Smithsonian Institution Press, 1988).

42 "Break the Internet: Kim Kardashian," PaperMag, accessed August 26, 2019, papermag.com/break-the-internet-kim-kardashian-cover-1427450475.html

43 Raphael Patai, *The Arab Mind* (New York: Scribner, 1976).

44 Zine Magubane, "Which Bodies Matter? Feminism, Poststructuralism, Race, and the Curious Theoretical Odyssey of the 'Hottentot Venus,'" *Gender and Society* 15, no. 6 (2001): 816–34. See also Sander Gilman, "Black Bodies, White Bodies: Toward an Iconography of Female Sexuality in Late Nineteenth-Century Art, Medicine, and Literature," in *Race, Writing, and Difference*, edited by Henry L. Gates, Jr. (Chicago, IL: University of Chicago Press, 1985), and Lyons, "The Two Lives of Sara Baartman." More recent African American feminist studies have moved beyond the analysis that Magubane so effectively critiques. See Jennifer C. Nash, "Strange Bedfellows: Black Feminism and Antipornography Feminism," *Social Text* 26, no. 4 (2008): 51–76.

45 Jacobus X, *Untrodden Fields of Anthropology* (New York: Falstaff, 1937).

46 See Clifton Crais and Pamela Scully, *Sara Baartman and the Hottentot Venus: A Ghost Story and A Biography* (Princeton: Princeton University Press, 2009); Ara Wilson, *The Intimate Economies of Bangkok: Tomboys, Tycoons, and Avon Ladies in the Global City* (Berkeley: University of California Press, 2004); Margaret Mead, *From the South Seas: Studies of Adolescence and Sex in Primitive Societies* (New York: Morrow, 1939). Also note that even the idea of "consent" here signifies a violence for the way in which it demands the production of the "consenting individual"; something akin to the way in which Native North Americans were repeatedly induced to "sign" treaties that took possession of their territories. See Elizabeth Povinelli, *The Empire of Love: Toward a Theory of Intimacy, Genealogy, and Carnality* (Durham, NC: Duke University Press, 2006).

47 Ann Laura Stoler, *Carnal Knowledge and Imperial Power: Race and the Intimate in Colonial Rule* (Berkeley: University of California Press, 2002), 9–13.

48 See Chow, "All the Natives," 28–30.

49 Pete Sigal, *The Flower and the Scorpion: Sexuality and Ritual in Early Nahua Culture* (Durham, NC: Duke University Press, 2011).

50 Frantz Fanon, *Black Skin, White Masks* (New York: Grove Press, 1967), 63–82.

51 Here we point to the example of Povinelli's *Empire of Love*, discussed below.

52 Mirelle Miller-Young and Jennifer Nash make similar theoretical moves in their recent books on pornography and African American women. See Miller-Young, *Taste for Brown Sugar*; Nash, *The Black Body in Ecstasy*.

53 Bronislaw Malinowski, *The Sexual Life of Savages in North-Western Melanesia: An Ethnographic Account of Courtship, Marriage and Family Life Among the Natives of the Trobriand Islands, British New Guinea* (New York: Eugenics Publishing Company, 1929), 256–57.

54 Malinowski, *The Sexual Life of Savages*, 257; emphasis added.

55 Malinowski, *The Sexual Life of Savages*, 258.

56 Malinowski, *The Sexual Life of Savages*, 261.

57 Malinowski arranged to have the famous sexologist Havelock Ellis write a preface to the book. Ellis writes that the book shows us that "the savage man is very like the civilized man, with the like vices and virtues under different forms, but we may even find that in some respects the savage has here reached a finer degree of civilization than the civilized man. The comparisons we can thus make furnish suggestions even for the critical study of our own social life." Malinowski, *The Sexual Life of Savages*, xiii. Lyons and Lyons term Malinowski a "reluctant sexologist." Andrew P. Lyons and Harriet D. Lyons, *Irregular Connections: A History of Anthropology and Sexuality* (Lincoln: University of Nebraska Press, 2004), 155–84.

58 Helena Wayne, *The Story of A Marriage: The Letters of Bronislaw Malinowski and Elsie Mason* (New York: Routledge, 1995).

59 We wish to thank Erika Robb Larkins for bringing this book cover to our attention, and for pointing out the illustration's similarities with Harlequin Romance novels of the same period.

60 Paula Rabinowitz, *American Pulp: How Paperbacks Brought Modernism to Main Street* (Princeton, NJ: Princeton University Press, 2014), 25.

61 In a somewhat ironic example of the ethnopornographic methods that we seek to promote, we found this map when Pete traveled to London to do some research on a new project that links modern sexual pleasure to colonial voyeurism. On the same trip, he planned to attend some fetish events, so he went shopping at a store for latex clothing and picked up "The London Fetish Map," where he found this advertisement.

62 Gunter Senft, "'Noble Savages' and the 'Islands of Love': Trobriand Islanders in 'Popular Publications,'" in *Pacific Answers to Western Hegemony: Cultural Practices of Identity Construction*, ed. Jürd Wassmann (Oxford: Berg Publishers, 1998), 388–89.

63 Savage Memory, home page, accessed August 21, 2019, http://www .savagememory.com/.

64 This vision of himself through the Trobriands' eyes seems contradicted in a certain manner by his diary, which expressed immense hatred toward his subjects. See Bronislaw Malinowski, *A Diary in the Strict Sense of the Term* (New York: Harcourt, Brace, & World, 1967).

65 Key in this respect is the place of Napoleon Chagnon, author of *Yanomamö: The Fierce People*, an extraordinarily popular ethnographic text—though from an author rejected by much of the establishment in professional anthropology. Chagnon tells us that the men were "hideous" and "filthy." They constantly competed to have sexual intercourse with women. And they scared him immensely. Chagnon, in telling us that the men were "hideous" and focusing our attention on their violence (they had drawn arrows, aimed, of course, at Chagnon), filth, and drug use, wants us to witness his fear, though from the safe distance of the living room couches upon which we sit to read his book. He wants us to experience the excitement and exhilaration of first contact—he wants to thrill us. And indeed, he is

better at it than most ethnographers, which is one reason his book has sold over a million copies. One must further remember that this excitement is an only slightly veiled sexual excitement, as we find that the entire book focuses on the competition between men over women and sexual activity. And the near constant focus on the naked bodies of the Yanomami places the reader in close proximity with the ethnographer. In other words, the reader becomes seduced as he imagines himself seeing, touching, and smelling everything taking place while he becomes part of this sexual competition over women, part of a sexual scene (we masculinize the reader here because we suggest Chagnon's primary audience as that of the Western man). Chagnon, *Yanomamö.* See also Patrick Tierney, *Darkness in El Dorado: How Scientists and Journalists Devastated the Amazon* (New York: Norton, 2000). We cannot, of course, characterize Chagnon as an average anthropologist. In fact, a recent article in the *Nation* somewhat oversimplistically suggests that cultural anthropologists have rejected Chagnon all along, and that he belongs more properly to sociobiology. It is true that, almost since the publication of the ethnography in 1968, many anthropologists have condemned Chagnon's work. And, more recently, anthropologist Marshall Sahlins resigned his membership in the National Academy of Sciences to protest the fact that Chagnon was voted a member. See Peter C. Baker, "Fight Clubs: On Napoleon Chagnon," *Nation,* accessed August 26, 2019, http://www.thenation.com/article/fight-clubs-napoleon-chagnon/. See also Chagnon's recent book *Noble Savages: My Life among Two Dangerous Tribes—The Yanomamo and the Anthropologists* (New York: Simon and Schuster, 2013).

66 Diane M. Nelson, *A Finger in the Wound: Body Politics in Quincentennial Guatemala* (Berkeley: University of California Press, 1999).

67 Povinelli, *Empire of Love.*

68 Neil Whitehead, *Dark Shamans: Kanaimà and the Poetics of Violent Death* (Durham, NC: Duke University Press, 2001), 1.

69 See Whitehead, *Dark Shamans.*

70 Whitehead, *Dark Shamans,* 14.

71 Whitehead, "Post-Human Anthropology," 4.

72 Whitehead, "Post-Human Anthropology," 11.

73 See the music videos on Blood Jewel's Facebook page: https://www.facebook.com /Blood-Jewel-171140362935107/, accessed May 10, 2019.

74 On the earlier understandings of sadomasochism, see Geoff Mains, *Urban Aboriginals: A Celebration of Leathersexuality* (Boston, MA: Alyson Publications, 1984); Mark Thompson, ed., *Leatherfolk: Radical Sex, People, Politics, and Practice* (Boston, MA: Alyson Publications, 1991).

75 See Kathryn Bond Stockton, *Beautiful Bottom, Beautiful Shame: Where "Black" Meets "Queer"* (Durham, NC: Duke University Press, 2006); Amber Jamille Musser, *Sensational Flesh: Race, Power, and Masochism* (New York: New York University Press, 2014). See also Margot Weiss, *Techniques of Pleasure: BDSM and the Circuits of Sexuality* (Durham, NC: Duke University Press, 2011).

76 Zeb Tortorici, "Queering Pornography: Desiring Youth, Race, and Fantasy in Gay Porn" in Susan Driver, ed., *Queer Youth Cultures* (Albany: State University of New York Press, 2008), 199–220.

77 Zeb Tortorici, "Auto/Ethno/Pornography," *Porn Studies* 2, no. 2–3 (2015): 265–68.

78 Whitehead, "Post-Human Anthropology," 4.

PART I —
VISUALIZING RACE

Exotic/Erotic/Ethnopornographic

Black Women, Desire, and Labor
in the Photographic Archive

One of the first courses I taught as a new assistant professor a decade ago was a media production course called "Black Feminist Multimedia." In this class I joined the students in creating short films that engaged issues of identity and politics through black feminist analyses of race, gender, class, nation, and sexuality. My feeble attempt at navigating the video editing software Final Cut Pro aside, I created a ten-minute-long video titled "Desiring Ourselves" using images I had culled from a recent research trip to Paris, France, where I had met a dealer of colonial French photography of African women and girls. Overlaying the photographs with text, my own spoken word poetry, and an unlicensed track from the great Nina Simone, my video attempted to explore the intertwining of violence and desire, along with questions of subjecthood, self-reflexivity, and erotic sovereignty,[1] that made the images so powerful to me personally as an intellectual and a black woman living the legacy of racialized sexuality that emerges from the colonial encounter. Eventually I posted the video on YouTube and received a few hundred likes and comments. Until one day when the video was gone. It had vanished from YouTube.

With no warning at all, my film was removed by the website for violating Google's terms of service regarding pornography and obscenity. In taking up material that in the original context of its production as part anthropological inquiry into the sexual behaviors and practices of the native woman and part economy of visual materials to satisfy the salacious curiosity of French photographers, audiences, and others, my censored video ultimately exposed at least two levels of meaning attached to this archive of "ethnopornography." First, the representation of the native body, and in this case the black female body, is always already pornographic. As such the black female body is a problem of representation evacuated of merit, a primitive counterpoint to the values of civility, beauty, and innocence upheld in the bourgeois body.[2] In fact, even when we (scholars, educators, artists) attempt to resignify the symbolic power of the pornographic gaze by manipulating the images, or to rethink issues of objectification, commodification, and violence indexed upon the native woman's body in colonial photography, this already pornographic body sutures (some of) us to the position of pornographer, just as it is itself wedded to the place of mimetic pornographic *thing*. How do we contend with the ways in which empire shaped pornography and pornography shaped empire? And more significantly for myself as a supposed (and admitted) black feminist pornographer,[3] I wonder how we might begin to use our analyses and creative tools to challenge the distortions, myths, and obfuscations about the Other that ethnopornographies circulated?

The late-nineteenth-century explosion of sexualized images of black women occurred at the nexus of ethnological, technological, and commercial interests. Emerging primarily from European colonial Africa, and traveling across the Atlantic to the United States and Latin America, a prurient ethnographic scientific gaze produced and consumed images of black women, black men, and those from other colonized, presumably racially inferior groups in Africa, Asia, the Americas, and Australia. An economy of images and desires trafficking in fascination and fear shaped how in the nineteenth century colonial imagination black women became "eroticized/exoticized,"[4] and important figures whose display in public commercial spaces and popular spheres (slave auctions, freak shows, museums, world's fairs) simultaneously titillated and disgusted white spectators. Photographic technology galvanized this circulation of desires by transforming the bodies of black women of the African Diaspora into erotic and exotic ethnographic sites for learned and professional study, particularly for anthropology and its subdiscipline, ethnography, as sciences seeking "authentic" images of racial others as if they would reveal a kind of essential truth about racial and cultural difference located in perceived anomalous sexual habits. This technologically enhanced gaze codified women of African decent as the most morally obscene, socially subordinate, and biologically deficient population, and hence ensured the rationale, impetus, and occasion for observers to *keep looking*. The advancement of photography as a form that could be duplicated, reproduced, shared, and sold inaugurated an important convergence of scientific and commercial uses of erotic and exotic photographic images that form an ethnopornographic marketplace.

Yet it is not the production of the black woman's body as pornographic object through the technology of photography—nor the scientific or commercial investments that overlapped in the colonial era—that solidifies black women's relationship to ethnopornography.[5] Ethnopornography offers a lens, a conceptual apparatus, and a method to think about the relationality and economy of images, techniques, discourses, bodies, subjectivities, desires, and state logics that brought the colonized under view in the domain of empire. Pornography did not arise on the margins of empire but was at its core. One could argue that empire was (and remains), in a sense, a kind of pornography. Empire prioritized possession, titillation, and fantasy, and it exploited the idea of the native's limitless sexual potency. Empire mapped the land it stole as a body consumable, appropriated a surveilling gaze, and mobilized the labor of colonized bodies to enact the drama of its imperious command. Yet the erotics of empire relied specifically on the administration of knowledge and relationships of domination; ethnography was a key method in maintaining discourses of power, truth, and control, while pornography facilitated ethnography's purview by opening up the sexual realm to view, providing networks to spread the idea of racialized sexual difference, and unleashing the imaginations and desires of Western audiences for more of what empire holds.

Although much attention has been given to the iconic role of the Hottentot Venus, the ur-text of atavistic animal-human black female sexuality for European scientists, the nineteenth-century photographic archive shows that black women were also figured in the preeminent medical-scientific classificatory projects of the United States.[6] For instance, in the 1850s, a series of daguerreotypes were taken of seven slaves in South Carolina as part of the modern empiricist scheme of categorizing and cataloging deviant groups. The daguerreotypes present five men, Jem, Jack, Fassena, Alfred, and Renty, and two women, Drana and Delia, naked or seminaked in a frontal and profile view soon to be formalized as the "mug shot." They were commissioned by Swiss-born scientist Louis Agassiz, the "most famous" natural scientist during his time and "star student" of Georges Cuvier, the French scientist that famously examined and later autopsied Sartjie Baartman, the best known of the many Hottentot Venuses. During his time as a professor at Harvard University, Agassiz engaged a community of scholars and elites in the widely held but debated theory of polygenesis, which posited that racial groups evolved from distinct and unequal species of humankind. A zoologist by training, Agassiz sought to capture images of human specimens to examine as racial "types"; typological images could be studied to decipher how the appearance and proportion of certain body parts explained intellectual, moral, and cultural differences between racial groups. Critical to his study was the innovation of photography, and in this case the use of the daguerreotype, as it captured a truer image of their specimens than illustrations had previously accomplished.

The daguerreotypes, ordered by Robert W. Gibbes and taken by Joseph T. Zealy, of the seven South Carolina slaves were not merely a product of the joining of medical and natural science and technology to organize a visual logic of race. They were also a form of voyeuristic violence. As Brian Wallis observes, "The typological photograph is a form of representational colonialism. Fundamentally nonreciprocal, it masks its subjective distortions in the guise of logic and organization. Its formations are deformations."[7] Typological photographs expose how black bodies became encoded by a body of scientific and cultural thought, through the "unalterable reasons of race," as "morally and intellectually inferior to whites."[8] The nakedness of the people documented in the photographs also exposes the differing gendering of racialized sexuality in what Mary Louise Pratt terms the "contact zones" of empire. In these images we observe a "social space where disparate cultures meet, clash, and grapple with each other," and the visual evidence of "highly asymmetrical relations of domination and subordination," of which gender is one dimension.[9]

The men are presented fully naked while Drana and Delia are shown with their calico homespun dresses pulled down to their waists. This differing nakedness offers a view into the desire of the white European and American scientists, the photographer, and the slaveholders located outside the frame of the image as it self-consciously confronts the gaze of the Other. For these elite white men the occlusion of female genitalia presented an ethnopornographic gesture whereby that which is not viewable in fact enhances the desire to look and to keep looking. Beyond mere voyeurism, this looking relationship provides a staged exposure in elaborating the *process* of undressing that belies any claims of modesty, civility, or respect for the enslaved women's privacy on the one hand and disavowal or repugnance on the other. Instead this partial nakedness ensured that the women remained firmly within an economy of desire and possession that concurrently traded in fear, disgust, and denial. Drana's photograph displays lines of scarring along pendulous breasts—part of the broader sexualized torture of enslaved men and women—showing that she had nursed enslaved babies for the profit of her owner.[10] The daguerreotypes thus present evidence of black female sexual labor under enslavement and a sexual political economy around their bodies.[11]

Moreover, with Drana and Delia's partial nakedness inviting scientific investigation, ethnopornography allows us to read the ways that the essential difference between black female bodies and white female bodies was signified. The chasm between nineteenth-century concepts of ideal white womanhood as essentialized purity, refinement, and aesthetic beauty, and conceptions of grotesque black womanhood are made apparent. Rather than act as aesthetic conventions of adornment, as seen in fine art and photographic portraiture, Drana and Delia's pulled-down dresses elicit an erotic charge through debasement, which again provides for the fantasy of the enslaved woman's sexual labor vis-à-vis concubinage, tourism, and trafficking. At that same time that an ethnopornographic frame reminds us to read the images for the relationships of power that give them context, my black feminist pornographic frame prompts a reading practice that considers how black women may have engaged with the pornographic codes, practices, and gazes taken up by Agassiz and his rowdy band of elite white male voyeurs. What did this visual project mean for the women in the photographs, and how might they have encountered it as an extension of their already ongoing sex work? Although art curator and critic Brian Wallis reads Drana and Delia as "calmly" revealing their breasts, their faces set like masks showing a deliberate "detached, unemotional, and workmanlike" expression, others, such as historian Molly Rogers, see tears in Delia's eyes.[12]

Indeed, looking closely at the frontal-view photograph of Delia, it appears that her eyes are welling up with tears and that she is on the very brink of crying. It is as if Delia is weighted down by an immense and irrevocable despair even as she tries to control her own body from revealing the surely complex emotions ignited by the setting of the photo shoot. The appearance of tears might also have been due to blurring during the nearly twenty-second process of capturing the image to each silver-covered copper plate of the daguerreotype, even though the iron headstand, known as the

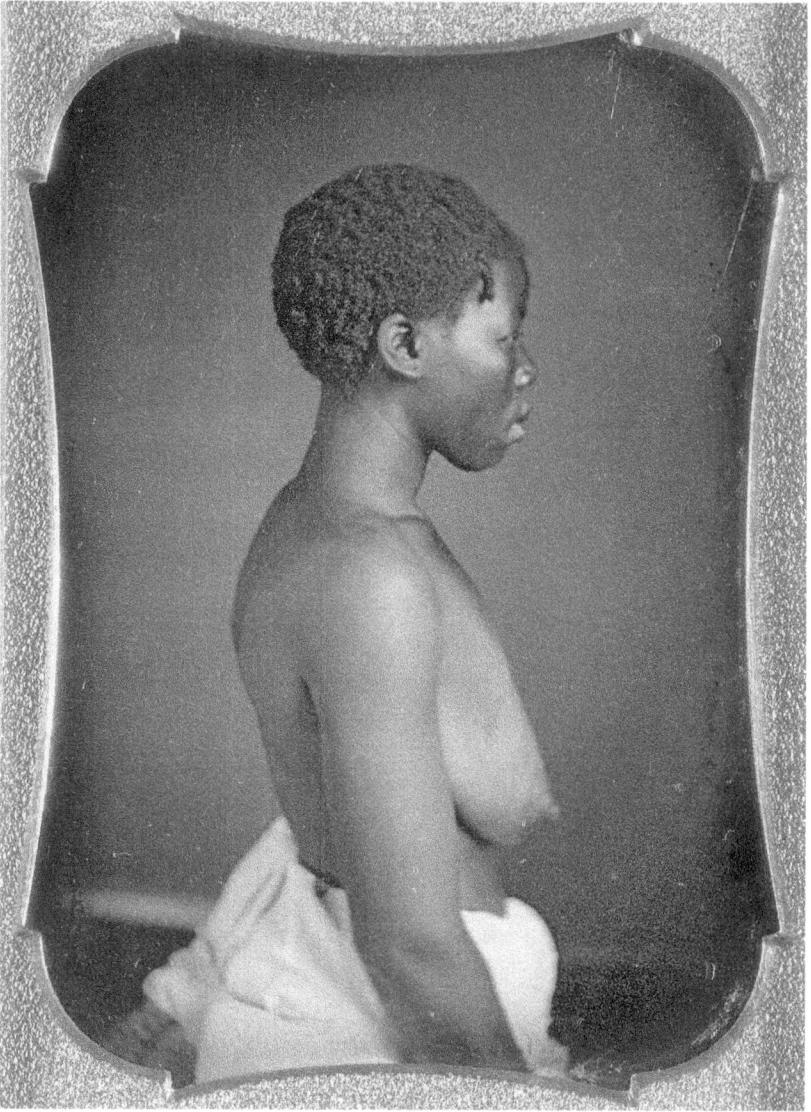

FIGURE I.I Drana (profile), daguerreotype by Joseph T. Zealy, 1850. Courtesy of the Peabody Museum of Archaeology and Ethnology, Harvard University, PM# 35-5-10/53042.

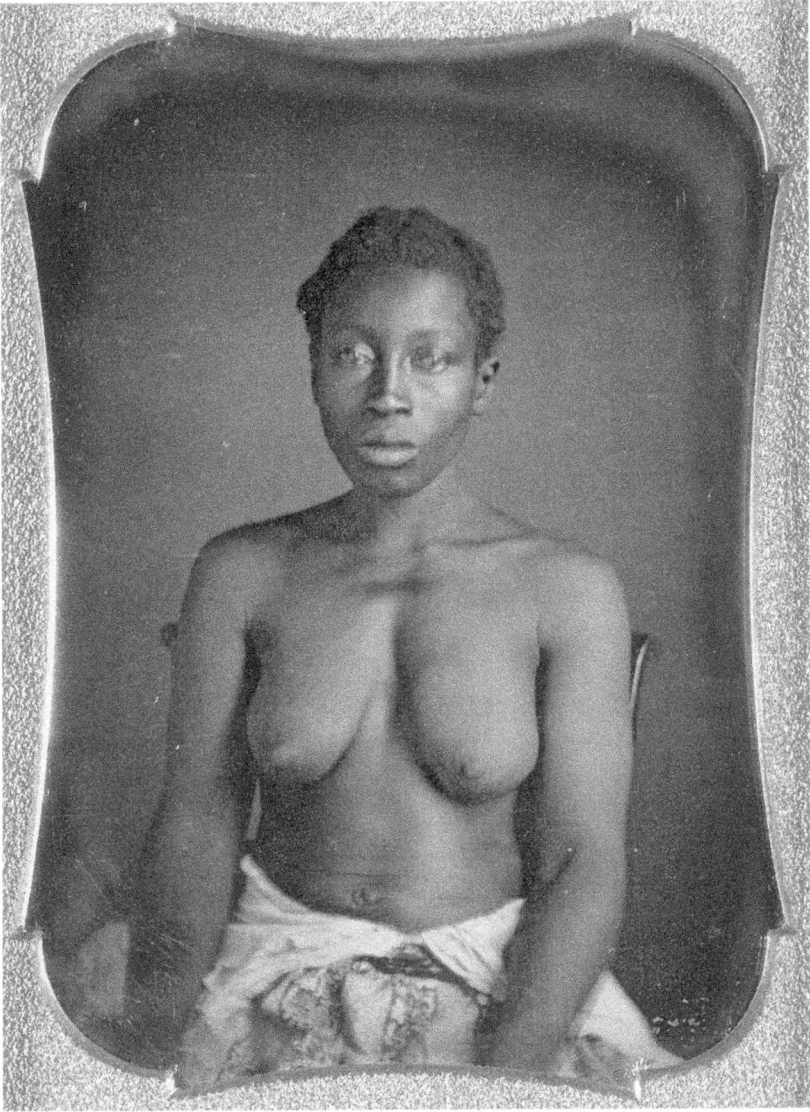

FIGURE I.2 Delia (frontal), daguerreotype by Joseph T. Zealy, 1850. Courtesy of the Peabody Museum of Archaeology and Ethnology, Harvard University, PM# 35-5-10/53042.

"iron instrument of torture,"[13] may have been used to keep the models still. Yet the technology itself could have powerfully registered for young Delia, a slave, like her father, Renty, at the Edgehill Plantation where the primary crop was cotton. Ordered to strip before a room full of men she did not know and who had total power over her life, and told to hold still with her neck in the iron brace, must have been frightening, intimidating, confusing, and uncomfortable, even painful.

It is impossible to know for sure what the diverse subjective experiences of the women in the images entailed, but here I assert that we pause to imagine what these women might have experienced and what their gazes back at the camera may have contributed to the ethnopornographic exchange. Through understanding the context of Agassiz's project, the shoot itself, and the inability of the enslaved to consent to what was being done to their bodies, while also remaining cognizant of the desire by slaves themselves to live sovereign sexual lives, it is conceivable to imagine that Drana and Delia—as two black women who became figures held captive by the convergence of visual power and pleasure—sensed the mighty weight of an imperial gaze upon them. This gaze may have felt scientific, cold, and distant, yet also probing, prurient, and interested. Perhaps these women understood the scientific gaze itself as part of the "careful stories" that were told that denied a clear, compelling erotic desire to plumb and evaluate Othered bodies.[14] Or perhaps they thought to say, "There was nothing—no secret—to be unveiled underneath my clothes. The secret was your phantasm."[15] Without their account of the experience we can only speculate about what was behind the gaze that the camera captured in that moment. Drana and Delia's need to strategically mask over—if Wallis is correct—detach from, or actively obscure their emotions can be understood in the context of their lack of power in the asymmetries of the ethnopornographic relationship. This strategy shows the embodied labor of representation for the objects of ethnopornographic display, and how ethnopornographic praxis is a contact zone for negotiations of dominance and oppression. I argue further that taking seriously the subjectivity and sexualized labor of the ethnopornographic subject means a necessary recovery of the slave or native point of view. Hence, the colonizing camera was not the only gaze in that studio.[16]

Agassiz's photographs were some of the earliest of American slaves. Later images depicted African Americans as nannies and house servants in portraits with their white owners, or working in the fields growing cotton, the dominant crop in the South in the years leading up to the Civil War, especially in the area surrounding Columbia, South Carolina, where

Joseph T. Zealy immortalized Drana and Delia in his photographic studio in 1850. Taken during the height of "daguerreotypomania" in the United States,[17] these photographs were markedly different from most images of African Americans or white Americans, who rushed to get their portraits taken as part of an emerging middle-class will to represent themselves. However, instead of being taken home in an intricately decorated, embossed leather holder and treasured, these images were brought to Harvard and presented at the Cambridge Scientific Club.[18] The elite white men of the club would have held the 3¼-by-4¼-inch daguerreotype plates in their hands while listening to Agassiz's lecture describing the ethnological roots of racial difference and comparative anatomical distinctions between those of African descent and those of European ancestry. To these men, the evidence of racial inferiority—whether they agreed with Agassiz's theories of polygenesis or not—would have been visible and tangible. The images of Drana and Delia, Molly Rogers posits, "resemble erotic and pornographic photographs."[19] "Such images were widely disdained in the nineteenth century, and yet they were still produced and consumed. Public nudity was associated with loose morals and so a person who was photographed without clothing was considered the lowest of the low socially. This was especially the case with black women."[20]

The Secret Museum

United States–produced ethnopornographic photography during the late nineteenth century and early twentieth largely consisted of images of Native American women, Asian immigrant women, and Pacific Islanders, but I have discovered in my years of research that a sizable circulation of black women's erotic images emerged from European colonies and imperial occupations in Africa at a time of rising fascination in the United States and Western Europe with the penetration of the African interior, the competitions for territory among nations, and the extraction of resources such as rubber, diamonds, cocoa, and minerals. A compendium of hundreds of ethnographic photographs from the period called *The Secret Museum of Mankind* reveals the vast extent to which imperial centers sought to map the bodies of their peripheries and how the popular interest in native peoples among Westerners was cultivated. The original text is of unknown origins, with no editor or year of publication listed, only a publisher called Manhattan House based out of New York. Booksellers suggest editions were published in 1925, 1935, and

1941, although the images are from the late nineteenth century up through the 1920s. Interestingly, a new edition was put out fairly recently by David Stiffler and Gibbs Smith Publishers of Layton, Utah, in 1999, which speaks to the ongoing market for such images. The text may be named after or linked to the Museum of Mankind in Britain, affiliated with the Ethnography Department of the British Museum.

And like ethnographic displays in museums, the text is divided into sections for each region of the colonial world. The extensive collection of images reflects the interplay as well as the intensely slippery boundaries between anthropological and ethnographic science, the colonial apparatus of surveillance, and mass-market pornography. Each image is accompanied by a caption, though it is unclear whether the origin of the caption emerged at the time the photograph was produced by colonial anthropologists and photographers or later, in Europe or America, when the photographs were most likely copied and reproduced.[21] The titles and captions are just as salient as the images, I argue, because they claim to decode the image while actually serving to encode it within a normalizing discourse embedded in exoticism, exploitation, and myth.[22]

For example, the photograph *Buttered Beauty of the Negroid North* presents a "girl of Tigré" who has "buttered," or oiled, her hair in an intricate design. The caption tells us that, "at night she sleeps with her head on a wooden rest." Because the image suggests that the presence of the girl, or more correctly, young woman, was a racial type—interchangeable with all the girls of Tigré, and even the "Negroid North" of Africa—she is presented in isolation. She is thus made to represent all the people—a community— that are not visible. The young woman's exposed breasts are presented frontally, while her face is placed in profile—an amalgam of the methods of taxonomic portraits much in use during the nineteenth century following the work of Cuvier and Agassiz. This pose of the model looking over her shoulder, and the placement of her necklace, allows the spectator a sense of access and the ability to observe the model's "buttered" chest, while the painted overlay of the photograph creates an unreal quality to the portrait.

This image is typical in its use of ethnopornographic framing to accelerate the erotic charge of the image for viewers. This description of how the young woman from Tigré uses oils to fashion her hair and how at night she sleeps with a wooden headrest highlights the fascinating difference of her primitiveness in relation to Western practices of grooming and habitation, while it also facilitates an imagined image of the model's body in repose, her skin soft, warm, and oily. The subtext of arousal through the con-

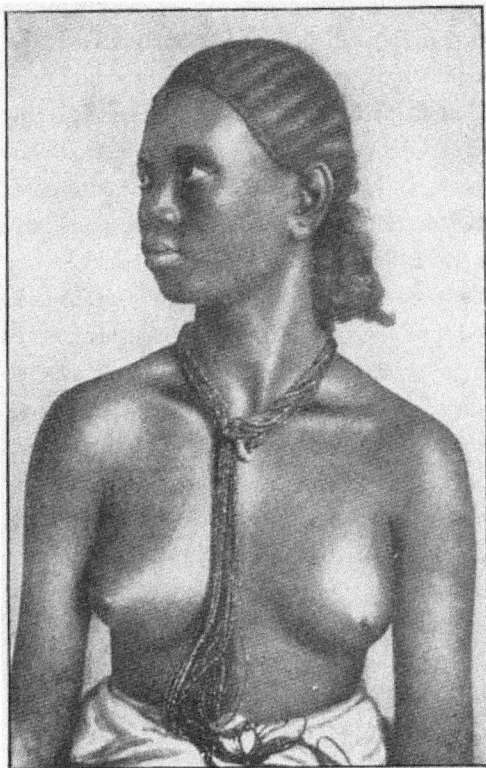

FIGURE I.3 *Buttered Beauty of the Negroid North.* The Museum of Mankind (Manhattan House, 1941 edition).

struction of the image of the young woman oiling her body in the private quarters of her room or hut is signified through the invisible icon of the headrest. This strategy infuses ethnopornographic images that, as Malek Alloula argues, reference the invisible but embedded fantasy of the native's limitless sexual life for the imperial observer. Like the photographs Alloula controversially reproduced of North African women with their nudity peaking through their veils,[23] referencing the fantasy of the harem, these colonial photographs of sub-Saharan African women suggest an imagined universe of abundant and deviant sexual practices and powers. "What is remembered about the harem," Alloula observes, "are the sexual excesses to which it gives rise and which it promotes. A universe of *generalized perversion* and of the *absolute limitlessness of pleasure*."[24]

By the 1880s the vast expansion of photography, through its transformation into a mass visual form, had broad implications for the production and consumption of eroticized images of black women in Africa and the Diaspora. Postcards became a primary form of visual communication important for their easy accessibility and affordability, especially for the working classes and rising middle class of the Industrial era. Because postcards communicated through photographs on the front and written messages on the back, they had mass-market appeal; they were "cheap, bright, multi-purpose and pervasive."[25] Between 1894 and 1919 nearly 140 billion postcards were sent worldwide, and an unknown but significant number of these had sexual themes.[26] According to Lisa Z. Sigel, sexual postcards of "domestic" bodies (i.e., white, European or American) could be sent through the mail only if they properly censored men's and women's genitals, but ethnopornographic postcards exposing the uncensored naked bodies of colonial or "foreign" subjects, both women and men, were allowable.[27] Ethnographic postcards featuring "natives" in their "natural" habitats were highly popular and profoundly affected how "foreign" bodies were seen within Western discourses of race, in ways similar to the small daguerreotypes of South Carolina slaves held in the hands of the men at the Cambridge Scientific Club, that were exceedingly tangible. Practices of capturing, circulating, and collecting postcards and other photographic artifacts of exoticized "primitives" were thus normalized for Western audiences.[28] In this way, postcards were an important technology in bringing women of African descent, and others, within the surveying, commercial, and disciplining power of a pornographic empire.

This visual economy of images voraciously consumed by scientific, bourgeois, and working-class audiences rendered indigenous peoples "anonymous and historyless subjects" and photographs of them collectible "image objects" and commodities.[29] Essential to the processes of imperial, capitalist expansion into non-Western lands, the photograph itself expanded the empire's ability to, as bell hooks would put it, "eat the other."[30] Mass-market photographic objects made black women newly viewable, and thus subject to novel forms of visual social control. Fatimah Tobing Rony usefully terms this quite obsessive consumption of the racial Other, made possible by ethnographic image making, "fascinating cannibalism."[31] Drawing attention to the combination of "fascination and horror" that the ethnographic evokes, Tobing Rony explains that "the cannibalism is not that of the people who are labeled Savages, but that of the consumers of the images of the bodies—as well as the actual bodies on display—of native people offered up by popular media and science."[32]

Ethnographic postcards employed a "staged nakedness"[33]—photographers manipulated the women's bodies, the settings, and the photographs themselves in order to emphasize a perceived exotic sexuality.[34] Through this heavy manipulation, the Western viewer confronted a spectacular differ-ence. The cannibalistic drive of a kind of sexual tourism reflected a growing hunger for information about "primitive" societies and their ways of life. While these images supported ideologies of white supremacy by indulg-ing the curiosity of people who saw themselves as more advanced than the savages, their main purpose was to depict how nonwhite people lived and to romanticize and exoticize the images in order to make money. Ethno-pornography thus involves the merging of the ethnographic and the com-mercial, a form of voyeuristic and titillating entertainment hidden behind the guise of scientific documentation and innocent curiosity about the lives of racial Others.

Ethnopornography exhibited African women as spectacles, and used their actual bodies and sexual labor to create marketable entertainment for Western appetites at the precise time when European countries were moving to explore, divide, and conquer the continent. Captured mainly by Western male photographers who traveled with military campaigns, sci-entific expeditions, or alone as entrepreneurs or tourists, or who were sta-tioned or took up residence in colonized areas, the photographs served as travel accounts "through which the world saw the indigenous people" of Africa.[35] The archive of ethnographic postcards from the late nineteenth century remains dispersed across the globe—emerging from time to time in Parisian flea markets, online collectors' forums, and the attics of some-one's grandfather's house. They are now artifacts of historical, asymmetri-cal power relations and violence that provide the context for each image of bare-breasted, young, native girls. Fetishistically made, circulated, and con-sumed, the images do not depict the violence of colonialism and imperialism but create a fantasy absent of violence and of history. Most of the postcards I discovered from the era were from French-colonized North Africa, though many images of French West African women and girls exist that were circu-lated in less commercial forms as paper-printed photographs.

I found a postcard in the streets of Paris sent from Tangier, Morocco, to Orleans, France, stamped in 1908 (fig. 1.4). It shows a young woman with short, soft curly hair presented in a traditional medium-view seated pose. Reminiscent of Agassiz's daguerreotypes of Drana and Delia, the photog-rapher has positioned the woman sitting with her hands in her lap and her dress pulled, billowing, down to her waist so as to expose her youth-ful breasts and part of her flat stomach. This effect of staged nakedness serves to heighten the woman's vulnerability to be visibly possessed for the photographer creating the image, the consumer purchasing the postcard, and the final viewer who receives it. Only in this image her body is not shown in a hard scientific frontal view; instead, in the softer erotic view of so many ethnopornographic postcards, she faces slightly away from the camera, and her gaze looks off into the distance, echoing formal tropes in Western painting and portraiture. The rows of beads around her neck and the plain background accentuate her body as the focal point of the image. To allure the viewer, the photographer painted color on the black-and-white image: her skin a deep brown; her patterned dress teal blue, pink, and brown; her beaded necklace pink; her eyelids blue; and her slightly parted lips are painted an impossibly bright, garish red. This coloring—particularly of the lips—creates an image of primitive luridness, and the added makeup marks the model's body as a sight of manipulation and ex-aggeration, a fantasy text.

The postcard includes the common ethnographic description that marked the women in these images within representations of racial types, such as "Types Indigènes—Une Négresse," "Jeune Négresse," "Jeune Béd-ouine," "Jeune Mauresque."[36] The caption describes the woman as a "Jeune Esclave Arabe," a young Arab slave. Like so many French postcards of the era, the youth of the girl is noted. This account of age—and many of the images I discovered in my research are of prepubescent girls and young women—is a particular fetishistic device, as it heightens the fantasy of vul-nerability, that the model's virginity could be taken by the viewer himself. The comments about the model's imagined status as a black African made into an Arab slave amplifies the quality of vulnerability—she is already owned, and therefore does not own herself.[37]

The back of the postcard is signed simply, "Cordiale poignee de mains, A. Boulet" (A cordial handshake, A. Boulet) (fig. 1.5). Boulet, perhaps a tourist, bureaucrat, or soldier working for the French colonial authority in Tangier, would have sent this card to his friend or colleague ("Monsieur Jean Mathè") as a gesture acknowledging his travels in a primitive land, and his fortunate access as a potential sex tourist to a variety of exotic women and girls. A hearty handshake—such an oddly short message—offers a joke or quip, a kind of bawdy humor referencing the girl in the image, her ex-posed breasts being nearly a handful and ripe to be held by eager hands.

The immense force of desire in this postcard (including the photograph and the note behind it) reinforces Tobing Rony's concept of "fascinating cannibalism" and what Malek Alloula describes as the construction of exoticized, primitive women as "available, consenting, welcoming, excit-ing, submissive and possessed."[38] While images of white women in post-

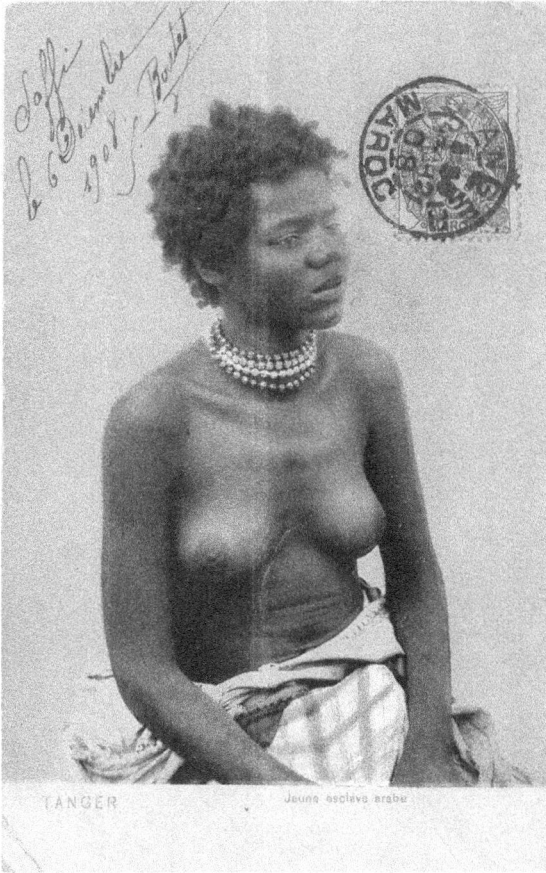

FIGURE I.4 1908 Postcard from Tangier to Orleans (front). Collection of Mireille Miller-Young.

cards from the Victorian era similarly frame them as passive, waiting, and available objects for men's viewing pleasure, women of color represented debased rather than idealized forms of womanhood. The messages written on the backs of these cards often use humor or dismissive remarks to comment on what Europeans at the time generally viewed as the barbaric and anachronistic culture of African people, which was deemed evident in the display of African women's (partial) nudity. These comments poke fun at the idea of African women's desirability but nonetheless show the vast networks through which a desire to consume their images was mobilized. Thousands of postcards of African women during the late nineteenth and early twentieth century ritually re-created the trope of the exotic Other,

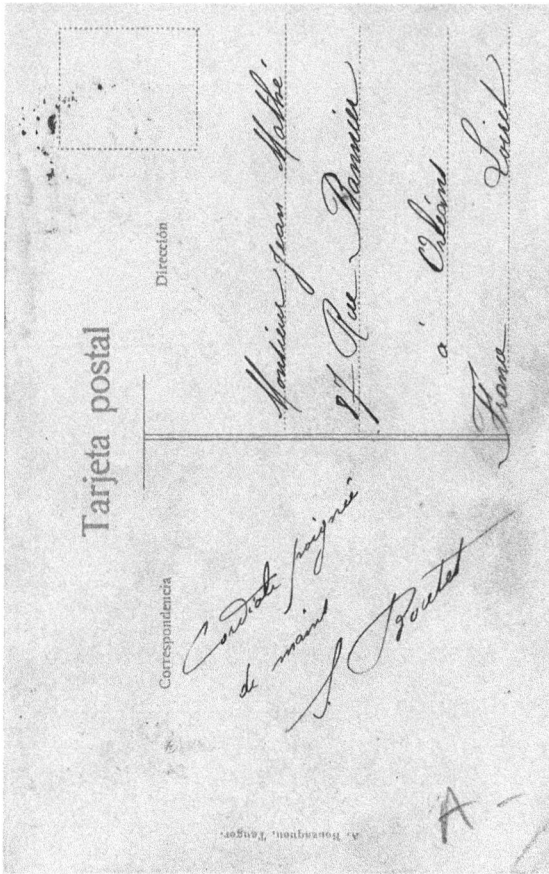

FIGURE I.5 1908 Postcard from Tangier to Orleans (back). Collection of Mireille Miller-Young.

and in the process they ritualized the use of an ethnopornographic gaze to see the imperial landscape expand.[39] Although postcards tended to render native bodies as novelty items for public consumption, there were other forms of ethnopornography that, being even more explicit, were disseminated in less public forums.

Some images taken by soldiers stationed in West Africa exhibit them posing with tribal girls and young women. Standing with their arms around girls' shoulders, hands grasping their nubile breasts, the soldiers are seen smiling directly at the camera, appearing confident and pleased. The shots are often poorly cropped, showing the amateur nature of the photographer and the makeshift or impromptu context in which the photograph was taken. For instance, in figure 1.6, the camera cuts off the man's head. Even if they may have been some of the primary spectators and consumers of postcard, white men, including photographers, soldiers, or colonial officials, who had sexual relations with the women and girls in the images were never visible in postcards. In their own photographs, however, they appear happy to be memorialized in the image and often take center stage. In addition, we can imagine that these shots may have been highly valued mementos for colonial visitors to Africa, as the apparent horizontal crease in the photograph above seems to reveal that someone carried this photograph on his person—perhaps in a shirt pocket—rather than keep it mounted in a frame or album. Alternately, the crease could represent the act of concealing—folding and stashing away—such a revealing and explicit image that places the man not simply as observer of native sexual display but as active consumer and participant in the construction of an interracial colonial sexual relationship.

These "selfie" photographs essentially brag about these men's access to native women—notably in ways that were not allowed for African men and European women—and as a result would have been exchanged and viewed in a more private and underground economy of ethnopornography. In this way, and in their frank acknowledgment of a colonial sex industry, these kinds of images were precursors to the hard-core images we see in later commercial pornographies.[40] Not only does the presence of these European men in the image confess the desire they had for African women—a desire that was normatively disavowed—their inclusion in these collective photographs shows that their interest went beyond a passive fetishization and actually amounted to a sexual relationship (perhaps sometimes violent or coercive but always unequal) with these women in which they wanted to see themselves as agents and actors. In figure 1.7, one man dressed in what is perhaps a military officer or administrator's crisp white uniform stands between two young women who wear matching waist beads, headscarves, and necklaces in front of a straw house. The man is holding the young women on either side of him by the waist, and just inside the doorway of the house we see a bed propped on wooden legs with checkered sheets and pillowcases. While I cannot decipher from this image if this man was visiting a house of prostitution, the placement of the bed and the touristic nature of the portrait raise the possibility.

Photographs of black women and girls in highly sexual poses and contexts, in huts or outdoor settings but also in makeshift studios, were taken not for the postcard trade but for a much more underground market in

FIGURE I.6 Grasping for Power, Hidden from View. Undated Photograph, Soldier with Hands on the Breasts of Two Women. Kinsey Institute for Research in Sex, Gender, and Reproduction, Art, Artifacts, and Photography Special Collection (KIDC 1123).

early pornographic images or for private keeping. Although many West African tribes did not view women as being "naked" without clothing—as long as they wore their prized waist beads or waist clothes they were considered decently attired—the fascination with these women's perceived nakedness by European standards read onto their bodies an obscenity and hypersexualization that was not organic to these communities. These photographs warp, deform, and exploit these women's unclothed bodies, simultaneously representing and misrepresenting the bodies and subjectivities of the colonized women whose bodies they portray. By transforming the meanings around their bodies, the photographs make the women naked through the fascinating cannibalism of a voracious ethnopornographic gaze. Such photographs showed women sitting with one knee up or both knees up and spread, reclining in an Odalisque pose with arms behind the head, the knees open, the camera positioned so as to provide a direct line to the coveted black vulva. Reminiscent of Cuvier's forceful desire to view the "Hottentot Apron"—which he was not able to do until Sartjie Baartman died and he dissected her—these photographers show a

FIGURE I.7 Revealing a Colonial Sexual Economy? Undated Photograph from Colonial West Africa, Soldier Posing with Two Young Women [M126]. Courtesy of Les Archives d'Eros.

cannibalistic and fetishistic obsession with the "Dark Continent" of African women and girls, especially below their waists, to the fount of mystery and locus of their assumed difference: the dark heart of Africa seemed to be found in their sexual parts.

These images reinforce the violence and exploitation of the ethnopornographic gaze as part of the imperialist project in Africa. They hypersexualize and pathologize black female bodies through a heavy desire that is as much about racialist fantasy, unequal power relations, and the erasure of the history and values of multiple civilizations as it is about visualizing sex. Multiple forces of subjection put women and girls in the position in which photographers used them for pleasure and profit. Yet some of the images can be read as holding more complicated scenarios than simply the abjection of women at the hands of horny and greedy men with cameras. We see moments, frozen in time by the photograph, in which these women appear to challenge the imperial gaze. They gaze back, even taking some pleasure or amusement in posing alone or with other women. We see them smile, scowl, make funny faces, relax, or make themselves comfortable. In

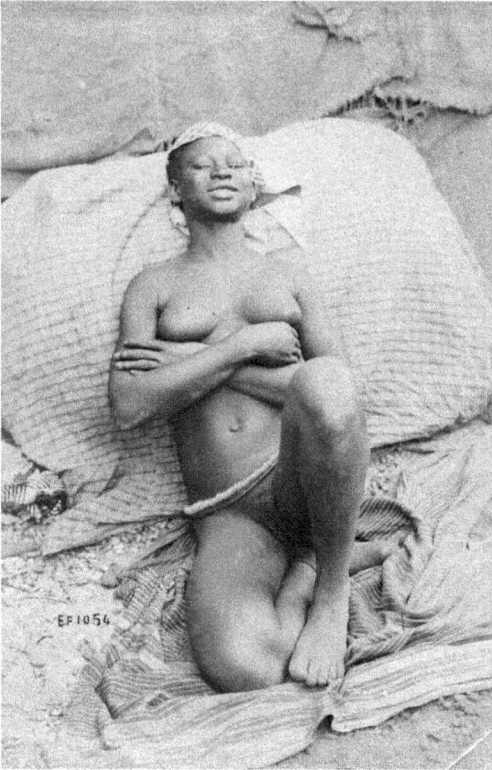

FIGURE I.8 A Voracious
Ethnopornographic
Gaze. Undated Colonial
Studio Photograph
[Mo24]. Courtesy of Les
Archives d'Eros.

the limited artifacts that remain we find evidence of contestation, curiosity, and playfulness in their expressions alongside demonstrations of disgust, sadness, solemnity, fear, suspicion, or boredom.

These complex and varied expressions suggest some level of consciousness and self-awareness by these women that they were performing sexuality for the camera and for someone else's fantasy. It also suggests a kind of erotic subjectivity in what amounts to a form of black women's sexual labor—the labor of erotic performance entailed black women to be "performers, and not just bodies."[41] Here, the faciality of the models matters to our analyses. Facial expressions give clues to the potential emotional and intellectual lives of the models, illuminating a possible range of attitudes and experiences, including curiosity.

These moments of returning the gaze are of course constrained and complicated by the overwhelming context of exploitation and repression in colonial Africa at the turn of the century, especially for women and girls who held the least power in most settings. We do not know to what ex-

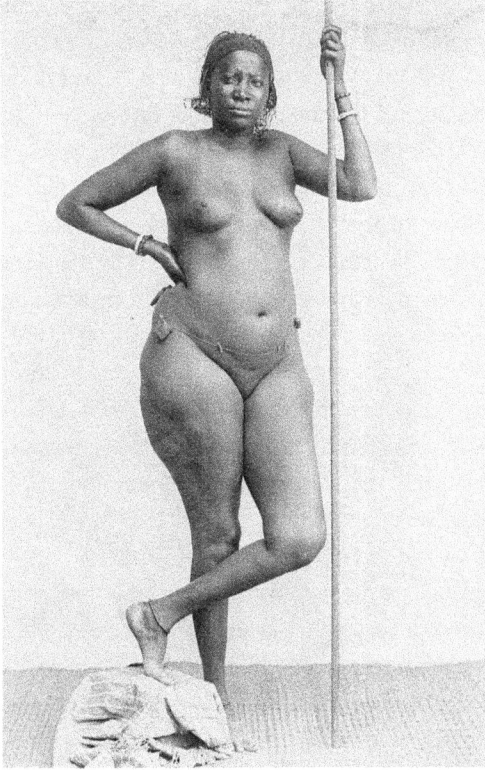

FIGURE I.9 Black Women
Do Gaze Back. Undated
Colonial Studio Photo-
graph [Mo2o]. Courtesy
of Les Archives d'Eros.

tent these autonomous glances and expressions amounted to any benefit, pleasure, or power for the women captured in time. It is unclear if the women were compensated for their modeling labor, but given the ongoing trade in sexual services in the postcolonial landscape, the enduring nature of sex tourism in relationships of vast inequality and in zones of imperial occupation and leisure, and the deep attachment that photographers and soldiers in the colonies had to their notions of capital exchange and currencies of erotic exchange, it is certainly possible that the models were compensated, either monetarily or with other resources or services. What is vital to confront, in addition, is the possibility of thinking about objectification beyond a one-way, unified, and assaultive gaze. Multiple gazes and subjectivities are possible and probable.[42]

This is not to deny the institutional and systemic power of the pornographic gaze, or to argue to its democratic nature,[43] but to propose instead that the objectifying force and heavy desire of the gaze could have been met with another gaze, and that this other gaze that acknowledged the ways ethnopornography kept viewers looking, and also looked back, constituted a subjective understanding of the myth of hypersexuality and the means by which one could put that conceptual vice to work. Thus I draw upon my theoretical interventions in my book *A Taste for Brown Sugar*, to argue that, indeed, using a black feminist pornographic reading practice allows us to posit the ways in which black women sex workers (including sexualized women drawn in unwittingly to the labor of sexual representation in ethnopornographies) engaged a politics of *illicit eroticism*.[44] By this term I am asserting that black women mobilized sexual myth and representation for their own uses, including to survive, to gain mobility, to profit, to be titillated, to critique the system, and even to explore the technical and political qualities of image-making devices such as the camera. A black feminist reading practice allows for the prospect of thinking about other types of gazes, black female gazes, as humanizing, sensual, complicit, or oppositional—it unlocks our analysis of black female subjectivity and unbinds these black female subjects from the weight of their representational work.[45]

An exclusive focus on critiquing how and why black female bodies were fetishized as objects of desire and disgust in pornographic visual regimes "all too often leaves in place the process by which" black women were constructed as objects.[46] Moreover, it denies the erotic and embodied political experience of models, as well as their sexual labor, as part of their anticolonial work. And so, too, it obscures rather than reveals the ways in which black women may have located the sexual economy of ethnopornography and the interracial interactions that produced this media as a site of pleasure, excitement, and expression.

Employing an ethnopornographic hermeneutic or method, scholars may begin to consider the ways in which the interplay of science, technology, and commercial interests with nationalist state imperatives to expand empire at any cost produce opportunities to think about these pornographic representations as contact zones for domination and subordination as well as for subversion and resistance. Beyond an easy claim for an always already oppositional gaze, I mean here to push our field to think about ethnopornography not simply as a technique for fixing power but also, when looking from the point of view of the subject of the image, for disrupting power. "People on the receiving end of European imperialism did their own knowing and interpreting," Mary Louise Pratt suggests, "sometimes . . . using the European's own tools."[47] And this is the reason that I have included pornographic images in my work. Rather than refusing the mantel of pornographer that is thrust upon those of us engaging

FIGURE I.10 Ethnopor-
nographic Disruptions.
Undated Colonial Studio
Photograph [M119]. Cour-
tesy of Les Archives d'Eros.

closely with these images (by Google, the public, our students, or other scholars), I embrace this identity because it means that I am making visible, tangible, or otherwise understood the very complicated dual work of violence and reappropriation, of exploitation and transformation, and of racist objectification and disruptive subaltern subjectivity.

Notes

1   I develop this concept in Mireille Miller-Young, *A Taste for Brown Sugar: Black Women in Pornography* (Durham, NC: Duke, 2014).

2   Ann Laura Stoller, *Race and the Education of Desire: Foucault's History of Sexuality and the Colonial Order of Things* (Durham, NC: Duke University Press, 1995), 6–7.

3   See my preface, "Confessions of a Black Feminist Academic Pornographer," in Miller-Young, *Taste for Brown Sugar*.

4 T. Denean Sharpley-Whiting, *Black Venus: Sexualized Savages, Primal Fears, and Primitive Narratives in French* (Durham, NC: Duke University Press), 7.

5 A number of important books by black feminist theorists have advanced my thinking about black women's representations in nineteenth- and early twentieth-century photography, ethnopornographies, and pornographies: Carla Williams and Deborah Willis, *The Black Female Body: A Photographic History* (Philadelphia, PA: Temple University Press, 2002); Deborah Willis, ed., *Black Venus 2010: They Called Her "Hottentot"* (Philadelphia, PA: Temple University Press, 2010); Jennifer L. Morgan, *Laboring Women: Reproduction and Gender in New World Slavery* (Philadelphia: University of Pennsylvania Press, 2004); Kimberly Wallace Sanders, ed., *Skin Deep, Spirit Strong: The Black Female Body in American Culture* (Ann Arbor: University of Michigan Press, 2002); Michelle Wallace, *Dark Designs and Visual Culture* (Durham, NC: Duke University Press, 2004); Nicole Fleetwood, *Troubling Vision: Performance, Visuality, and Blackness* (Chicago, IL: University of Chicago Press, 2011); Jasmine Nicole Cobb, *Picturing Freedom: Remaking Black Visuality in the Early Nineteenth Century* (New York: New York University Press, 2015); Jennifer Nash, *The Black Body in Ecstasy: Reading Race, Reading Pornography* (Durham, NC: Duke University Press, 2014).

6 The article that really opened up the field of study into the Hottentot Venus is Sander Gilman, "Black Bodies, White Bodies: Toward an Iconography of Female Sexuality in Late Nineteenth-Century Art, Medicine, and Literature," *Critical Inquiry* 12, no. 1 (autumn 1985): 204–42.

7 Brian Wallis, "Black Bodies, White Science: Louis Agassiz's Slave Daguerreotypes," in *Only Skin Deep: Changing Visions of the American Self*, ed. Coco Fusco and Brian Wallis (New York: Harry N. Abrams, 2003), 54–55.

8 George M. Frederickson, *The Black Image in the White Mind: The Debate on African American Character and Destiny, 1817–1914* (Middletown, CT: Wesleyan University Press, 1971), 2.

9 Mary Louise Pratt, *Imperial Eyes: Travel Writing and Transculturation*, (New York: Routledge, 1992) 7.

10 Shawn Michelle Smith, *Photography on the Colorline: W. E. B. Du Bois, Race, and Visual Culture* (Durham, NC: Duke University Press, 2004), 47.

11 Adrienne Davis, "Don't Let Nobody Bother Yo' Principle: The Sexual Economy of American Slavery," in *Sister Circle: Black Women and Work*, ed. Sharon Harley and the Black Women and Work Collective (New Brunswick, NJ: Rutgers, 2002).

12 Wallis, "Black Bodies, White Science," 40; Molly Rogers, *Delia's Tears: Race, Science, and Photography in Nineteenth-Century America* (New Haven, CT: Yale University Press), 247.

13 Ross J. Kelbaugh, *Introduction to African American Photographs, 1840–1950: Identification, Research, Care, and Collecting* (Gettysburg, PA: Thomas Publications, 2005), 16.

14 Walter Johnson, *Soul by Soul: Life Inside the Antebellum Slave Market* (Cambridge, MA: Harvard University Press, 2001), 149.

15 Rey Chow, "Where Have All the Natives Gone?," in *Displacements: Cultural Identities in Question*, ed. Angelika Bammer (Bloomington: Indiana University Press, 1994), 145.

16 Here I am indebted to the work of Walter Johnson (*Soul by Soul*) and his rich development of the subjective lives of the enslaved and careful work around agency in the context of slavery.

17 Johnson, *Soul by Soul*, 13.

18 Rogers, *Delia's Tears*, 241–47.

19 Rogers, *Delia's Tears*, 246.

20 Rogers, *Delia's Tears*, 246.

21 Catherine A. Lutz and Jane L. Collins, *Reading National Geographic* (Chicago, IL: University of Chicago Press, 1993).

22 Henrietta Lidchi, "The Poetics and Politics of Exhibiting Other Cultures," in *Representation: Cultural Representations and Signifying Practices*, ed. Stuart Hall (Thousand Oaks, CA: Sage Publications, 1997).

23 See Rey Chow's critique of Alloula's use of images in *The Colonial Harem* in "Where Have All the Natives Gone?," 145.

24 Malek Alloula, *The Colonial Harem* (Manchester, UK: Manchester University Press, 1987), 95; emphasis in original.

25 Lisa Z. Sigel, "Filth in the Wrong People's Hands: Postcards and the Expansion of Pornography in Britain and the Atlantic World, 1880–1914," *Journal of Social History* 33, no. 4 (summer 2000): 860. Sigel points out that postcards were much more accessible because they did not require a viewing apparatus—such as with stereoscopes and transparencies—and were far cheaper. After the 1890s postcards could be sent easily and inexpensively but with noted censorship. "Obscene" cards would have been placed in an envelope if they were mailed, retaining discretion, rather than sent directly, as government authorities began to police them.

26 Sigel, "Filth," 861.

27 Sigel, "Filth."

28 Sigel, "Filth," 861–62.

29 Deborah Poole, *Vision, Race, and Modernity: A Visual Economy of the Andean Image World* (Princeton, NJ: Princeton University Press, 1997), 140.

30 bell hooks, *Black Looks: Race and Representation* (Boston, MA: South End Press, 1992), 21–39.

31 Fatimah Tobing Rony, *The Third Eye: Race, Cinema, and Ethnographic Spectacle* (Durham, NC: Duke University Press, 1996), 10.

32 Rony, *Third Eye*, 10.

33 Sigel, "Filth," 862.

34 Sigel, "Filth," 862.

35 Aleta M. Ringlero, "Prairie Pinups," in Fusco and Wallis, *Only Skin Deep*, 186.

36 The translations from the French read, "Indigenous Types—A Negress," "Young Negress," "Young Bedouin," and "Young Moorish Woman." According to this website about French colonial texts, "Négresse" was not a direct translation for

black woman but was also not the same as saying "Negro" or the epithet "Nigger." It was less offensive than the latter but stronger and more demeaning than "Negro" or "black." See Washington State University Vancouver, accessed August 21, 2015, http://directory.vancouver.wsu.edu/people/sue-peabody/french-colonial-texts.

37 Slavery, having been abolished in the West by 1908, still continued in Morocco, so here we have an anachronistic sentiment toward the young slave.

38 Alloula, *Colonial Harem*, 122.

39 Sigel, "Filth," 864.

40 On the rise of modern hard-core pornography, see Linda Williams, *Hard Core: Power, Pleasure and the "Frenzy of the Visible"* (Berkeley: University of California Press, 1989).

41 Rony, *Third Eye*, 24.

42 Maria Sturken and Lisa Cartright, *Practices of Looking: An Introduction to Visual Culture* (Oxford: Oxford University Press, 2001), 87.

43 Lisa Gail Collins, "Historic Retrievals: Confronting Visual Evidence and the Imagining of Truth," in Willis, *Black Venus 2010*, 77.

44 Miller-Young, *Taste for Brown Sugar*.

45 On the binds of representation, see Celine Parrenas Shimizu, *The Hypersexuality of Race: Performing Asian/American Women on Screen and Scene* (Durham, NC: Duke University Press, 2007). On representational work, see Stuart Hall, ed., *Representation: Cultural Representations and Signifying Practices* (Thousand Oaks, CA: Sage Publications, Open University, 1997).

46 Rony, *Third Eye*, 24.

47 Pratt, *Imperial Eyes*, 7.

"Hung, Hot, and Shameless in Bed"

*Blackness, Desire, and Politics in a Brazilian Gay
Porn Magazine, 1997–2008*

"You've never seen anything sooooo big." This was the cover caption for
the February 2007 issue of *G Magazine*, Brazil's most successful publication directed at a gay male audience. The model was Iran Gomes, a recent
contestant on the hit reality show *Big Brother Brasil*. Iran wore a white suit,
silk shirt, and straw hat, with gold chains hanging from his neck. With one
hand jauntily placed in a pocket, the other seductively pulling aside his
shirt, his posture slightly slouched, he would have been recognizable to any
Brazilian as a *malandro*, a stock figure of Rio de Janeiro popular culture
since the early twentieth century.[1] Frequently imagined as dark-skinned,
the malandro is a chronically and willfully unemployed hustler who wears
gaudy jewelry, a white suit, and a straw hat and wanders about the urban
landscape composing samba songs, supporting himself through odd jobs
and cons. The subtext behind Iran's posture and vaguely sullen facial expression, along with the contrast between the shadowy background, the
suit, and his black skin, was clear. Black is exotic. Black is dangerous. Black
is sex. As one reader commented in an online message board dedicated to

the magazine, "These big black guys (*negões*) are extremely hung, hot, and shameless in bed."[2]

This chapter analyzes how desires and fantasies about blackness, through both their presence and absence, structured erotic and political representations of African-descended men in *G Magazine*. Between its founding in 1997 and sale in 2008, *G* was Brazil's best-selling publication targeted at an audience identified as "gay," a term appropriated directly from English with its connotations of a globalized identification based upon male same-sex desire. While articles on travel and fashion, as well as LGBT activism, occupied many of the magazine's glossy pages, the engine driving sales was the pornographic photographs (with erections) of straight-identified athletes, musicians, singers, and TV stars, their bodies on display for an implicitly upper- and middle-class audience. In keeping with Brazilian society's pervasive association between whiteness, beauty, and wealth on the one hand and blackness, ugliness, and poverty on the other, the magazine's cover models were overwhelmingly white. Afro-Brazilian men did appear on occasion, but when they did, the magazine's gaze was profoundly ethnopornographic, as it nearly invariably represented eroticized black and brown models as malandros, primitive natives, athletes, samba artists, or manual laborers, their racial and class "other-ness" granting them their value in a capitalist marketplace of same-sex desire.[3]

Yet this was only one facet of how the magazine's editors and readers gazed upon and appropriated black bodies. Paradoxically, alongside these racialized erotic representations, *G* self-consciously advanced a political discourse that claimed to challenge nationalist myths of racial democracy and promote an alliance between Brazil's black and LGBT movements. This tension between desire and identity politics seems odd, even jarring, at first glance. Yet it was at the heart of the magazine's representations of African-descended men and demonstrates that even as Brazil's black movement has successfully brought attention to racism and promoted policies to remedy inequality, erotic representation remains governed by racialized discourses so firmly rooted that even a well-intentioned, politically progressive magazine reinforced them as it represented black bodies as consumable fetishes for a white capitalist market.

If one were to examine only *G Magazine*'s "discourse of desire" via its sexualized photographic and written representations of African-descended men, it would be easy to condemn the magazine as simply another example of the silences and stereotyping that pervade global representations of African-descended people. However, focusing solely on the magazine's parallel "discourse of identity politics" could lead to the flawed conclusion that *G* was on the cutting edge of progressive racial politics. This chapter avoids such a dichotomous understanding through an empirical analysis of production and reception, as revealed through a broad range of sources. In addition to analyzing an eleven-year run of the magazine, including photographs, captions, reader-contributed erotic stories, personals ads, and letters to the editor, it uses social media, online interviews, and chat sessions with models. It also incorporates my own face-to-face interview with *G Magazine*'s owner, Ana Fadigas, and her editor, Klifit Pugini, to explore the complex interplay between the representation of race and the production of erotic and political meaning. At the same time as Fadigas and her editorial staff determined the types of models and images that were most likely to sell magazines, they also attempted to promote an antiracist discourse in which they asserted the magazine's solidarity with marginalized Afro-Brazilians and claimed to challenge their absence from Brazilian media.

Models contributed as active subjects by presenting their bodies as sites of desire and drawing attention to their own experiences of racism. Readers in turn participated as they communicated their desires as consumers, contributed content, and weighed in on the political discussion. These negotiations between editors, models, and readers sometimes reinforced and other times challenged Brazilian racial assumptions. While *G Magazine*'s endorsement of a progressive racial politics was unable to displace a discourse of desire that objectified black men as "hung, hot, and shameless in bed," it was also not simply a farce or an attempt to ameliorate the magazine's racially charged erotic representations. Rather, these seemingly contradictory discourses were emblematic of the broader debate about race that continues to rage in Brazilian society, with all the contradictions that entails as a nation that still prides itself on its cordial race relations and fluidity of racial categories grapples with the realization that the black and brown half of its population suffers from structurally enduring poverty and racial prejudice.

Despite nearly a century of studies of race in Brazil, it has only been in the last twenty-five years that scholars have seriously examined Brazilian mass media's gross underrepresentation and stereotyping of Afro-Brazilians. Joel Zito Araújo's 2000 book and 2002 documentary *A negação do Brasil* stand out for their nuanced analysis of both the drastic underrepresentation of Afro-Brazilians in prime-time TV soap operas, a genre that is complicit "with the persistence of the ideal of whitening and the desire of Brazilians to Euro-americanize," and the stereotypical roles that are usually assigned to the rare Afro-Brazilian characters.[4] Another rich area for analysis has been the experiences of African-descended women in a country that imagines the mixed-race woman (*mulata*) as the ideal of sexualized beauty while simultaneously casting darker-skinned black women as unattractive and unworthy of romantic relationships.[5] Yet although the representation of blackness in media and the sexualization of Afro-Brazilian women have been addressed extensively, the ways in which Afro-Brazilian men are represented and sexualized in Brazilian popular culture have received virtually no attention at all.

If studies of race in Brazil have seldom examined black male sexuality, studies of male sexuality in Brazil, particularly nonnormative sexualities, have paid little attention to race. For example, anthropologist Richard Parker, in his pioneering study of gay male culture in urban Brazil, argues that race is "generally secondary to, or at best function[s] in concert with, the more sharply dividing cleavages that organize sexuality around the lines of social class."[6] Don Kulick, in his superb ethnography of transgendered sex workers in Salvador, never addresses their color, although his photographs reveal them to be predominantly African-descended, nor the role that race might play in their marginalization.[7] The most important exception to this trend was Nestor Perlongher's study of *michês* (stereotypically "masculine" sex workers) in 1987, in which he identified pervasive racial prejudice among both clients and michês, even though over half of the sex workers he observed were Afro-Brazilian.[8] More recently a new generation of Brazilian anthropologists has studied race and male homosexuality in the neoliberal marketplace. Isadora Lins França has studied the intersection of class, masculinity, and race among working-class Afro-Brazilian men in a gay samba club in São Paulo.[9] Similarly Camilo Braz has examined how a variety of social cleavages, including race, structure interactions between men in São Paulo sex clubs.[10] And Osmundo Pinho has offered tantalizing hints into the ways that paid gay porn websites fetishize and commercialize a mixed-race, hypersexual "Brazilian-ness."[11]

With its analysis of written sources such as print and social media, personal ads, and visual representation, combined with my interview with *G Magazine*'s founder and longtime owner and editor, this chapter proposes a more nuanced analysis of the layers of desire, stereotyping, political conviction, and market considerations that structure the erotic representation and reception of blackness. It stands apart from most earlier work on Brazil by identifying race, not social class, as the focal point for social divisions. That is, rather than arguing that African-descended men are marginalized because they are poor, it maintains that there is a set of racially based stereotypes that structures erotic representation and desire in Brazil that operates parallel to but separate (and in very different ways) from social class.[12] It also innovates by looking beyond underrepresentation and stereotypes to examine how these interact with politics.

In contrast with the Brazilian literature, the relationship between race and (homo)sexual visual representations has been explored in great depth by scholars of black cultural studies in the Anglophone world. Going back at least to Kobena Mercer's provocative critiques of Robert Mapplethorpe's famous photographs of black men, which itself builds on a far older tradition of black scholarship that dates to Frantz Fanon, scholars have turned a sharp eye to how black men are sexualized by both white and black artists and authors.[13] Yet these works seldom look beyond the United States and United Kingdom. With over 100 million people who identify as black or brown, Brazil has the world's second-largest African or African-descended population, trailing only Nigeria. With its 350-year use of enslaved labor on sugar and coffee plantations and in gold mining, its peaceful and gradual process of abolition, the lack of any system of legal segregation similar to Jim Crow, mass black and brown migration from north to south in the twentieth century, and a national discourse that glorifies rather than demonizes racial mixture, Brazil offers a fascinating point of comparison to and departure from the United States and helps clarify which manifestations of and challenges to racism and inequality are uniquely Anglo-American and which might be diasporic, perhaps even global. As this chapter's title makes clear, Brazilian sexualized representations of black men are immediately recognizable to North Americans. The ways in which Brazilians recognize and interpret racism and racialized representations, particularly in the context of racial democracy, can be strikingly, even uncomfortably, different.

Finally, I would like to reflect on my role as I have looked at these images for a decade, grinned as I have shown them to shocked and titillated audiences at academic conferences, and write about them now. This project began in 2006, my first year as a doctoral student, in a seminar on Afro-Brazil at Duke University. I had just returned from six months in Brazil and brought back several copies of G Magazine, which I'd intended to show off to my gay friends in the United States. During the week our seminar discussed the absence of Afro-Brazilians in Brazilian media, I brought a copy of the magazine with me to class, with a white, green-eyed cover model in the process of removing a suit and dress shirt. The caption said, "This is the type of guy you marry!" At the urging of the professor, John D. French (my advisor), I made *G Magazine* the object of my research in a seminar with Pete Sigal on the history of sexuality. Yet as I have presented the project to that class and conferences and invited talks in both the United States and Brazil, I have found myself forced to reckon with the same issues over and over, issues that relate to my own implication in producing and reproducing the ethnopornographic gaze.

First, as I have shown these images and put black bodies—specifically, "big (hard) black dicks"—on display for an audience of largely white academics, have I not reproduced the same ethnopornographic gaze that structures racialized representation in *G Magazine*? Indeed, when we consider the added dynamic of relatively privileged North Americans of any color casting our gaze upon Brazilian Others, is my own gaze not even more complicit with racial, class, and national structures of inequality? Is the point a critical discussion of Brazilian representations of black men, or am I using black bodies to win attention as "that guy who showed naked black guys"? Over the years, I have experimented with several ways to address this. Sometimes I have passed the images out as a handout; other times I have shown them on the screen for only a few seconds, replacing them quickly with a blank slide. For this chapter, however, I have chosen not to show them at all. In part, this is because *G Magazine* was sold in 2008 and ceased publication a few years later. The company it was sold to is also now defunct, complicating my efforts to obtain permission to reproduce the images. Yet I also leave the images out because I want to ensure that my reproduction of black bodies is not the focus. Besides, I am confident in interested readers' ability to execute an online image search if the fancy strikes.

Second, there is the question of what it means not only for an American historian to examine and reproduce pornographic images of black Brazilian bodies but also how my own race and sexual preference fit into the analysis. I am a gay, white man who has dated several black and brown Brazilian men over the years, and my gaze here is informed by the sexual and romantic relationships I have had with these men who are stereotyped as "hung, hot, and shameless in bed," as well as the pleasure and desire I feel when I look at the images in *G Magazine*. Consequently, my own analysis is not just an analysis of the ethnogpornography that pervades *G Magazine*; it is intensely and inescapably ethnopornographic itself. I have no illusions of an idealized objectivity, for, as the introduction to this volume shows, such claims only further the ethnopornographic "Othering" of black bodies. There is no way for me to escape this, but I would be remiss if I did not acknowledge it. This is an analysis of white discourses about blackness, written by a white, gay, cisgender male who often finds himself attracted to darker-skinned Brazilians. Undoubtedly the account of a black or brown Brazilian gay, cisgender male scholar would complicate the ethno-pornographic gaze in very different ways.[14]

G Magazine: A Pioneer in Brazilian LGBT Media

Launched in 1997 in São Paulo, *G Magazine* distinguished itself by combining soft-core pornography (a staple of earlier gay publications) with information on the gay bar scene in major cities, travel information, fashion tips, body care, workout recommendations, advice columns, and frequent forays into activism. Its format proved popular, but even more importantly, *G* possessed the initial capital to pay famous actors and athletes to pose nude. In August 1998, *G* succeeded in recruiting a well-known *novela* (prime-time soap opera) actor as a cover model.[15] This was followed in January 1999 by the controversial appearance of the African-descended soccer star Vampeta, who played for Corinthians, the most popular football club in São Paulo, if not Brazil, and who would later play on Brazil's 2002 World Cup championship team.[16] The combination of full-frontal nudity (with erections), nonsexually oriented material, and, above all, icons of popular culture was wildly successful. By 2005, owner Ana Fadigas claimed that *G* averaged 110,000 copies sold per month, nearly half the 240,000 copies per month sold by the Brazilian version of *Playboy*.[17] By January 2008, when Fadigas astutely sold the magazine as more and more Brazilians gained access to the internet and its endless variety of pornography, *G* had released over 120 issues and become a staple of urban Brazilian gay culture.

G was popular for at least four reasons. First, it combined pornography, which previous gay lifestyle magazines lacked, with travel, fashion, activism, and other nonexplicit content, which previous pornographic magazines lacked. Second, its format was glossy, professional, and eye-catching. Third, it marketed a cosmopolitan, fashionable, internationally oriented, healthy "gay lifestyle" at a time when male homosexuality was becoming increasingly tolerated in Brazil, as evidenced by the spectacular growth of what would become the world's largest gay and lesbian pride parades and the increasing visibility of gay men and lesbians in the media and entertainment. Fourth, and by far most important, it offered its readers the opportunity to see athletes, actors, reality show participants, and other icons of pop culture nude, from the front, with erections. In a 2003 online survey of users of *G*'s website, 59 percent of respondents indicated that their first choice for a cover model was "someone famous, just to see him nude," while only 20 percent preferred "someone attractive, not just his body, but also his face."[18] *G* thus benefited from the same desire that drives the market for celebrity porn—the desire to see what beautiful and famous people have underneath their clothes, for the viewer to gaze upon their image and experience its reciprocal gaze.[19] As the photograph looks back at the viewer, it penetrates him through its seductive gaze—the famous person "enters" the viewer.

The magazine's appeal was increased for many of its readers by the fact that virtually all the cover models were assumed to be (and identified as) heterosexual. The interviews with the models nearly always remained ambiguous, however, using gender-neutral language and carefully avoiding questions about sexual orientation. In one issue, the interviewer asked Iran Gomes (the man dressed as a malandro referenced in the introduction), "Do you often use your body to seduce someone?" Iran responds, "That's normal, isn't it? I've passed by that men's area of *Posto 9* [the gay section of Ipanema Beach in Rio de Janeiro]—then there comes the applause, everyone looking at you."[20] Thus, readers all "knew" that the models were straight, but the magazine avoided any mention of wives or girlfriends and left the interviews ambiguous enough for readers to participate in a fantasy of a sexually attainable straight man.[21]

African-Descended Models in *G Magazine*: Underrepresentation and the Gay Market of Desire

Scholars and black activists alike have long noted the near absence of African-descended people in Brazilian media, even though in the 2010 census over half of Brazilians identified as brown or black. *G Magazine* followed this pattern—as of January 2008, when Fadigas sold the magazine, out of a total of 139 cover models, 121 were white, with only 16 black or brown men. (The two remaining models were of Asian descent.) This is notable not only because of the inflated number of white models compared to the population but also because among the African-descended models, most had prominently "African" phenotypical features; only 4.3 percent of the models demonstrated a visibly mixed ancestry.[22]

Most of the Afro-Brazilian models appeared in the earlier issues of the magazine, through May 2001. But from June 2001 to April 2007, only five Afro-Brazilian models appeared on the cover, and the magazine once published thirty-three consecutive issues with white cover models, many of them blonde and blue-eyed. This decrease in African-descended models coincided with an editorial decision to refine the magazine's image by reducing its emphasis on sex and nightlife. As the magazine grew in popularity and the editors experimented with various types of models and gauged reader responses, both through letters and sales data, it is possible that they reduced the number of African-descended models accordingly. Marcelo Cerqueira of the Grupo Gay da Bahia (GGB), a gay rights organization in Salvador, expressed this view in an interview with *Revista Gold*, reproduced on the GGB's website. "Here in Brazil, editors of magazines directed at the gay public say that *negros* on the cover do not sell magazines."[23] When I interviewed her in 2008, Fadigas agreed, claiming that when she put a black man on the cover, she knew that unless he was very famous, that issue would sell 30–40 percent fewer issues than one with a nonfamous blonde model, but that she insisted on having, on average, one black model per year, because she believed it was important to open up space for Afro-Brazilians in media.[24] *G* was invested in an effort to project a modern, fashionable image of a Brazil that mimicked Euro-North American gay life. Due to the centuries-old association of blackness with lower-class status in Brazil, which squares well with Western standards of beauty that define attractiveness according to European norms, *G* had little space for Afro-Brazilian models.

Letters to the editor indicate that some readers were concerned with the relative absence of African-descended models. The force of these letters was blunted, however, by their publication alongside ones asking for older models, hairier models, more pictures of feet, and more photos of *bunda* (ass). Whiteness, sculpted bodies, and youth remained the norm; any departure from that norm, including blackness, was relegated to the status of fetish.[25]

Considering the near absence of blackness in Brazilian media, the low proportion of black models in *G Magazine* was unsurprising. Although this certainly showed how the dominant aesthetic in Brazilian gay culture assumed whiteness as normative, it is more instructive to explore how *G* represented Afro-Brazilians when they did appear and, in so doing, ask how such representations circulated in the gay marketplace of desire. The following pages analyze images of models, interviews, letters, and erotic stories to explore the representation of Afro-Brazilians as desirable in *G*, suggesting how these representations can be interpreted within the context of the sexual marketplace and transnational sexualized representations of black men.

King of a Free Nation—Créo Kellab

The May 2000 issue of *G* featured Créo Kellab, a model and theater actor who had appeared in minor roles in novelas. The cover proclaims him "king of a free nation," and the first page of the photo essay contains a short paragraph to set the stage for the images that follow. "Although he has faced the jungle of the big city with all its competition, it's in the middle of nature that Créo Kellab exhibits his astonishing black beauty in all its fullness."[26] The photographs portray a dreadlocked Créo next to (and in) a river in the rainforest, wearing only tribal jewelry and carrying a brightly colored spear. It is unclear if Créo is "king of a free nation" in the jungles of Africa, or if he is the leader of a maroon community (*quilombo*) in Brazil.[27] Regardless, the representation implies that the black man is "in his element" in the jungle. Ultimately, the urban jungle of Rio de Janeiro, where he actually lives, is not where Créo belongs; the most appropriate environment for the exhibition of his "astonishing black beauty" is the real jungle, surrounded by rocks, trees, and water—a black man in his native habitat.

The placement of Créo in the jungle highlights his supposed savagery and closeness to nature. In most of the images, he appears barely conscious of his nudity, and his penis is erect only in one or two images, heightening the sense that he is a native in his natural environment. However, although Créo may appear unconscious of his own nudity, he is not unconscious of his sensuality and ability to seduce the reader. For despite his unselfconscious nudity, Créo is not merely a primitive object upon whom viewers direct their devouring gaze. Rather, as Todd McGowan points out, "The gaze is not the look of the object, but the point at which the object looks back. The gaze thus involves the spectator in the image, disrupting her/his ability to remain all-perceiving and unperceived."[28] The photos also temper the innocence of his unselfconscious nudity with the spear he carries. Long and erect, it communicates the message of aggression and danger that his penis does not—this "savage" in his native habitat possesses the ability to hunt the reader down with his spear, to penetrate the reader with his weapon and gaze alike.

Reader responses printed in the letters to the editor in the months after Créo's appearance were generally positive, yet they focused almost without exception on his color, referring to him as "a god of black beauty," and "well-hung, doing justice to the fame of the *negros*."[29] A female reader stated that the essay took her breath away with "the perfect and inspiring forms of this *negro* stud."[30] Yet another called Créo "a true representative of this delicious race . . . not only beautiful [but also] charming, hot, and erotic to the maximum."[31] These comments gave voice to racialized beliefs about the sexuality of African-descended men that circulate well beyond Brazil, and it was precisely these supposed characteristics that made black men desirable for these readers. Such references to color occurred only when the models were not white; white models might be referred to as "Greek gods," but no one made them representatives of their race.

You've Never Seen Anything Sooo Big—Iran Gomes

In February 2007, *G* featured former *Big Brother Brasil* reality show contestant Iran Gomes on the cover. As stated previously, the cover caption proclaimed, "You've never seen anything sooo big," establishing from the beginning that it was first and foremost Iran's (black) penis that merited attention and made him a commodity in the gay marketplace of desire. Although all gay pornography exhibits a rather predictable focus on the penis, this preoccupation became an obsession in *G*'s images of Iran. In one picture it hangs innocuously from the open fly of his white pants as he holds onto and leans away from a lamppost on a Rio de Janeiro street. In another, he clutches it, fully erect, as if debating where to aim a weapon, while gazing directly at the camera and, by extension, at the viewer. This direct gaze, together with the hand grabbing the erect penis, invites the viewer to fantasize being penetrated, being possessed, by this aggressive black man and his "big, black dick." In still another, he caresses the tip with his finger as he gazes dreamily at it, eyes nearly closed. Once again, the penis is the focal point—Iran directs his gaze at it and touches it gingerly, while its dull blackness contrasts sharply with the shininess of the rest of his body. In others, Iran holds his hand just next to his flaccid penis, not quite touching it, as if to remind the viewer that, though soft, it is nevertheless ever at the ready.[32] In most of these images, Iran wears the gold jewelry of the malandro—and little else.

The setting is also telling. All the images show Iran on the streets and in the bars of Rio de Janeiro at night. In contrast to Créo Kellab, who although he lived in the city belonged in the jungle, Iran is represented as being completely in his element in the city, evidenced by his carefree posture and cool,

relaxed demeanor. The urban setting is directly connected to his representation as a malandro. After the abolition of slavery in 1888, formerly
enslaved Afro-Brazilians migrated en masse to urban centers, especially
Rio de Janeiro. They built shantytowns on the steep hills (*morros*) overlooking the city, where they developed a community structure that existed
alongside yet was largely separate from the city below, where white elites
dreamed of recreating Paris in the tropics.[33] Due to their marginal status
the residents of the morros often found themselves excluded from the formal economy. Jobs were scarce and prejudice common; thus, it is not surprising that many African-descended and working-class men did, in fact,
wander about the city looking for odd jobs or resorting to petty crime to
support themselves.[34] By the 1930s, the figure of the malandro, with his
white suit, silk shirt, straw hat, and gold jewelry, had become a Rio de Janeiro icon. He became a constant theme of the songs of the samba culture
that was emerging in Rio in the 1930s, and through the growing influence
of radio, the malandro of the samba lyrics soon became a national icon
as well.[35] The malandro is intimately associated with not only Rio de Janeiro but also blackness. All the attributes of the racialized malandro are
transferred to Iran in the photographs—the clothes, the jewelry, the urban
setting, but above all, the focus on danger and a legendary sexual prowess
with the power to seduce and conquer.

Readers' responses to Iran were similar to their responses to Créo Kellab
seven years earlier. On the now-defunct social networking website Orkut
(a precursor to Google+, at the time the most popular social networking
site in Brazil), readers expressed their opinions on the message boards of
the *G Magazine* community, a group organized for fans to share images
and discuss the magazine. Even before the magazine hit newsstands, once
it had become known that Iran was to be the February cover model, members speculated about what his images might reveal. "When the magazine
comes out, could someone post his pictures? He's delicious, and he must
be hung."[36] Once the magazine hit newsstands on February 1, several posters to the site, both male and female, speculated about what it would be
like to be penetrated by Iran's admittedly large penis. "It's the biggest dick
in the history of *G*; anyone who bottomed for him would risk rupturing
internal organs."[37] This led to a discussion of precisely how large it was
and whether large members were a universal characteristic of black men,
along with what other sexual characteristics black men might possess. One
poster exclaimed, "I only hook up *negões* [big black guys] because they are
extremely hung, hot, and shameless in bed. . . . I only go out with *negros*. In

addition to being hot, they're also passionate and make me delirious. Who here has already enjoyed a really well-endowed *negão*?"[38] In response, another poster gushed, "*Nossa Senhora* [Our Lady], where would I be without these *negões*? I adore a *mulato*, or, better yet, a *negro*. I've hooked up with four, and of the four, I think the smallest was 20 centimeters."[39]

It is from statements like these, which unlike the letters were not filtered through an editorial staff, that it is easiest to capture the way readers exoticized black men as Other. Readers looked upon the black penis with a mixture of fear, awe, and pleasure. While some posters feared it as something that could cause physical injury, others expressed a strong (and not necessarily contradictory) desire to be penetrated by Iran's penis (or one similarly big and black). Furthermore, through the various discussions concerning Iran and *negros*, it again becomes clear that the *negro* was viewed as someone or something fundamentally Other. It never appeared to occur to any of the posters that black or brown men might buy the magazine or post on the message board; rather, African-descended men were an Other by whose enormous penises the presumably white posters dream of being penetrated, either literally or metaphorically.

Immense Penises and Insatiable Sex Drives—African-Descended Men in Erotic Stories

Paralleling their relative absence from the magazine covers, African-descended men seldom appeared in reader-contributed erotic stories; however, when the stories did mention race, it was nearly always because one of the characters was *mulato* (mixed race) or *negro* (black). When African-descended men did appear, particularly when they were dark-skinned, they were even more racialized than the cover models, represented as brutishly strong, extraordinarily well-endowed, aggressive, sexually insatiable ravishers of meek, smooth, young white men.[40] The stories were nearly invariably told from the perspective of a white "bottom" who lusted after a black "top," and the Afro-Brazilian character was never well-developed— one story does not even give his name, instead alternately referring to him as the negro, the *negrão* (a variant of *negão*), the *afro*, and the taxi driver.[41] The negro (or in one case, mulato) was always the active partner who penetrated the white character with his "immense" penis.

The following story, titled "Sexta-feira 13—O Terror" ("Friday the 13th— The Terror"), is representative. At the end of the semester at a trade school, the students throw a costume party on Friday the 13th. The unnamed protagonist relates that all semester he had his eye on Pepeu, "a strong mulato the size of a wardrobe," but that Pepeu never looked twice at him, even though he was "blonde, tan, and [had] an ass that could make girls envious and turn any man on." He encounters Pepeu drunk at the costume party, and Pepeu immediately makes known his desire to penetrate him. They move to a bathroom stall, where the mulato reveals his "immense dick, as hard as a rock . . . thick and dark." "Famished," the "uncontrollable *macho*" sucks and invades the protagonist's ass "with an animalistic fury," devouring his little body. Pepeu penetrates him once, but as soon as they finish, the insatiable mulato is ready to do it again. The blonde, tan protagonist concludes with, "I doubted that fuck, already the second, would be the last. The night was going to be a terror."[42] This story, then, repeats practically every popularly-held belief about black male sexuality and would be easily recognizable in the United States—Pepeu is masculine, well-endowed, sexually insatiable, and, of course, the top.

Erotic stories in *G* featuring white characters or characters whose race was not specified also referred to penis size, but instead of possessing incredibly "immense" penises, white men were simply "well-endowed," "big and thick," or "really big."[43] Unlike Pepeu, however, whose penis was immense, hard, thick, *and* dark, white men were never described as having large *white* penises. This phenomenon is reminiscent of popular attitudes toward the black penis in the United States, where the same intimate association between size and blackness holds true. In his analysis of the place of the black penis in North American gay culture, Dwight McBride states, "It is virtually unimaginable that one might hear in [a gay pornographic] film, 'Give me that big white dick.' . . . The nomenclature of size is so integrated with blackness that when it comes to the pornographic idea of the penis in the imaginary, it is nearly impossible to think of disaggregating the two."[44] Or, as Scott Poulson-Bryant succinctly puts it, "The size is the color. The color is the size."[45]

Regardless of the race of the characters, erotic stories were nearly always told from the perspective of the passive partner, either in the first person or in the third person with an omniscient narrator. In the same way that the direct gaze of the models in the photographs generated a fantasy of possession and penetration by the model in the viewing subject, the near exclusive focus in the erotic stories on the experience of the passive partner likewise encouraged the reader to place himself in the position of the protagonist, to imagine himself seduced and penetrated. The immense, insatiable, uncontrollable, and always penetrating, never penetrated figure of the negão was especially well-suited to such a fantasy.

"The Problems a Negro Faces": *G Magazine* and Racial Politics

To summarize, in the context of desire, African-descended men were distinguished in *G Magazine* primarily by race-based markers, which expressed themselves through several different themes or motifs—the sexually aggressive, sinister urban figure and the primitive native, among others. Yet this discourse of desire was only one form that discourses about race took in *G*. Paradoxically, even as the magazine underrepresented African-descended men and portrayed them according to long-standing transnational stereotypes, it also issued strident critiques of Brazilian racism, lamented the socioeconomic marginalization faced by Afro-Brazilians, and pointed out the limited space afforded them in the country's media. On occasion, this political discourse even bled over into erotic representations of African-descended men, representing them quite differently from the manner described above. While the photographs, as the most sexualized feature of the magazine, acted as a site only for desire, columns, interviews, letters to the editor, and erotic stories exhibited both erotic and political discourse. Editors, models, and readers all participated in this parallel political discourse and combined it with the discourse of desire. The results did not cancel out the stereotypical representations the magazine employed; indeed, in a magazine that was bought primarily for its photos, it could never fully supplant sexualized discourses. Nevertheless, they showed that old understandings of Brazil as a racial democracy and black men as aggressive and savage must now share space with admissions of Brazil's deep-seated racism and more humanized depictions of African-descended men.

The editors of *G* encouraged political content about race in the magazine first and foremost by granting African-descended models much greater exposure than they had in other Brazilian pornographic magazines. It could at first appear absurd to claim that *G* granted heightened visibility to African-descended models; after all, between 1997 and 2008, 87 percent of the cover models were white. However, for a Brazilian pornographic publication, 12 percent was actually a high percentage of African-descended cover models. The percentage of African-descended models in the Brazilian version of *Playboy* during the same period was far lower. Out of 155 *Playboy* cover models between October 1997 and January 2008, 150 (96.8 percent) were white, with only five (3.2 percent) black or visibly mixed women. The Afro-Brazilian *Playboy* models were usually at the lighter end of the color spectrum and their hair was usually straightened. Although *G* once published thirty-three consecutive issues without featuring an African-descended cover model, Brazilian *Playboy* once published *two hundred* consecutive issues, from 1980 to 1996, without featuring one cover model with African phenotypical features.[46] This far higher percentage of African-descended models in *G* could have been for two non–mutually exclusive reasons. First, *G* could have believed that its target market, gay men, was more open to African-descended models than *Playboy*'s market. Second— and this was the argument made by the magazine's founder—*G* could have been making a political statement by including African-descended models, attempting to express solidarity with the black struggle in Brazil.

The first possibility is intriguing but difficult to prove. My examination of a selection of the personals ads published in *G* between 1997 and 2000 revealed that although 70.3 percent contained a racial description of the person placing the ad, only 17.1 percent of men who placed personals ads specified that they sought men of a particular race.[47] In contrast, a 1984 study of personals ads in the United States found that 42 percent of North American men posting in gay personals specified a racial preference, as compared to much lower percentages of heterosexual men, heterosexual women, and lesbian women.[48] And anyone who has spent any time at all on gay dating apps today knows how often white gay men in the United States say, "Sorry, no blacks. Not a racist, just my preference!" This could mean that Brazilian gay and bisexual men were less preoccupied with race than their North American counterparts, but it was more likely just the result of Brazilian racial etiquette and its desire to avoid the appearance of prejudice. It is telling, after all, that many of the ads requested a photograph, thus enabling the solicitant to reject respondents who did not fit their racial or other aesthetic preferences.

The second possibility, that *G* included African-descended models as a political statement, finds more definitive support within the magazine. *G* occasionally published columns or made editorial comments that expressed the magazine's support for the black struggle and its opposition to all forms of discrimination. For example, in a column titled "Black and Homosexual: A Double Dose of Prejudice," Marcelo Cerqueira asserted that new spaces were opening for those whose racial or sexual identities once consigned them to marginality. "Our era is witnessing the affirmation of identities which for centuries were denied or stigmatized: to be *negro* was shameful, to be gay, a hideous crime. Today, 'Black is beautiful!' [in English] and, 'It's cool to be gay!' Human rights have come to include all the 'minorities,' including the ex-slaves and the ex-sodomites."[49]

Yet at the same time, Cerqueira affirmed, "In Brazil, being black alludes to a sad past of exploitation, official racism, slave labor, and forced exile from Mother Africa in the New World."[50] Cerqueira knew that racial discrimination still existed, but the only examples he gave were of immigration agents at airports in Portugal, Chile, and the United States scrutinizing his passport more carefully than they did those of white Brazilians. By the end of the column, however, he admitted that prejudice was not confined to the past or to other countries. "Despite not having much pride in our Brazil, so unjust, corrupt, violent, and prejudiced, it is here that I have chosen to transform our land into a happier, more fraternal, more joyful society, where neither skin color nor sexual orientation are reasons for division, insecurity, or suffering."[51]

Cerqueira thus moved successively from claiming that modern society affirmed formerly marginal identities like never before to admitting that although slavery and official racism were in the past, their memory remained, to asserting that although racism existed, it existed primarily in other countries, and, finally, to expressing disillusionment with Brazil and its social problems, of which racial prejudice was only one. Ultimately, neither the consignment of racism to the past nor its displacement to other countries made Cerqueira forget the prejudice African-descended Brazilians still experienced at home. Yet he held out hope that Brazil could still become the kind of country he dreamed of, that it could turn into the racial democracy it claimed to be. As Robin Sheriff has argued, racial democracy is not simply a myth or form of false consciousness that deceives Brazilians into believing that equality actually exists; rather, it is a yet-unrealized dream of equality that Brazilians believe should and can exist.[52]

Furthermore, Cerqueira directly tied the struggle for racial equality to the struggle for equality for sexual minorities, a connection that the gay rights movement in Brazil and abroad had consistently attempted to make. By linking gay rights to the struggle for racial equality—and by publishing a column by Cerqueira, himself a black gay activist—*G* attempted to posit the Brazilian gay rights movement as a natural ally of Brazil's black movement. In so doing, it exposed its readers to the discourse of the black movement and helped reinforce what many Brazilians have come to accept—that racism and prejudice remained widespread in Brazil. By stating that being black and gay exposed one to a "double dose of prejudice," G equated the prejudice felt by gay men to that experienced by black men—a problematic claim, to be sure, since white gay men in Brazil and elsewhere still enjoy racial and class privilege, but nonetheless an acknowledgment of the black struggle in Brazil's "racial democracy."

Interviews with models were another politicized medium through which G attempted to establish its consciousness of racism and inculcate that consciousness in its readers. When Afro-Brazilian models appeared in the magazine (except as athletes), G tended to draw attention to the limited space for them in Brazilian media and entertainment. Interviews were also the most obvious means through which black or brown models participated in political discourse. In an interview with *Big Brother Brasil* contestant Alan, the issue of race comes up repeatedly. Born in the Baixada Fluminense, a sprawling mass of working-class suburbs north of Rio de Janeiro, Alan moved with his parents to Angra dos Reis, a gritty coastal city, when he was eleven. When speaking of his teenage years, Alan recalls that although he attended the best high school in the city, his classmates always saw him as "the *neguinho* [little black kid] who came from the Baixada," indicating that race and class were jointly responsible for his marginalization. People began to accept him only when he started playing basketball for a local team, and as he played sports and built up his body, "that neguinho stuff came to an end."[53]

After being voted off *Big Brother Brasil*, Alan had the opportunity to act in several television commercials, all destined for a foreign market. "In Brazil, it's the same as ever—I don't do commercials." The interviewer asks, "Why? Prejudice?" Alan, however, in a classic manifestation of Brazilian racial etiquette, is reluctant to make such a harsh accusation. "I don't know if that's what it is." The interviewer presses the issue, "The products sold out there exist here too." Emboldened, Alan responds, "Absolutely. For example, you don't see a negão doing a toothpaste commercial, a shaving cream commercial, here in Brazil. And I've done three commercials like this for other countries. In the United States, if the toothpaste commercials don't show a negão brushing his teeth, people won't buy it. There is more exposure [for blacks] there. But not here. As far as teeth go, for example, damn, our teeth are the best. Even so . . ."[54] Finally, when the interviewer asks who his idols are, Alan lists not Brazilian heroes but Martin Luther King Jr. and Malcolm X, "those who taught me to pursue my goals."[55]

Alan expresses a willingness to discuss prejudice but is astute enough to realize that it has seldom done Afro-Brazilians much good to complain about it. The interviewer suggests that his absence from commercials in Brazil may be due to prejudice, and when he equivocates, the interviewer presses him, reminding him that these same products are also sold in Brazil. The interview repeatedly compares the space afforded black men in Brazil negatively with the space available in the United States. Whereas in the United States consumers will reputedly not buy toothpaste unless a black man appears in the commercial, in Brazil, Alan has not managed to appear in one commercial. His idols are the heroes of the North American civil rights movement, implying (incorrectly) that Brazil does not have similar role models who can teach young black men to pursue their goals.

The interview with Créo Kellab similarly draws attention to the prejudice directed at black men in the media and entertainment industries. The interview contains no questions, instead providing a narrative of Créo's career with quotations from the actor interspersed throughout. Créo grew up in Minas Gerais, the son of "a black man who was at the margins of society, who sold fish." He moved to Rio de Janeiro at the age of eighteen to pursue a theater career, but, in the words of the editorial staff, "Créo was not aware of the problems a black actor faces."[56] As Créo recalls,

> For me, prejudice is something that is in people's heads. But soon I realized that there was no one with black skin on the cover of magazines. I would try out for the role of a young man who falls in love with a girl. No one would say so, but it could never be a negro. This hurt me a little. . . . Even so, I used my fear and innocence to become stronger, to conquer things. . . . In the beginning, I was just a black guy who wanted to work. But after I made a place for myself, I started to bother some people. . . . Thank God I had matured by then and learned to let certain situations slide.[57]

Créo qualifies his allegations of racism by stating, "Prejudice is something that is in people's heads," that is, it is an individual problem, not a structural problem. He also asserts that when faced with prejudice, sometimes the best response is to be mature and "let certain situations slide." At the same time, Créo exhibits in his interview a conscious desire to increase awareness of the problems faced by Afro-Brazilians in entertainment. In an online chat between the actor and his fans organized by a Brazilian digital media conglomerate, Créo urged the chat participants to not only look at his photos in *G* but also read the interview in order to find out about where he came from and the difficulties he had faced, "because it's complicated for a black man to get on the cover of any magazine. Even as a professional, an actor."[58]

Créo clearly viewed his appearance in *G* as a unique opportunity for a black man to gain access to a medium normally inaccessible to African descendants, and he repeatedly referred to the difficulties he faced as a black actor. At the same time, by quoting Créo's statement that he never saw Afro-Brazilians on the cover of magazines, *G* emphasized that he *was* on the cover of *this* magazine, thus highlighting its own cooperation with the struggle of Afro-Brazilians to carve out a space for themselves in media and entertainment. As a prominent voice of one oppressed group (homosexuals), *G* represented itself as standing in solidarity with another (blacks). This may have served as an attempt to establish solidarity between the LGBT movement and the black movement. It is also possible that *G* used this political discourse to offset the potential negative effects of its racialized discourse of desire and its underrepresentation of African-descended models. That is, an occasional column about the plight of gay Afro-Brazilians, along with a focus in interviews on prejudice in the media and entertainment industry, helped protect the magazine from charges of racism as it racialized and hypersexualized black men while displaying white models out of all proportion to their percentage in the Brazilian population.

Perhaps this was at the prompting of the editorial staff, and perhaps it was spontaneous on the part of the models, but either way, it is significant that these explicit challenges to Brazil's most treasured national myth received such prominent, albeit occasional, attention in Brazil's premier gay publication. Whatever the editors intended, even when models attempted to qualify or soften their critiques of racism in Brazil, the interviews *did* open discursive space that held the potential to destabilize the Brazilian system of racial etiquette that demands silence about racism and questions the patriotism of those who doubt the reality of racial democracy. The fact that this occurred alongside blatantly racialized visual representations blunts its effects, particularly for foreign readers who may be more shocked by such unapologetic peddling in stereotypes (something not uncommon in Brazilian media), but it does not eliminate them. The interviews show that the African-descended models who posed for *G* were not simply powerless victims whom the magazine subjected to racialized stereotypes to spur sales. Rather, these men were active subjects who, within certain limitations, were themselves engaged in the production of meaning.

Indeed, there is evidence that the models helped select the actual nude photographs that appeared in the magazine. In so doing, they were capable of appropriating images such as the malandro and the "king of a free nation" and using them to create an exotic, desirable image of themselves. For example, in the February 2007 issue that began this chapter, it appears that Iran had a role in selecting the malandro motif. In his profile on the *Big Brother Brasil 6* website, Iran gave his occupation as *sambista*—that is, composer of sambas. A longtime member of Salgueiro, a Rio de Janeiro samba school that participates in annual Carnaval festivities, Iran composed songs for the school after his appearance on *Big Brother Brasil*.[59] As a member of Salgueiro, Iran gained a reputation as a womanizer, so much so that his teammates on the school's soccer team reportedly joked that they preferred not to shower with him after a game because "that guy is the man—he screws all the women. You can't let your guard down around him, or he'll try to fuck you too."[60] When his teammates told Neneo, a visiting sambista, about Iran's reputation, Neneo and fellow samba composer Paulo Rezende were inspired to write a song titled "Meu Ébano," about a seductive, passionate, dark black malandro, that later played on the 2005 novela *América* and became a national hit.[61] Thus, when *G* portrayed Iran as a malandro, it did not solely use a racialized stereotype to stimulate desire in its readers; rather it used an image that he himself had long cultivated. As the magazine's owner pointed out in our interview, for Iran, the malandro motif was an affirmation of pride in his blackness, not a stereotype, and when he was asked to appear in *G*, he insisted on being portrayed as a malandro and would not be dissuaded.[62] When the magazine depicted him as sexually aggressive, grabbing his penis as though aiming a weapon, it used an image that Iran was proud of; no one even knew that he was the inspiration for "Meu Ébano" before he revealed this detail on *Big Brother Brasil*.

Finally, readers also contributed to the political discourse in *G*, although their contributions were less obvious than those of the editors and models. Readers did occasionally complain about the underrepresentation of black men in the magazine. As one reader put it, "In a country with such rich ethnic diversity as ours, your photo essays are becoming more and more tiresome due to the repetitive tone of the models, who always follow one ethnic and aesthetic pattern. Sometimes it seems like we are reading a gay magazine from Argentina [imagined as white by Brazilians]. We [in Brazil] have white, brown, *mulato*, Indian, black guys—all marvelous. You could diversify more."[63]

The implication that a magazine with predominantly white models would be more appropriate in another country and was thus not authentically Brazilian was repeated by other readers. "Is this magazine pro-apartheid? Are we in Sweden? Do you think that attractive black men don't exist?"[64] It is possible that these letters reflected genuine concerns with underrepresentation, but it is also possible that their authors were merely using political discourse to demand a type of model that they personally found more desirable. Some letters, after all, did use more explicitly erotic language to request more black male models. "It's always good to see boys who can make your mouth water, well-endowed and handsome black guys who truly complete the magazine."[65] Still, it is notable that when political discourse did appear in letters, it revolved exclusively around the presence or absence of black men. No readers complained about the conventions according to which they were represented when they did appear. Ultimately, the political discourse contained in the letters was predicated upon and influenced by the discourse of desire, which portrayed black men as attractive based on racialized sexual characteristics.

Conclusion

This chapter ends in much the same way as it began, with a representation that at first glance is racially charged, even stereotypical, but this time one that destabilizes such representations. "A Todo Vapor" ("Full Vapor"), unlike other erotic stories in *G*, was told from the perspective of a black character. "I had the luck—and I take pride in this, even with the prejudice that ravages Brazil, and also the gay world—to be born black." Miguel has recently purchased a new apartment, and he frequently uses the building's gym. One evening he decides to visit the sauna and discovers that it is the setting for orgiastic encounters between the building's male residents. Miguel knows the unique allure he possesses as a black man and is proud of his ability to elicit desire. "The white guys I screwed around with [envied] the ease with which I could develop my chest and biceps. Mixing the '*barbi*' look with the *ginga* of a *capoeirista*, I know how to drive guys crazy wanting to try out the delights of this *negão*."[66] Nevertheless, once the orgy begins, Miguel defies the sexual characteristics usually associated with black men. He performs oral sex on two other men and allows another to penetrate him anally with a finger. He does not become the center of attention as the exotic black man; rather, he is simply another participant in the orgy. His race comes up only once, when one of the other men comments, "I love a negão like you."[67] This story is unique for its combination of overt political discourse with a discourse of desire in which hypersexual black men possess unique seductive qualities. Moreover, the discourse of desire, while present, is not dominant, and Miguel participates in activities that do not belong to the repertoire of expected black male sexual behavior. The story thus indicates that it is possible to envision a black man who uses racialized stereotypes to his own advantage but does not restrict himself to prescribed roles.

G Magazine was thus the site of two contradictory yet complementary, nearly separate but occasionally overlapping discourses of desire and politics. They are fused in a way that is often clumsy, even jarring, but they are there all the same. In the discourse of desire, photographs of and erotic stories about black models elicited a specific type of desire in their viewers. Through their penetrating gaze, hypersexualization, and association with exotic types such as the malandro and the primitive native, these representations of black models were intended to make the reader want to be dominated and penetrated by them. In the gay marketplace of desire, this made the black man desirable as the exotic Other to a white standard of male beauty. Through their letters, readers revealed that these were the images of black men that they found desirable, with no objection to such racialized representations. Indeed, during our interview, Fadigas appeared shocked that anyone might take offense at her magazine's representations of black men and claimed there were certain themes that simply worked better with black models. To deny this, to represent everyone the same way—this would be prejudice, she told me.[68]

At the same time, editors, models, and readers participated in a parallel political discourse that recognized the existence of pervasive racism in Brazil. This political discourse did not replace the racialized discourse of desire; rather, it served another purpose by attempting to associate the gay rights movement with the black movement and raise awareness of racism in ways that would have been impossible in Brazil only a generation earlier. These two discourses highlighted the success of the black movement in dramatically raising public awareness of racial prejudice and underrepresentation in cultural representations, but they also showcased the continued impermeability of desire to politics. As the locus of the discourse of desire and the primary engine that drove sales of the magazine, the photographs never questioned the racialization of black men as exotic Others. Only rarely, in a few interviews and erotic stories, did African-descended men emerge from such roles and become something other than the Other, or at least more than simply the Other. Whatever the successes of the black movement, the political discourse of equality remains largely unable to touch the deeply engrained discourse of desire that structures erotic representation. And looking beyond Brazil, at a political and historical moment in which discussions about race in the United States have brought fresh attention to well-meaning white "allies," we are reminded that whether we are progressive magazine editors, ethnographers with a genuine desire to protect and learn from indigenous cultures, or white gay guys who have dated black Brazilians and write articles about "big black dicks," sympathy for the struggles faced by marginalized groups does not shield us from our own ethnopornographic desire. Politics don't trump desire, but does desire trump politics?

Notes

I would like to thank Pete Sigal for his invaluable input at every stage of this project, dating to a graduate seminar at Duke University in 2007, as well as John D. French, Ara Wilson, and James N. Green for their mentoring, support, and comments on various drafts. Thanks as well to the innumerable panelists, commenters, and attendees who lent me their perspectives at the Duke-UNC Latin American Studies Consortium Afro-Latin and Nation-Building, Popular Culture, and Marginalities working group; the Brazilian Studies Association; the Latin American Studies Association; the Conference on Latin American History; the Department of Latin American and Latino Studies at the University of California, Santa Cruz; and the Universidade Federal do Rio de Janeiro. Many friends in Brazil, particularly Laura Dias and Wagner Almeida, have offered me their own deep insights into the sexualization of black men in Brazil. Ana Fadigas, the founder of *G Magazine*, and Klifit Pugini, the magazine's longtime editor, generously took the time to meet with me nearly a decade ago and offer an inside look at their editorial decisions. The research trip in 2008 during which I conducted that interview was funded by the Center for Latin American and Caribbean Studies at Duke University, through a Mellon Foundation field research travel grant.

1   *G Magazine* 113 (February 2007).
2   Orkut, "Communities," *G Magazine*, accessed February 20, 2007, http://www.orkut .com/CommMsgs.aspx?cmm=2041528&tid=2514963010553268732. While all links to Orkut Communities in this essay were valid as of 2007, Orkut, once Brazil's most popular social media network, faded into obscurity as Facebook increased in

popularity. Google, Orkut's parent company, shut Orkut down in 2014 but saved some of its fan pages ("Communities") in an online archive, which was deleted in May 2017. See "Google vai apagar definitivamente arquivo de comunidades do Orkut," *Folha de S. Paulo*, April 29, 2017, http://www1.folha.uol.com.br/tec/2017/04/1879806-google-vai-apagar-definitivamente-arquivo-de-comunidades-do-orkut.shtml.

3 In contrast to the United States, which was long governed by the "one-drop rule," the Brazilian racial system is a color continuum with many intermediate categories between *branco* (white) and *preto* or *negro* (black). Only those with the strongest African phenotypical features have traditionally been described as negros, while those with brown skin but more European phenotypical features have often been described with a host of intermediate terms, depending on specific characteristics and personal preference. The Brazilian census (and more than a few scholars) has simplified this system by referring to anyone who is not branco or negro as *pardo* (brown). However, since the 1980s, recognizing that pardos and negros experience similar economic disadvantages and racial prejudices, activists in the *movimento negro* (black movement) have promoted a classification system in which anyone with African phenotypical features is considered negro, which carries a connotation similar to "black" in the United States. For the best work in English on the Brazilian racial system, see Edward E. Telles, *Race in Another America: The Significance of Skin Color in Brazil* (Princeton, NJ: Princeton University Press, 2006). See also Stanley R. Bailey, *Legacies of Race: Identities, Attitudes, and Politics in Brazil* (Stanford, CA: Stanford University Press, 2009). In this essay, the terms "African-descended," "Afro-Brazilian," "black," and "negro" will refer to anyone whose physical appearance indicates African descent as evidenced by skin color and phenotypical features. This does not constitute a denial of the uniqueness of Brazil's racial classification system; rather it acknowledges the fact that "negro" has become increasingly common to refer to all Afro-Brazilians. The owner and editor of *G* used "negro" in our 2008 interview in much the same sense.

4 Joel Zito Araújo, *A negação do Brasil: O negro na telenovela brasileira* (São Paulo, Brazil: Editora SENAC, 2000), 305; Joel Zito Araújo, *A negação do Brasil*, documentary film (São Paulo: SENAC, 2000), 92 minutes. See also Silvia Ramos, ed., *Mídia e racismo* (Rio de Janeiro, Brazil: Pallas, 2002); and Samantha Nogueira Joyce, *Brazilian Telenovelas and the Myth of Racial Democracy* (Lanham, MD: Lexington Books, 2012).

5 See Erica Lorraine Williams, *Sex Tourism in Bahia: Ambiguous Entanglements* (Champaign-Urbana: University of Illinois Press, 2013); John Burdick, *Blessed Anastácia: Women, Race, and Popular Christianity in Brazil* (New York: Routledge, 1998); Sueli Carneiro, "Black Women's Identity in Brazil," in *Race in Contemporary Brazil: From Indifference to Inequality*, ed. Rebecca Reichmann (University Park: Pennsylvania State University Press, 1999), 217–27; José Jorge de Carvalho, "The Multiplicity of Black Identities in Brazilian Popular Music," in *Black Brazil: Culture, Identity, and Social Mobilization*, ed. Larry Crook and Randal Johnson

(Los Angeles, CA: UCLA Latin American Center Publications, 2000), 261–96; and Donna M. Goldstein, *Laughter Out of Place: Race, Class, Violence, and Sexuality in a Rio Shantytown* (Berkeley: University of California Press, 2003).

6 Richard Parker, *Beneath the Equator: Cultures of Desire, Male Homosexuality, and Emerging Gay Communities in Brazil* (New York: Routledge, 1999), 122. See also José Fábio Barbosa da Silva, "Homossexualismo em São Paulo: Estudo de um grupo minoritário," in *Homossexualismo e outros escritos*, ed. James N. Green and Ronaldo Trindade (São Paulo, Brazil: Editora UNESP, 2005).

7 Don Kulick, *Travesti: Sex, Gender, and Culture among Brazilian Transgendered Prostitutes* (Chicago, IL: University of Chicago Press, 1998). See also João Silvério Trevisan, *Perverts in Paradise*, trans. Martin Foreman (London: GMP, 1986); and Peter Fry, "Male Homosexuality and Spirit Possession in Brazil," in *The Many Faces of Homosexuality: Anthropological Approaches to Homosexual Behavior*, ed. Evelyn Blackwood (New York: Harrington Park Press, 1986), 137–53.

8 Nestor Perlongher, *O negócio do michê: Prostituição viril em São Paulo* (São Paulo, Brazil: Editora Brasiliense, 1987). For a partial exception to the rule, see James N. Green's pathbreaking 1999 history of Brazilian homosexuality. Green notes that in gay communities, "skin color can determine social positioning," and "sharp class divisions and a racial hierarchy have precluded substantial integration" between members of different socioeconomic and social groups. See James N. Green, *Beyond Carnival: Male Homosexuality in Twentieth-Century Brazil* (Chicago, IL: University of Chicago Press, 1999), 284.

9 Isadora Lins França, *Consumindo lugares, consumindo nos lugares: Homossexualidade, consumo e subjetividades na cidade de São Paulo* (Rio de Janeiro, Brazil: EDUERJ, 2012).

10 Camilo Albuquerque de Braz, *À meia luz . . . : Uma etnografia em clubes de sexo masculinos* (Goiânia, Brazil: Editora UFG, 2012).

11 Osmundo Pinho, "Race Fucker: Representações raciais na pornografia gay," *Cadernos Pagu* 38 (2012): 159–95. See also Adriana Nunan, *Homossexualidade: Do preconceito aos padrões de consumo* (Rio de Janeiro, Brazil: Editora Caravansarai, 2003).

12 On the stereotyping of blackness in Brazil, not only sexually but also more broadly, see Viviane Barbosa Fernandes and Maria Cecília Cortez Christiano de Souza, "Identidade Negra entre exclusão e liberdade," *Revista do Instituto de Estudos Brasileiros* 63 (2016): 103–20.

13 See, along with his many other publications on the topic, Kobena Mercer, "Reading Racial Fetishism: The Photographs of Robert Mapplethorpe," in *Welcome to the Jungle: New Positions in Black Cultural Studies* (New York: Routledge, 1994), 171–219.

14 See, for example, the fascinating work of Darieck B. Scott on black-authored comics in the United States. Scott, "Big Black Beauty: Drawing and Naming the Black Male Figure in Superhero and Gay Porn Comics," in *Porn Archives*, eds.

Tim Dean, Steven Ruszczycky, and David Squires (Durham, NC: Duke University Press, 2014), 183–212.

15 *G Magazine* 11 (August 1998).

16 *G Magazine* 16 (January 1999). The publicity generated for *G* by Vampeta's appearance in the magazine is reminiscent of the publicity generated for *Cosmopolitan* by Burt Reynolds's nude centerfold in 1972. Of course, Reynolds's nudes were "discreetly posed," while Vampeta's nudes showed him from the front, with an erection; and Reynolds posed for a women's magazine, while Vampeta posed for a men's magazine. See David Allyn, *Make Love, Not War: The Sexual Revolution, an Unfettered History* (Boston, MA: Little, Brown and Co., 2000), 232.

17 Camila Marques, "*G Magazine* muda e público atinge quase a metade da *Playboy*," *Folha de S. Paulo*, May 26, 2005, http://www1.folha.uol.com.br/folha/ilustrada/ult90u50966.shtml, accessed 1 March 2007.

18 "Conta pra gente," *G Magazine* 67 (April 2003), 15.

19 On celebrity porn, see Adam Knee, "Celebrity Skins: The Illicit Textuality of the Celebrity Nude," in *Framing Celebrity: New Directions in Celebrity Culture*, ed. Su Holmes and Sean Redmond (New York: Routledge, 2006), 161–76.

20 *G Magazine* 113 (February 2007), 48.

21 In addition to its cover models, *G* also included a "Desejo" (Desire) section each month with a less-known nude model, whose profession was usually listed as model, go-go boy, or dancer. The magazine also occasionally recruited lesser-known athletes such as volleyball players and boxers. It often contained a "Replay" section with additional nude photographs of recent cover models. Finally, it usually contained a "Fetiche" (Fetish) section with themes such as soldiers, policemen, manual laborers, BDSM, and, of course, black men.

22 My statistics here contain an inherent classificatory problem. The census asks Brazilians to self-select their racial category, while my classification of *G Magazine* cover models is based upon my own subjective criteria. However, this problem is mitigated by the fact that the race of very few *G* models would be open to negotiation, even in Brazil—models in the magazine nearly always exhibit markedly European or markedly African phenotypical features, with very few (other than several professional soccer players) falling anywhere in between.

23 Marcelo Cerqueira, "Sexo, raça e relação entre homens gays," undated interview with *Revista Gold*, accessed 24 March 2007, http://www.ggb.org.br/musica_carnaval.html.

24 Ana Fadigas, interview with the author, July 17, 2008. Fadigas also pointed out that the magazine was primarily interested in attracting famous Brazilians and that other than athletes, most famous Brazilians are white.

25 This tendency is not unique to *G Magazine* or Brazilian gay pornography. As Richard Fung has noted, referring to North American gay pornography, "If we look at commercial gay sexual representation, it appears that the antiracist movements have had little impact; the images of men and male beauty are still of *white* men

and *white* male beauty." See Richard Fung, "Looking for My Penis: The Eroticized Asian in Gay Video Porn," in *Asian Canadian Studies Reader*, ed. Roland Sintos Coloma and Gordon Pon (Toronto, ON: University of Toronto Press, 2017), 88.

26 Alessandra Levtchenko, Alfredo Sternheim, and Ana Paula Elias, "Negro é lindo," *G Magazine* 32 (May 2000), 43–58.

27 Due to the efforts of the movimento negro to raise awareness about the history of African-descended people, the maroon communities called *quilombos* loom large in the national consciousness. The 1988 Constitution contains a provision granting land to communities descended from quilombos, and Zumbi, leader of an enormous seventeenth-century quilombo in the modern-day state of Alagoas, has been promoted as a national hero. On the historical Zumbi, see Robert Nelson Anderson, "The Quilombo of Palmares: A New Overview of a Maroon State in Seventeenth-Century Brazil," *Journal of Latin American Studies* 28, no. 3 (1996): 545–66. On the movimento negro, including its appropriation of Zumbi as a symbol of resistance, see Michael G. Hanchard, *Orpheus and Power: The Movimento Negro of Rio de Janeiro and São Paulo, 1945–1988* (Princeton, NJ: Princeton University Press, 2001).

28 Todd McGowan, "Looking for the Gaze: Lacanian Film Theory and Its Vicissitudes," *Cinema Journal* 42, no. 3 (2003): 28–29.

29 "Cartas," *G Magazine* 33 (June 2000).

30 "Cartas," *G Magazine* 34 (July 2000).

31 "Cartas," *G Magazine* 34 (July 2000).

32 J. Levis and Ane O'Connor, "Graaaaaande brother!"*G Magazine* 113 (February 2007), 30–47.

33 Nicolau Sevcenko, *Literatura como missão: Tensões sociais e criação cultural na Primeira República*, 2nd ed. (São Paulo, Brazil: Brasiliense, 1985), 28–34.

34 Lisa Shaw, *The Social History of the Brazilian Samba* (Aldershot, UK: Ashgate, 2000), 9.

35 Bryan McCann, *Hello, Hello, Brazil: Popular Music in the Making of Modern Brazil* (Durham, NC: Duke University Press, 2004), 52–58.

36 Orkut, "Communities," *G Magazine*, February 1, 2007, http://www.orkut.com /CommMsgs.aspx?cmm=2041528&tid=2513324854160506824.

37 Orkut, "Communities," *G Magazine*, February 6, 2007, http://www.orkut.com /CommMsgs.aspx?cmm=2041528&tid=2514205361100382190.

38 Orkut, "Communities," *G Magazine*, February 10, 2007, http://www.orkut.com /CommMsgs.aspx?cmm=2041528&tid=2514963010553268732.

39 Orkut, "Communities," *G Magazine*, February 12, 2007, http://www.orkut.com /CommMsgs.aspx?cmm=2041528&tid=2514963010553268732.

40 Mulatos fall at the darkest end of the pardo category and can also be classified as negros depending on their social class and personal preference. Even if defined as pardos, mulatos look sufficiently African-descended so as to be unable to deny it. See Burdick, *Blessed Anastácia*, 31.

41 "Passivo por vocação," *G Magazine* 32 (May 2000).

42 "Sexta-feira 13—O Terror," *G Magazine* 61 (October 2002), 87.

43 See, for example, "Hombre," *G Magazine* 50 (November 2001), 94; "O esporte faz muito bem," *G Magazine* 59 (August 2002), 87; "O padeiro," *G Magazine* 58 (July 2002), 87.

44 Dwight McBride, *Why I Hate Abercrombie & Fitch: Essays on Race and Sexuality* (New York: New York University Press, 2005), 109–10.

45 Scott Poulson-Bryant, *Hung: The Measure of Black Men in America* (New York: Doubleday, 2005), 75.

46 Playboy Covers of the World, accessed March 10, 2008, http://www.pbcovers.com.

47 "Procurados," *G Magazine* 2 (November 1997), *G Magazine* 5 (February 1998), *G Magazine* 6 (March 1998), *G Magazine* 15 (December 1998), *G Magazine* 16 (January 1999), *G Magazine* 18 (March 1999), *G Magazine* 22 (July 1999), *G Magazine* 25 (October 1999), *G Magazine* 30 (March 2000), *G Magazine* 31 (April 2000), *G Magazine* 34 (July 2000), *G Magazine* 36 (September 2000).

48 Kay Deaux and Randal Hanna, "Courtship in the Personals Column: The Influence of Gender and Sexual Orientation," *Sex Roles* 11, nos. 5–6 (September 1984): 369.

49 Marcelo Cerqueira, "Negro e homossexual: Preconceito em dose dupla," *G Magazine* 58 (July 2002), 98.

50 Cerqueira, "Negro e homossexual."

51 Cerqueira, "Negro e homossexual."

52 Robin Sheriff, *Dreaming Equality: Color, Race, and Racism in Urban Brazil* (New Brunswick, NJ: Rutgers University Press, 2001), 222–24.

53 *G Magazine* 81 (June 2004), 48.

54 *G Magazine* 81 (June 2004).

55 *G Magazine* 81 (June 2004).

56 *G Magazine* 32 (May 2000).

57 *G Magazine* 32 (May 2000).

58 "Bate-papo com Créo Kellab, modelo e ator," May 9, 2000, http://www1.uol.com.br /bparquivo/integra/bp_creo_kellab.htm.

59 "Ex-BBB Iran compõe samba para o Salgueiro," *O Fuxico*, August 8, 2006, http:// ofuxico.uol.com.br/Materias/Noticias/2006/08/28710.htm.

60 "Iran inspirou sambista a compor grande de Alcione," *O Dia Online*, February 20, 2006, http://exclusivo.terra.com.br/bbb6/interna/0,,OI886560-EI6120,00.html.

61 "Iran inspirou sambista."

62 Fadigas interview.

63 "Cartas," *G Magazine* 62 (November 2002).

64 "Cartas," *G Magazine* 6 (March 1998), 64.

65 "Cartas," *G Magazine* 22 (July 1999), 79–80.

66 The point is that Miguel is muscular and attractive and has a swaying, self-confident gait when he walks. A *barbi*, taken from the English "Barbie doll," is gay Brazilian slang for a muscular, attractive gay man who, as an effeminized Barbie doll, is the epitome of male beauty. A *capoeirista* is a performer of *capoeira*, an Afro-Brazilian combination of martial art and dance. A *ginga* is "the basic body

movement in *capoeira*" and "is derived from the word for swaying from side to side," but it also "refer[s] to the signature way in which an individual carries themselves while walking." Definition of "ginga" from John D. French, *Sharing the Riches of Afro-Brazilian History and Culture* (Durham, NC: Duke University African and African American Studies Program and the Consortium in Latin American Studies at UNC Chapel Hill and Duke University, 2003), 40.

67   "A Todo Vapor," *G Magazine* 18 (March 1999): 72–73.

68   Fadigas interview.

The Ghosts of *Gaytanamo*

Popular online sources, from Urban Dictionary to TV Tropes, posit the existence of "Rule 34." Rule 34 states, "If it exists, there is porn of it—no exceptions". In 2007, this "rule" was applied for the first time to an institution integral to the War on Terror: the Guantanamo Bay detention camp. The gay video porn studio Dark Alley Media released their feature-length film *Gaytanamo*. The film follows the abduction of a German tourist by US security forces and his subsequent torture and sexual adventures in Gaytanamo/Guantanamo. According to the studio's description, "Dark Alley mixes political parody, classical music and scorching sex in *Gaytanamo*."[1]

Dark Alley Media claims that *Gaytanamo* was "the most controversial porn film of 2007."[2] Though their claim may be hyperbolic, it may not be far from the mark. The film was widely reviewed by a variety of LGBT outlets, some of which focus solely on porn and some of which do not. All commentators who wrote of the film mention the controversy surrounding the film. Some praised the film. The blog *GayPornucopia!* downplays criticism of the film and describes it as "a genuinely hot fantasy scenario" and being "1 part political parody and 100 parts incredible sex".[3] Gay porn reviewer Vincent Lambert praises *Gaytanamo* in a review that begins, "The political gets very personal in Dark Alley Media's latest release, *Gaytanamo*, a gay porn epic that's both sexually explosive and politically charged."[4]

Some found the film distasteful, mostly those outside of the porn review websites. The oldest LGBT newspaper in the country, the *Washington Blade*, titled their review "New Lows in Bad Taste," in which the film is described as "paying nominal homage" to Guantanamo Bay, and that Dark Alley Media is busy "fisting their way out of the Geneva Convention."[5] NarcissusAU, author of the blog *Synthetic Ego*, described his reaction to the film as "unsettled." His introspection continues, "Whilst my initial reaction was to smirk somewhat (as it is a very smart play on the word) I soon became uncomfortable with a porn video which sets its torture in an actual real life torture camp. . . . Does this make me a hypocrite?"[6] Commenters across many websites variously described *Gaytanamo* as "sickening," "trivializing," and "immoral." An anonymous reviewer on the blog *Queerty* wrote that they found the film to be "absolutely inappropriate and offensive." They go on to say that "sensationalizing and sexing up what is happening in Guantanamo Bay is like making a porn called 'Gay-Auschwitz.' . . . These are human beings who are being tortured, their lives destroyed. And you are dismissing them and capitalizing on their horror. If you have any sense of decency, you would withdraw this film and either scrap it or re-title it immediately."[7]

What is striking about the last review/condemnation is that it, like some of the other comments scattered around various blogs, mentions the "human beings who are being tortured, their lives destroyed." One of the most striking features of *Gaytanamo* is that none of the characters or actors is Arab or Muslim, the very men who make up the detainee population of Guantanamo Bay. This absence is noticeable and draws my attention to what is *not* in the film rather than what is.

In her seminal book *Hard Core*, Linda Williams discusses pornography's obsession with the quest for visible evidence of pleasures and bodies, even at the expense of realism or more arousing scenes. She terms this pornographic principle "maximum visibility."[8] As it is an inherently visible medium, those who study visual pornography are often concerned with what is on-screen, with what is contained within a film or set of films. What happens when porn studies strays from the visible, when more attention is paid to what and who are *not* on-screen?

BEATRIX McBRIDE

My project aims to interrogate the absences, rather than the visibilities, within and without the gay porn film *Gaytanamo*. The bodies of Arab and Muslim men, the men who populate the real Guantanamo, are conspicuously absent from *Gaytanamo,* the porn film that claims to parodize the detainee camp. I contend that the absence of these men constitutes more than a mere absence; it constitutes a haunting, specifically an ethnopornographic haunting. According to Avery Gordon, haunting "is an animated state in which a repressed or unresolved social violence is making itself known, sometimes very directly, sometimes more obliquely."[9] The Arab and Muslim men imprisoned in Guantanamo are still there in the physical world. When they are absented from the pornographic fantasy of Guantanamo, a trace remains, as anyone watching the film knows that they are still imprisoned in Guantanamo. This trace constitutes such a haunting, as they are the bodies upon which the US government has inflicted an "unresolved social violence" and they cannot be so easily disappeared in fiction. What, then, is an *ethnopornographic* haunting? In the introduction to this volume, Sigal, Tortorici, and Whitehead define ethnopornography as "the production of an eroticized facticity" about people different from oneself.[10] I will argue that *Gaytanamo*, through its absenting of Arab and Muslim men, constructs an ethnopornographic narrative and absence that produces an eroticized facticity about *both* those who are and are not present in the film.

Questions of ethnopornographic absence and haunting in pornography animate and drive this project. What happens to a porn studies analysis when the focus shifts from what *is* on-screen to what *should* be on-screen but is not? In this venture, I align myself with gay porn studies scholar John Champagne, who implores us to "stop reading films." Champagne argues against the practice of close-reading gay porn films and for a focus on the social context of the films.[11] As I will later outline, Champagne argues that attention to social context can tell us about the potential political implications of gay porn. Through analyzing the hauntings within *Gaytanamo* and the absences surrounding it, I aim to sidestep the reliance on the visible in porn studies in an attempt to see the unseen social context that so often falls out of view in such practices of reading only presences. Ethnopornographic representations of such spaces of state violence, including what they do and do not contain, have much to tell us about the sexualized and racialized contours of the War on Terror.

A Detour, a Description

Gaytanamo opens on a rooftop in a city. Classical music plays throughout the credits sequence, as do brief flashes of the sex scenes to come. Three men, two of them masked, all presumably government agents (as they are dressed in fatigues), spy on Danny Fox, a German tourist.[12] They then kidnap him, tie him up, and drive him to what looks like an abandoned warehouse, "Gaytanamo." The setting of the warehouse, or "Gaytanamo," is a rundown, nondescript former industrial site. The lighting inside is darkened throughout the film, and red light bulbs are frequently used. The warehouse interior sports numerous exposed beams and pipes. Inside, the main interrogator, known as "Violator," verbally and physically abuses Danny, berating, pinching, slapping, and punching him. After a brief conversation with an underling in a hallway, Violator decides to torture Danny by forcing him to watch gay porn. The interrogators are dressed all in black, while Danny is now naked, tied to a chair. The interrogators threaten to staple Danny's eyelids open if he does not watch voluntarily. The scene that he watches involves Owen Hawk and Dominik Rider (a white man and a Latino man, respectively). The sex is standard for gay porn, including oral sex (both fellatio and analingus), masturbation, and anal sex in a variety of positions. During this scene, the viewpoint shifts from being inside the sex scene (which Danny is watching on a television) to Danny masturbating. Violator then returns, asking Danny if he knows why he is there, all the while intimidating him with a gun, whipping him with a rope, and generally abusing him. When Danny continually does not answer, Violator returns to the hall with his comrade, who suggests that they use a hallucinogenic drug that will make Danny tell the truth. After they drug him, Danny hallucinates three different sex scenes: one starring Tim Rusty and Tony Diamond (a white man and a black man), a second featuring Matthias von Fistenberg and Demetrius (two white men), and a third starring Owen Hawk and Jason Tyler (two white men). All three of these scenes contain the same standard variations of sex acts as the first sex scene, with the occasional dildo thrown into the mix. In each sex scene, if the performers wear any clothing at all, said clothing consists of either a jockstrap and/or black boots. All of the sex scenes seem to take place in similar surroundings, rooms in a dimly lit warehouse. In the end, despite the surfacing of new evidence that Danny might be innocent, Violator has him thrown into "the hole . . . until we find new evidence to show he's guilty." In the hole, a dark industrial room with no carpet and no furniture,

Danny encounters a naked Sebastian Cruz (a white man). They have sex, employing the standard sequence of sex acts as outlined above, after which the film ends.[13]

Porn Studies, the Visible, and Absence

The centrality of the visible in porn studies goes back to its modern origins. Linda Williams, one of the founders of contemporary porn studies, uses Michel Foucault's discussion of *scientia sexualis* in her book *Hard Core: Power, Pleasure, and the "Frenzy of the Visible."* According to Williams, Foucault describes *scientia sexualis* as "a hermeneutics of desire aimed at ever more detailed explorations of the scientific truth of sexuality . . . *scientia sexualis* . . . constructs modern sexualities according to a conjunction of power and knowledge that probes the measurable, confessable 'truths' of a sexuality that governs bodies and their pleasures."[14] Williams claims that "a desire to see and know more of the human body . . . underlies the very invention of cinema" and therefore of hard-core pornography.[15] She terms knowledge produced by hard-core porn a "frenzy of the visible." For Williams, one of the primary organizing principles of hard-core porn's frenzy of the visible is "maximum visibility," or the principle that visual porn, as a site of knowledge production of pleasure and the body, strives to show ever more of those bodies and pleasures. Visibility remains front and center, summarized by Williams's assertion that hard-core porn "obsessively seeks knowledge, through the voyeuristic record of confessional, involuntary paroxysm, of the 'thing' itself."[16] When so many scholars within porn studies see Linda Williams and *Hard Core* as foundational touchstones, it is no surprise that so much of the field is constructed around the visual and the visible.

Williams does, however, gesture toward the invisible. One of her main arguments is that porn may be "the key genre" for answering the question of how women's bodies have been constituted as a primary site of knowledge, especially concerning sexual difference.[17] In this, she notes something curious about the principle of maximum visibility, which is that "while it is possible, in a certain limited and reductive way, to 'represent' the physical pleasure of the male by showing erection and ejaculation, this maximum visibility proves elusive in the parallel confession of female sexual pleasure." She and those whom she cites describe the place of female pleasure as "secret" and "invisible." She even goes so far as to argue that this drive toward knowledge of female pleasure is a central organizing feature of hard-core porn, stating that "the history of hard-core film could thus be summarized in part as the history of the various strategies devised to overcome this problem of invisibility" and "the woman's ability to fake the orgasm that the man can never fake . . . seems to be at the root of all the genre's attempts to solicit what it can never be sure of: the out-of-control confession of pleasure, a hard-core 'frenzy of the visible.'"[18] Williams's bold and somewhat totalizing statements show that, for her, a question of invisibility is at the heart of the entire genre, at the heart of the "frenzy of the visible" itself.

The issue of visibility and invisibility is different, though, from the question of presence and absence. One popular textbook, Gillian Rose's *Visual Methodologies*, has this to say about the topic in its discussion of discourse analysis: "Finally, discourse analysis also involves reading for what is not seen or said. Absences can be as productive as explicit naming; *invisibility* can have just as powerful effects as visibility."[19] This elision belies the differences between invisibility and absence. Invisibility implies that something is present, only unseen. Absence, however, is when the thing is not there. When Linda Williams discusses female pleasure in hard-core porn, she is specifically discussing its invisibility, rather than its absence. Though the question of the presence of female pleasure is often ambiguous and ambivalent, she claims that pornography is looking for proof of something that is there, just unseen. The case of *Gaytanamo* is one of absence, not invisibility. It is not that Arab and Muslim men are somewhere in *Gaytanamo*, only unseen. It is that Arab and Muslim men are absent from a space in which they are present in the real world. How, then, to think about absence in porn, rather than invisibility?

For the question of absence, I turn to Avery Gordon's *Ghostly Matters: Haunting and the Sociological Imagination*. Gordon uses the concepts of haunting and ghosts to discuss socially violent absences. As she describes,

> Haunting was the language and the experiential modality by which I tried to reach an understanding of the meeting of force and meaning, because haunting is one way in which abusive systems of power make themselves known and their impacts felt in everyday life, especially when they are supposedly over and done with (slavery, for instance) or when their oppressive nature is denied (as in free labor or national security). Haunting is not the same as being exploited, traumatized, or oppressed, although it usually involves these experiences or is produced by them. What's distinctive about haunting is that it is an animated

state in which a repressed or unresolved social violence is making itself known, sometimes very directly, sometimes more obliquely.[20]

Gordon argues that haunting is political in nature and serves to call our attention to oppressive power systems that might otherwise be obscured. Haunting occurs through the calling attention to a loss or an absence that is the result of these oppressive power systems. I argue that haunting is an important lens through which to analyze the absences of Arab and Muslim men in *Gaytanamo*, as haunting allows us to think about how absences are political and part of larger systems of social violence.

Earlier, I described the haunting as "ethnopornographic." How, then, does the "ethnopornographic" come into play? If ethnopornography were only about "the production of an eroticized facticity," one could argue that most, perhaps the overwhelming majority of, pornography produces such an eroticized facticity. Scholars and activists, including those within porn studies and those who are ardently antiporn, have argued that pornography attempts to produce "facts" and/or to "educate" people about bodies, sexualities, and desires. What makes it ethnopornography is that the eroticized facticity produced is "regarding people deemed different from" the person engaged in the study. My argument is that it is through *ethnopornographic* absence and haunting that *Gaytanamo* produces eroticized facticities about those very people and bodies who are absented from the film. Such ethnopornographic haunting not only produces knowledge about those absented but, through the absence, produces and reinforces knowledge about the people and bodies who are actually in the film.

The actual Guantanamo Bay detention camp exists as part of a larger system of US post-9/11 national security and the War on Terror. The oppressive nature of this system is often denied in official discourses, instead positing that Guantanamo is necessary to protect American citizens and interests worldwide from the possibility of terrorist attacks.[21] In reality, Guantanamo is a prison camp wherein exceptional discourses and practices of indefinite detention are the norm.[22] In a symbolic sense, Bruce Bennett argues, "The prison at the Guantanamo Bay naval base in Cuba has become one of the most symbolically dense sites of the 'war on terror.' Images of the prison have come to communicate not merely the technical processes by which the U.S. military detains selected prisoners of war, but the relationship of the U.S.A. with the rest of the world, a visual rendering of power—cultural, imperial, military, legal and physical."[23]

In his article, Bennett argues for the power of and potential for critical political engagement with photojournalistic images that come out of Guantanamo, specifically of the Arab and Muslim prisoners held there. He argues that what those images both show and do not show is worthy of our engaged attention. By absenting Arab and Muslim men from *Gaytanamo*, the film denies the real-world oppressive nature of Guantanamo, allowing it to be eroticized as a space of gay sexual pleasure. The ethnopornographic haunting, though, comes through the fact that people watching *Gaytanamo* know that Guantanamo is populated by Arab and Muslim men, yet those men are not on-screen. Those men then constitute the ghosts of what I am calling ethnopornographic haunting. Gordon argues that "the ghost is primarily a symptom of what is missing. It gives notice not only to itself but also to what it represents. What it represents is usually a loss, sometimes of life, sometimes of a path not taken."[24] The Arab and Muslim men who *should* be in the space, but are not, haunt the film, as their ethnopornographic absence is necessary for the continued fantasy of *Gaytanamo*. The ghosts of *Gaytanamo*, the Arab and Muslim men missing and absent in the film, represent the violence and oppression of Guantanamo and the broader War on Terror, as well as "knowledge" about the bodies and sexualities of Arab and Muslim men. In what follows, I will use queer of color critique, particularly that of Jasbir Puar and Sara Ahmed, to argue for an ethnopornographic haunting within and constituting *Gaytanamo*.

Fantasy, Orientation, and Disorientation

Fantasy plays a central role in hard-core pornography, gay, straight, or otherwise. Linda Williams claims, "In cinematic hard core we encounter a profoundly 'escapist' genre that distracts audiences from the deeper social or political causes of the disturbed relations between the sexes; and yet paradoxically, if it is to distract effectively, a popular genre must address some of the real experiences and needs of its audience."[25] Hard-core porn portrays a world of endless sexual energy, abundance, and excess. As an example, Williams notes that in some hard-core porn, sexual coercion is always portrayed as pleasurable, with the victim eventually finding pleasure in the coercion itself. Therefore, the fantasy of the impossibility of rape is enacted.[26] Susanna Paasonen also discusses the role of fantasy in porn, particularly in the domestic "pornotopias" of online amateur porn, including how the family home becomes constructed as a space of sexual freedom and abundance.[27] When it comes to gay porn, fantasy is also paramount in its constitution and consumption. Richard Dyer, in analyzing the gay porn film *Inch by Inch*, highlights the use of pastiche and fantasy in gay porn to facilitate erotic enjoyment. According to Dyer, the film creates a fantastical space, set in the real world, in which gay male sexuality is uncontrollable, unbridled, and endless.[28] Gay porn also serves to create a fantasy world in which gay sexuality is celebrated, unabashed, and visible, unlike the everyday reality of homophobia and heterosexism.[29] Gay porn often goes further and imagines all-male stereotypically masculine and heterosexual spaces, such as prisons, the military, sports teams, locker rooms, and/or dormitories as completely overrun with gay sex. Gay porn reimagines these spaces as removed from the world of heterosexuality, where men's "true" desires for each other can come to surface, into fruition.[30] Fantasy and the fantastical are central aspects in hard-core pornography that allow its representations to function as supposedly apart from the real world.

Gaytanamo not only presents a pornographic fantasy but specifically presents a racialized ethnopornographic fantasy, as the real-world Guantanamo is an extremely and violently racialized space. Scholars who study the representations of people of color in pornography have noted the centrality of fantasy to such representations. Both Mireille Miller-Young and Jennifer Nash, in their analyses of black women in pornography, discuss racialized ideas of black women's sexuality that are portrayed in pornography, including hypersexuality and aggressiveness. While Miller-Young focuses on how black porn actresses navigate these representations in the porn industry, Nash discusses the potential power of racial fantasies for black women's freedom, counter to standard black feminist narratives of fantasy as wound.[31] Darieck Scott and Kobena Mercer, on the other hand, have argued that, in gay male erotic and pornographic imagery, black men are stereotyped and reduced to an animalistic sexuality, often specifically focused on the trope of the exaggeratedly oversized black penis.[32] These stereotypes in gay porn serve to create a fantasy that orients viewers toward a status quo vision of black male sexuality. All four of these scholars refer to the long history of racist stereotypes of black men and women's sexualities in how such representations function in the context of pornography.

A few scholars have discussed fantasies and stereotypes about Arab men in gay porn, something that is directly relevant to discussions of *Gaytanamo*. Royce Mahawatte and Karim Tartoussieh have argued that the overwhelming majority of gay porn featuring Arab men has portrayed them in a particularly Orientalist fashion. Arab men are portrayed as animalistic, bestial, depraved, and sexually voracious, focused on their own pleasure above all else. These stereotypes are taken directly from Orientalist narratives of Arab male sexuality.[33] These stereotypes and narratives then work to shore up the idea of a "civilized" white manhood that is opposed, yet sexually attracted to, the sexuality of Arab men. Such films are an example of ethnopornography. These films produce an erotic "knowledge" of Arab men that may have little, if any, correspondence in the world outside the film. This "knowledge" then sticks to the bodies of Arab men and can have important potential real-world consequences, as all other Orientalist knowledge does. These analyses, though, still focus particularly on porn in which Arab men are present and visible. What, then, is the place of fantasy in the absence of Arab and Muslim men in *Gaytanamo*?[34]

If one takes as a given that gay porn regularly fantasizes about all-male hypermasculine spaces and the potential for gay sex within them, then one can see that that is clearly what is occurring in *Gaytanamo*. The space of Guantanamo is appropriated into the fantasy of the space of Gaytanamo, a secret War on Terror military detention facility in which gay sex and fantasy are commonplace, even expected, especially by the audience. The audience of *Gaytanamo* is primed to fantasize about the space as one overflowing with gay sex and sexuality. The audience and the film, then, are *oriented* toward this space of sexual fantasy. In fact, most of the sexual action of the film takes place in a fantasy within the fantasy. Most of the sex scenes are either on a screen in the film, as part of the "torture" of Danny Fox, or they are Fox's own hallucinations while drugged. The absence of Arab and Muslim men in *Gaytanamo* is therefore necessary to keep the ethnopornographic fantasy of Gaytanamo intact. To include Arab and Muslim men in the space of Gaytanamo would serve to *disorient* the fantasy by aligning it too closely with reality. Seeing Arab and Muslim men tortured within the fantasy of Gaytanamo would serve to disorient that fantasy, as the viewer would know that such torture happens in the real-world space of Guantanamo. Part of the fantasy of *Gaytanamo* is that it represents a self-contained, unreal space of gay sexual pleasure, albeit one that is loosely based on an actual physical space. This space allows for the production of knowledge and reality that is counter to that which is outside of the film, therefore participating in a project of ethnopornography. The inclusion of Arab and Muslim men might orient the film too much toward the well-known images of sexualized torture at Abu Ghraib prison in Iraq, or toward the indefinite detention of such men in Guantanamo, many of whom are still there.

Ahmed additionally argues, taking from Frantz Fanon, that bodies of color may have particularly disorienting effects. She claims that "an effect of being 'out of place' is also to create disorientation in others: the body of color might disturb the picture—and do so simply as a result of being in spaces that are lived as white, spaces into which white bodies can sink." Ahmed also notes that "some bodies more than others have their involvement in the world called into crisis."[35] The film *Gaytanamo* is by no means an entirely white space that is disoriented by any bodies of color. There are white, black, and Latino men in the film in various sexual combinations. Notably, the film does not specify the races of the men in the film in the title or any of the promotional material, which is significant, as gay porn tends to classify films with casts of more than one race as "interracial" porn. The nonevent of a multiracial cast, a cast composed of men of a variety of racial backgrounds, in the film constructs a multicultural sexual space of gay porn. Puar, in discussing the work of Rey Chow, describes liberal multiculturalism as "the careful management of difference: of difference within sameness." She goes on to describe how logics of liberal multiculturalism dictate that certain people and bodies of color get folded into a nationalist imaginary, which ends up bolstering white supremacy through the conscription of those people and bodies as exceptional and as docile enough not to upset the racial status quo.[36] There are certain bodies of color, however, that could disorient such a vision within *Gaytanamo*. The ghosts of the Arab and Muslim men who are imprisoned in Guantanamo haunt this multicultural ethnopornographic fantasy. To include them would disrupt the fantasy by bringing the real-world violence of Guantanamo and the War on Terror into the film. The hypervisibility of Arab and Muslim Americans post-9/11 during the War on Terror makes their absence in the film even more conspicuous.[37] The only way to construct a potentially multicultural sexual space in Guantanamo is to absent the people who are actually imprisoned there, thereby taking the racialized violence out of the equation.[38] But they are never truly and completely gone. They still haunt the space, as the knowledge of their absence creates ghosts of them.

Gay Porn and Homonationalism

Terrorism and queer sexuality are tightly intertwined in this film, held in tension by the absence of specific racialized bodies, as they constitute each other. During the first interrogation scene, when Violator first encounters

Danny Fox in the confines of Gaytanamo and speaks to him in Hebrew, the film provides the audience with subtitles.[10] Violator repeatedly calls Danny a "faggot," while at the same time saying that he is Igor Yugo, the leader of a terrorist group that Violator has been hunting for ten years. By referring to Danny as both a faggot and a terrorist in the first scene, he constructs Danny as both simultaneously. Jasbir Puar and Amit Rai argue that the image of the terrorist is always sexually deviant and the image of the faggot is generally lacking in patriotism.[39] However, despite being tightly intertwined, they are not necessarily viewed as one and the same throughout the entire film. One instance of the opposition of terrorism and queer sexuality in the film is during a conversation between Violator and another interrogator:

VIOLATOR: He's not talking.

OTHER INTERROGATOR: Igor's a jihadist; he will never give in to the normal forms of interrogation.

VIOLATOR: You're right. We must resort to a more intense form of persuasion.

OTHER INTERROGATOR: What do you have in mind?

VIOLATOR: What does a jihadist hate more than anything?

OTHER INTERROGATOR: Our free way of life!

VIOLATOR: Besides that.

OTHER INTERROGATOR: Women?

VIOLATOR: Close. Homosexuals. Tie him up to a chair, staple his eyelids open, and expose him to graphic homosexual intercourse until he can no longer take it. We will break him sooner than you think.

In this scene, the idea of a "jihadist" and that of a homosexual are conceived of as being mutually exclusive, as completely incompatible. It is noteworthy that this is the only place in which anything remotely related to Islam appears in the film. When it does appear, it is attended by Orientalist stereotypes, that Muslims are inherently homophobic and misogynist.[40] During the next scene, Danny Fox is "tortured" by being made to watch gay porn. As he watches, however, he becomes erect and masturbates. The other interrogator even helps him by stimulating his nipples while he masturbates. At the end of the scene, his ejaculation comes along at the same time as the men he's watching. The sequence of masturbation and ejaculation is very important. As Linda Williams has noted, ejaculation, or the money shot, is one of the most significant features of hard-core pornography as it is the culmination of the sexual scene and the visual proof of masculine pleasure.[41] In *Gaytanamo*, this money shot is a moment when the claim that Danny Fox is a "terrorist" most falters. By using the "torture" to get off, he subverts its intended use. He takes the "torture" and transforms it into something pleasurable. This act and scene constructs the homosexual and the terrorist as mutually exclusive categories, in and through each other. If Danny Fox were actually a terrorist or "jihadist," the torture would have worked and he would have been disgusted and told them everything they wanted to know. The fact that it did not work, in a very specific, sexual manner, is evidence that not only is Danny Fox queer but he is also *not* a terrorist.

In a later scene, the interrogators drug Danny with "sulfuric transmuglobin," a fictional compound that is supposed to make one tell the truth after causing intense hallucinations. Danny's hallucinations consist of three different gay sex scenes. After these scenes, the audience meets the two interrogators again. This time, the second interrogator tells Violator that there is new evidence that Danny might be innocent. He holds up the evidence, saying that all they found in his bag was not a bomb but a long, black dildo. In the moment before he shows the evidence, the audience could be led to believe that the queer hallucinations themselves are evidence of innocence. This innocence, then, is constructed through queer sexuality. Also, the black dildo, indicating that Danny is in some way queer, is the physical evidence of his innocence, further constructing innocence through queerness. This evidence works only through an ethnopornographic rendering of the absent Arab and Muslim men as not only not queer but specifically as virulently homophobic, so much so that anything related to being gay, such as a large black dildo or a gay porn film, would be felt as torture. Afterward, Danny is thrown into "the hole" with another presumably innocent man, Sebastian Cruz, where they immediately have sex. Once again, queer sex and sexuality are proof of innocence of terrorism.

The innocence of the white queer man, and the innocence of queerness, can be achieved only through opposition to the figure of the terrorist and the absence of the particularly racialized presence of Arab and Muslim men. The figures of the Arab and Muslim and the terrorist are implicitly one and the same in the film. The term "jihadist" is a heavily racialized term in the US context, almost always meaning a terrorist primarily influenced by Islam. Additionally, Arabs and Muslims are conflated with each other throughout the mainstream media.[42] By putting the white queer man in the position where the Arab or Muslim men would be in the real Guantanamo Bay, the film constructs him as out of place. He is not supposed to be there, as is evidenced by his own sexuality and the lack of hard evidence against him. In the film's narrative, he functions as a homonationalist figure. Jasbir Puar coined the term "homonationalism," the fact that some or certain bodies signify homonormative nationalism."[43] Homonationalism invokes the rehabilitation of *some* lesbian, gay, and queer bodies and identities in the War on Terror through a nationalist opposition to racialized and foreign "Others" and "enemies." Puar claims as "a primary facet of homonationalism" "that of the whiteness of gay, homosexual, and queer bodies and the attendant presumed heterosexuality of colored bodies."[44] In particular, she is speaking to how queer and Arab bodies and identities are relegated to separate and distant spaces. This makes it appear to be impossible to be both queer and Arab at the same time. White American queers get folded into the multicultural nationalist narrative within homonationalism, as they become perceived as safe and docile for the aims of the US nation-state, as positioned against Arabs and Muslims. As mentioned earlier, this homonationalist multiculturalism plays out in *Gaytanamo*. By absenting Arab and Muslim men from the narrative, the white queer man can then be recuperated as *not* a terrorist, in opposition to those who are not present, yet haunt the film. The homonationalist multicultural narrative remains intact, though it does so only through the knowledge that the white queer man is not supposed to be there *because Arab and Muslim men are "supposed" to be there*. Their ghosts make his innocence possible, make his queerness recuperable. They continue to haunt the film right up until the end, as the punishment given to Danny Fox is the same as that given to Arab and Muslim men in Guantanamo. Even though there is hard evidence that he is innocent, his interrogators put him in "the hole . . . until we find new evidence to show he's guilty." Though his innocence is crafted in the narrative of the film and by hard evidence, he is still never truly "innocent." There is always the potential for new information to be found, new evidence to be uncovered by the interrogators and the government. Fox's innocence also does not affect the outcome of his capture and torture; he is still subjected to the same punishment. This is a cinematic representation of indefinite detention, a fact of life for many in

Guantanamo. As Lisa Hajjar, among many others, has noted, there are still hundreds of Arab and Muslim men held in Guantanamo with no real idea of whether or not they will ever be tried in any sort of court of law, much less if they will ever be released, regardless of guilt or innocence.[45] Hajjar notes that the treatment of the detainees in Guantanamo falls outside of any accepted ideas of legality or justice, either domestic or international. Their punishment, despite their absence, haunts Danny Fox and reminds the viewer of the unjust nature of Guantanamo itself.

At the same time that this final scene depicts a very real treatment that many suffer in Guantanamo, it reinscribes the whiteness of *Gaytanamo*. Both Danny Fox and Sebastian Cruz are white, and at least one is held without cause or evidence. Importantly, this is the only sex scene in the film that takes place in the "reality" of the film. All of the other sex scenes, including those featuring men of color, take place on a TV screen as torture or within the drugged mind of Danny Fox. The only men in *Gaytanamo* who get to have sexual pleasure in the "real world" are two white men. This scene reorients the fantasy back to the safety of white queerness through two moves: the total absence of Arab and Muslim men, and the relegation of all other men of color to the realm of a fantasy within a fantasy. The re-orientation toward whiteness occurs simultaneously with the enactment of real-world punishment on-screen. While viewers are reminded of such injustice, the potential political weight of that knowledge is blunted by the reorientation toward white queer fantasy.

Conclusion: Porn, Haunting, and Ethnopornographic Engagement

In *Ghostly Matters*, Avery Gordon names three characteristic features of haunting. She states,

> We have seen that the ghost imports a charged strangeness into the place or sphere it is haunting, thus unsettling the propriety and property lines that delimit a zone of activity or knowledge. I have also emphasized that the ghost is primarily a symptom of what is missing. It gives notice not only to itself but also to what it represents. . . . We are in relation to it and it has designs on us such that we must reckon with it graciously, attempting to offer it a hospitable memory *out of a concern for justice*. Out of a concern for justice would be the only reason one would bother.[46]

For Gordon, haunting and ghosts have a distinctly political quality. In particular, haunting has to do with social violences, "it always registers the harm inflicted or the loss sustained by a social violence done in the past or in the present."⁴⁷ The violence of the War on Terror, including indefinite detention at the Guantanamo Bay prison, is ongoing. It remains in the present, even as the War on Terror, national security, and global events take new shapes and forms. The ghosts of *Gaytanamo*, the Arab and Muslim men absent in the film yet present in Guantanamo, remind us of the ongoing nature of the War on Terror and of their indefinite detention without trial. They haunt the corridors and torture rooms and cells of *Gaytanamo* because *we know they should be there, though they are not.* No one can deny the reality of Guantanamo and the reality of the indefinite detention of the men imprisoned there, regardless of one's political position. The ghosts and the haunting point to the social violence of Guantanamo, even within the confines of a porn film. In Gordon's words, they "unsettle" the delimited "zone of activity" of the sexual fantasy. Such unsettling is congruent with Sara Ahmed's notion of "disorientation." To unsettle is to disorient, to make things strange.

But the ghosts, as Gordon claims, are not dead; they are very much alive. The Arab and Muslim men in Guantanamo are still alive, waiting for a potential justice that may or may not come. If reckoning with haunting, according to Gordon, is "out of a concern for justice," how are we then to reckon with haunting in a gay porn film about Guantanamo? I argue that the haunting and ghosts of *Gaytanamo* serve to unsettle sexual fantasies that would absent the racialized violence inherent in Guantanamo from the scene of the fantasy. The ghosts remind us that real people exist in a real place, the real place on which the porn is based. They nag at us subtly, yet surely. We know their presence and we know that our sexual arousal is facilitated through ignoring their existence and plight. This is not to say that anyone who watches *Gaytanamo* necessarily derives pleasure from the War on Terror; this is instead to say that we should remain on guard. We should remember that the ethnopornographic absenting of Arab and Muslim men from *Gaytanamo* only serves to bolster a broader agenda of multicultural homonationalism. *Gaytanamo* is an example of ethnopornography that renders knowledge and "facts" about the erotic lives of the absent Arab and Muslim men, as well as the white main characters. Such ethnopornographic knowledge production has ramifications, as it can influence and change how people think about racial and sexual "Others," potentially for better or for worse.

What, then, is the place of haunting and ghosts in porn studies more broadly? I believe that attention to absence, attention to what should be in a film but is not, can help us to think through the political consequences and meanings of contemporary hard-core pornography. As many porn scholars have argued over time, pornography is a reflection of the broader culture, just like any media form or genre. As Gayle Rubin notes in her critique of antipornography feminism "Misguided, Dangerous, and Wrong," the antiporn feminist focus on porn alone, apart from other media, was and is misguided. She notes that "by 1978 feminists had already spent a decade identifying and criticizing the ideologies that justified male supremacy and that permeated virtually all of Western literature, high art, popular media, religion, and education."[48] She argues that to single porn out as being particularly misogynist, while the rest of cultural production could be argued as equally misogynist, is to miss the point about transforming broader structures of power and oppression. We can take Rubin's argument to also mean that pornography, just like every single other media genre and form of cultural production, is a reflection of the broader culture and society that creates it.

One of the major interventions of porn studies throughout its existence as a field is that pornography is a legitimate subject of scholarship and should be treated like other media genres in terms of the rigor and critical inquiry applied to it. This was one of the key interventions of Linda Williams in *Hard Core* and continues to animate the field. If porn is another genre of media and should be treated as such, porn studies scholars must also engage with the politics woven into pornography. Historically, this attention to the political has been primarily concerned with the politics of censorship and antipornography forces, such as antipornography feminists, religious fundamentalists, and right-wing politicians. More recently, scholars of pornography have moved into more complex issues of the political. For example, Mireille Miller-Young and Jennifer Nash's books on black women in pornography, though different in methodology, purpose, and conclusion, are both manifestations of a concerted engagement with the complex politics of porn. The contributors to the anthology *Porn Archives* write about porn and political topics as diverse as race, history, technological development, and war. This is not to say that these authors are the only scholars paying heed to the varied and complicated political issues of pornography, but they are simply examples in a broader constellation of scholarship.

Haunting, for Gordon, requires an attention to questions of justice, even if that sense of justice seems an impossibility. The absences, the ghosts, the haunting makes us aware of social violences, calls our attention to them. The sense of the impossible justice of theories of haunting are what is at stake in these readings of absence in porn. It is not close reading that will get at the meaning of what this text offers us but the context, the ultimate lack of freedom and justice and the violences done to Arab and Muslim men through indefinite detention, among other state practices. *Gaytanamo* itself does not offer us any solutions. The final scene is one of foreclosure of the possibility of freedom. The nonresolution of the film, though, speaks to the systemic oppression that none of us are outside of. The torture and injustice of spaces such as Guantanamo are ongoing, seemingly without end. The ghosts of *Gaytanamo* call our attention to such political and ethical concerns as they haunt the film.

One of the underdeveloped areas of porn studies is absence. I suggest that an attention to absence in and around pornography can reveal much about the construction and constitution of pornography as a politically engaged media form, as *ethnopornography*. What *isn't* there is often just as important as what *is*. Absences sometimes work to hide important issues while they can also work to expose others. Ethnopornographic absences work through negation to produce knowledge about those not present, those without a voice, which always produces more knowledge about those that are on-screen. I find that the framework of ethnopornographic haunting and ghosts serves as a politically engaged model for how to think about absence within pornography. If porn studies scholars and scholarship are to remain politically engaged, an attention to absence through ethnopornographic haunting will be crucial to maintaining "a concern for justice."

Notes

1   "*Gaytanamo*," *Dark Alley* DVD. 2010. http://darkalleydvd.com/product. php?productid=16200.

2   "*Gaytanamo*."

3   "The Controversy over Gaytanamo Gay Torture Sex," *GayPornucopia!*, May 4, 2007, https://web.archive.org/web/20070921131253/ http://www.gaypornucopia. com/2007/05/04/the-controversy-over-gaytanamo/

4   Vincent Lambert, "New Release: Gaytanamo," April 23, 2007, http://vincentlambert.blogspot.com/2007/04/new-release-gaytanamo.html

5   "New Lows in Bad Taste," *Washington Blade*, January 5, 2007.

6 Narcissusᴀᴜ, "Good Taste? . . ." *Synthetic Ego*, March 24, 2007, http://syntheticego. blogspot.com/2007/03/good-taste.html

7 "Gaytanamo Draws Fire," *Queerty*, April 4, 2007, https://web.archive.org/web/ 20070429004946/http://www.queerty.com/queer//gaytanamo-draws-fire -20070404.php

8 Linda Williams, *Hard Core: Power, Pleasure, and the "Frenzy of the Visible"* (Berkeley: University of California Press, 1989), 48–49.

9 Avery Gordon, *Ghostly Matters: Haunting and the Sociological Imaginary* (Minneapolis: University of Minnesota Press, 2008), xvi.

10 Introduction, this volume.

11 John Champagne, "'Stop Reading Films!': Film Studies, Close Analysis, and Gay Pornography," *Cinema Journal* 36, no. 4 (1997): 76–97.

12 Throughout this chapter, I refer to the actors and characters in *Gaytanamo* by the actors' stage names, as the characters do not have their own individual names within the film.

13 In the original version of *Gaytanamo*, released in 2007, all sex scenes employ condoms. Another version was released in 2009, *Gaytanamo Raw*, which was shot with bareback, condomless sex.

14 Williams, *Hard Core*, 34.

15 Williams, *Hard Core*, 36.

16 Williams, *Hard Core*, 49.

17 Williams, *Hard Core*, 4.

18 Williams, *Hard Core*, 49–50.

19 Gillian Rose, *Visual Methodologies*, 3rd ed. (Los Angeles: Sage Publications, 2012), 219.

20 Gordon, *Ghostly Matters*, xvi.

21 Judith Butler, *Precarious Life: The Powers of Mourning and Violence* (New York: Verso, 2004), 50–51.

22 Lisa Hajjar, *Torture: A Sociology of Violence and Human Rights* (New York: Routledge, 2013), 5–6.

23 Bruce Bennett, "X-Ray Visions: Photography, Propaganda and Guantanamo Bay," in *Controversial Images: Media Representations on the Edge*, ed. Feona Attwood, et al. (Basingstoke, UK: Palgrave Macmillan, 2013), 67.

24 Gordon, *Ghostly Matters*, 63–64.

25 Williams, *Hard Core*, 154–55.

26 Williams, *Hard Core*, 164. Williams's analysis does not take into account extreme porn in which the victims are not portrayed as enjoying rape and/or sexual coercion, as this genre came to prominence only in the years after *Hard Core* was published. For examples of analysis of films from this genre, see "Rough Sex" by Eugenie Brinkema in *Porn Archives*, ed. Tim Dean, Steven Ruszczychy, and David Squires (Durham, NC: Duke University Press, 2014), 262–83; and "'Choke on It, Bitch!': Porn Studies, Extreme Gonzo and the Mainstreaming of Hardcore," by

Stephen Maddison in *Mainstreaming Sex: The Sexualization of Western Culture*, ed. Feona Attwood (London: I.B. Tauris, 2009), 37–54.

27 Susanna Paasonen, *Carnal Resonance: Affect and Online Pornography* (Cambridge, MA: MIT Press, 2011), 107–108.

28 Richard Dyer, "Idol Thoughts: Orgasm and Self-Reflexivity in Gay Pornography," in *More Dirty Looks: Gender, Pornography and Power*, ed. Pamela Church Gibson (London: British Film Institute, 2004), 103–104.

29 Michael Bronski, *Culture Clash: The Making of Gay Sensibility* (Boston: South End Press, 1984), 161–62.

30 John Mercer, "In the Slammer: The Myth of the Prison in American Gay Pornographic Video," *Journal of Homosexuality* 47, no. 3/4 (2004): 151–66.

31 Mireille Miller-Young, *A Taste for Brown Sugar: Black Women in Pornography* (Durham, NC: Duke University Press, 2014), 177–78; Jennifer C. Nash, *The Black Body in Ecstasy: Reading Race, Reading Pornography*, (Durham, NC: Duke University Press, 2014), 150–51.

32 Darieck Scott, "Big Black Beauty: Drawing and Naming the Black Male Figure in Superhero and Gay Porn Comic" in *Porn Archives*, ed. Tim Dean, Steven Ruszczycky, and David Squires (Durham, NC: Duke University Press, 2014), 183–212; Kobena Mercer, "Looking for Trouble," in *The Gay and Lesbian Studies Reader*, ed. Henry Abelove, Michèle Aina Barale, and David M. Halperin (New York: Routledge, 1993), 350–59.

33 Royce Mahawatte, "Loving the Other: Arab-Male Fetish Pornography and the Dark Continent of Masculinity," in *More Dirty Looks: Gender, Pornography and Power*, ed. Pamela Church Gibson (London: British Film Institute, 2004), 127–136; Karim Tartoussieh, "Muslim Digital Diasporas and the Gay Pornographic Cyber Imaginary," in *Between the Middle East and the Americas*, ed. Ella Shohat and Evelyn Alsultany (Ann Arbor: University of Michigan Press, 2013), 214–30.

34 I argue that an explanation can be found in Sara Ahmed's ideas of orientation and disorientation in her book *Queer Phenomenology: Orientations, Objects, Others*. Ahmed argues that, in connecting disorientation with queerness, "disorientation could be described here as the 'becoming oblique' of the world" (162). She also argues that disorientation is "an effect of being 'out of place'" (160). This model of disorientation has direct bearing on absence in *Gaytanamo*.

35 Sara Ahmed, *Queer Phenomenology: Orientations, Objects, Others* (Durham, NC: Duke University Press, 2006), 159–60.

36 Jasbir Puar, *Terrorist Assemblages: Homonationalism in Queer Times* (Durham, NC: Duke University Press, 2007), 25–27.

37 Nadine Naber, "Introduction: Arab Americans and U.S. Racial Formations," in *Race and Arab Americans before and after 9/11: From Invisible Citizens to Visible Subjects*, ed. Amaney Jamal and Nadine Naber (Syracuse, NY: Syracuse University Press, 2008), 1–45.

38 Though this chapter makes a limited foray into the relationship between multiculturalism and porn, the question of multiculturalism or the multicultural, in any

of its formulations, for pornography has not been taken up within porn studies. Several articles and books discuss racialized pornography of many variations, but an engagement with concepts of multiculturalism has not occurred.

39 Jasbir Puar and Amit Rai, "Monster, Terrorist, Fag: The War on Terrorism and the Production of Docile Patriots," *Social Text* 72, vol. 20 (2002): 118–48.

40 Puar, *Terrorist Assemblages*, 19–20.

41 Williams, *Hard Core*, 117.

42 Evelyn Alsultany, Arabs and Muslims in the Media: Race and Representation after 9/11 (New York: New York University Press, 2012), 9–10.

43 Puar, *Terrorist Assemblages*, 10.

44 Puar, *Terrorist Assemblages*, 38–39, 44.

45 Hajjar, *Torture*, 5–6.

46 Gordon, *Ghostly Matters*, 63–64.

47 Gordon, Ghostly Matters, xvi.

48 Gayle Rubin, "Misguided, Dangerous, and Wrong: An Analysis of Anti-Pornography Politics," in *Bad Girls and Dirty Pictures: The Challenge to Reclaim Feminism,* ed. *Alison Assiter and Avedon Carol* (London: Pluto Press, 1993), 19.

Under White Men's Eyes

Racialized Eroticism, Ethnographic Encounters,
and the Maintenance of the Colonial Order

> My mother used to say that the black woman is the white man's mule and the
> white woman is his dog. Now, she said that to say this: we do the heavy work and
> get beat whether we do it well or not. But the white woman is closer to the master
> and he pats them on the head and lets them sleep in the house, but he ain' gon'
> treat neither one like he was dealing with a person.
> —Interview with Nancy White

1 A white American man says to me, "You know, they [African men] only
   want to fuck you because they hate you." I think but do not say, "No.
   They want to fuck me because they hate you."[1]

2 My boyfriend, a black American man, asks me to talk to him during our
   intimate moments about the racial implications of our union, about our
   bodies. He wants to generate and amplify the idea that my body should
   not belong to him, that in giving in to him, in giving myself to him, I am
   defying the social order. He says that he craves these ideas; they make
   him feel powerful and strong.

3   Discussing erotic subjectivity in my graduate seminar, the class is split on the idea of ethics. "Fucking for facts," one student calls it. "It's ethical only if you marry the person," says another. "But somebody gave you a grant, you're obligated to be professional." "There's always a power imbalance." "Love is love, it doesn't matter where you are." "It depends if you are a man or a woman." "You can't count out the idea of race." "How do you know if they want you for you?"

4   I organize a panel addressing erotic subjectivity at a professional conference. My home discipline, ethnomusicology, has historically been reluctant to engage fully with the subject of erotic subjectivity. On this panel, six female ethnomusicologists speak frankly about the ways that race and sexuality have structured their ethnographic work, writing, and institutional experiences. It was a gratifying intellectual experience for me that was somewhat dampened by a few male colleagues whose thoughts demonstrate why these conversations are difficult to have in the first place. Two white male colleagues say that they feel marginalized by our conversation because they cannot immediately relate to those experiences, and suggest that the topic is unnecessary. One man criticizes my personal story for the details I include, and those that I don't; he suggests that I was both promiscuous and deceptive.

Later, I reflect upon each of these moments and the histories they represent: The white man believed that hate fuels the intimacy and arousal between African men and white women. That the history of colonialism has been so thoroughly internalized that there is no room left for emotional, physical, or spiritual union apart from the web of violence that comprises the discourse of the black sexualized body.

My black American boyfriend was strengthened in emotional and sexual power by the idea of our difference, a difference structured by the histories that have regulated my body and his. By breaking through those histories, or confronting them through direct engagement, a kind of balance is restored for him and a corrective narrative emerges in which he has agency to name and define.

The students struggle with institutional legitimacy, the discourse of power imbalance that they have inherited from anthropology classes and fieldwork ethics. A part of them want direct answers about what they should do, what they can write about, and what people will think. They recognize that there are complicated answers to complicated questions, and they know that they too will be theorizing these issues as they process them through their ethnographic encounters. They point to the constraints both professional and personal of intimate encounter, and how to situate those experiences within our work. They rightly point out that it matters, in fact is crucial, how one's gender, sexuality, and race intersect in these conversations. It matters, indeed, not only how we see ourselves but also how the world—comprised of located culturally intelligible lenses—interprets our bodies.

Thinking about negative or critical responses to a professional presentation is useful insofar as it provides an opportunity to examine the context into which we are speaking. Some forms of critique are valuable, obviously, and others reveal more about the critic and the discipline than anything else. But taken beyond the context of an isolated criticism, we can see that particularly when these criticisms rely upon tactics of shaming or accusation, they represent a history of determining whose experiences are given priority and value within the field. I considered our panel successful not only because of the conversations that were had during the discussion but also because many people came to me throughout the week to share similar experiences and thoughts on our topic. However, the response from those colleagues, and my initial reaction to them, showed me how one becomes trampled by voices that do not edit themselves, who feel entitled to the priority of their experience and knowledge, and who will call upon gendered forms of criticism to shame and silence dissent.

Taken alone, each one of these moments and my reflection upon them represents a historical conflict, institutional parameters both of educational possibilities and of intellectual freedom, and the imagination of bodies and of intimacy. However, they represent somewhat myopic perspectives of the spectrum of arousal and desire that occurs between people. They offer no insight into the power exchange of sexual encounter, or the histories that individuals bring into their sexual lives. And they offer no resolution to the questions of individual subjectivity within these narratives. Within these moments, people are reduced, *products of these histories*, rather than agents within them. We become comprised entirely of discourse—figurines acting out historical scenes of violence. And we are confined in the ways that we can speak back to this discourse. In order to make these moments productive, they need to be set in dialogue with each other.

These configurations lead to some specific questions about the connections between the racialized sexualized subject, intimate encounter, and ethnography. In particular, for me, questions arise about the connections between ethnomusicology, ethnography, and ethnopornography. For instance, what methodological overlap can be found in the history of ethnomusicology as a discipline and the circulating imagination of the encountered Other? What disciplinary mechanisms enable the continued neglect of these histories and the erasure of counternarratives? As I will discuss later, there is disciplinary anxiety about the erotic when it is manifested in intimacy or desire. This anxiety runs counter to the methodological imperative of the ethnographic encounter, such that the disjuncture reproduces specific power hierarchies that have developed alongside and within ethnomusicological thought and method. These reproduced power hierarchies have the effect of silencing dissent, amplifying dismissive voices, and generating ethnographic methodologies that embolden those who benefit from such imbalance.

In analytical terms, how can we best situate the overlapping categories of body, self, and the context through which those realities become manifest? When my black American boyfriend focuses in on racial difference as a means to arousal he is choosing to activate the historical narratives that have defined our bodies, and in doing so reimagines his position of power vis-à-vis those narratives. In order to situate this example, it is crucial not to generalize and give the impression that all black men fantasize along these terms. Such a generalization is both violent and reductive, and serves no purpose here. While I think that performing the theater of dominance and subjugation through those terms might serve as a relief, for him, even temporarily, from a state of aggression that characterizes daily life in a hostile racial environment, it does not mean that that performance is neutral or meaningless. I'm going to avoid an individualized psychological portrait of this man because I think the specifics of his needs and situation are not necessarily instructive in elucidating the psychosexual dynamics that drive such a performance. I think, too, that they are not unique, but rather representative of particular types of sexual encounters. I hope that in using such an example, the ways that the racialized body is eroticized will become more evident, as will the circumstances through which the body shapes our experience of subjective consciousness. I'd also like to point out that in this relationship, although not in every relationship, these moments did not define the union; they were isolated performances. I think that characterizing them as theatrical is useful because they existed apart from both daily experience and moments of intimacy that felt more closely tied to other areas of psychosexual connection.

It can be challenging to have these conversations for a number of reasons, primarily for me because the way that my body is understood as both racialized and sexualized is not only always shifting over time and context but also changes from encounter to encounter. Focusing in specifically on my ethnographic experiences in West Africa from 2008 to 2017 will locate the frame of my analysis quite a bit, but there are myriad factors that simply cannot all be attended to here. What is represented here is really my perception of the context through which race and sexuality become meaningful aspects of ethnographic research rather than a precise account of all the possibilities of what other people thought and felt. People clearly do not necessarily articulate around race in every encounter, though it is still an important quality of the experience.

In this chapter I explore the erotic as a framework of analysis through an account of a few experiences conducting field research on the northwestern border of Ghana and Burkina Faso. I interrogate how the explorations of the erotic body, the lived realities of desiring and being desired, and the practices that surround the gendered, racialized, sexualized subject shed light on anthropological knowledge. Although race and sexuality are a meaningful aspect of all ethnography, I prioritize a discussion of encounter between white women and black men in Africa because I am proceeding from my own subjective consciousness and experience. Additionally, generalizations about race and gender offer much less analytical fruit than located and specific case studies, though there are certainly broader implications to be drawn from such examples. Furthermore, the ethnopornographic gaze is already crafted through white heterosexual patriarchal machinery, making corrective accounts more necessary. Finally, the social construction of black men and white women is animated uniquely by such a gaze, and is a source of anxiety in very particular ways.

I begin with an examination of erotic subjectivity as it has been discussed in anthropology, pointing in particular to areas in which I plan to intervene. I then offer thoughts on two types of ethnographic encounter: one of violence/subjugation and one of desire/love. I choose these broad categories of analysis because I think that the borders between viewing and surveillance, desiring and objectifying, and being desired and being observed, are barbed and irregular, particularly as we negotiate the cultural expectations inherent in ethnographic work. In fact, the relationship between these encounters should highlight the proximity between what is pleasing and empowering, and what is prohibitive and violent. I draw from Audre Lorde's theories of the relationship between the pornographic and the erotic in order to help situate located experiences along these lines.[2] I engage her thinking in conversation with that which approaches theories of how an ethnopornographic gaze is generated and reproduced. Ultimately, I hope to complicate worn notions of difference, while examining how colonial ideas of both black men and white women's bodies remain intact and operative. The reproduction of these ideologies can be potentially subverted through a critique that provides a nuanced analysis of power, race, and sexual encounter. I conclude with a reflection that demonstrates how these scenes reveal the ethnopornographic gaze as a multidirectional entanglement. As we seek to navigate ethnographic terrain, both in research and in writing, we are bound up in colonial histories, in disciplinary expectations, in institutional regulation, and in interpersonal complexity.

Erotic Subjectivity and Gendered Ethnography

As an interpretive frame, erotic subjectivity can be understood as an epistemological position through which the political dimensions of sensuality are made real. Previous anthropological accounts of erotic subjectivity have fruitfully explored intimate encounter as a meaningful aspect of ethnography and as a subject position.[3] These works have productively demonstrated that sexual encounter is a way of knowing;[4] it is a social relationship that is given meaning through culturally grounded interpretive parameters, and is dependent upon an exchange of power, and is therefore always political.

We are directed toward a relationally constructed understanding of subjectivity as we traverse the landscape of desiring and being desired, as well as the culturally specific terms through which desire is produced. Field research becomes a process not only of getting to know another but also of relearning ourselves. The ways in which we experience ourselves as gendered, sexualized subjects must be reexperienced, reexplored, and reconstructed as we seek to connect with others and to learn how they live within their bodies. Negotiating these parameters is always a relational process. Other scholars have productively shown how conflict as well as passion and everyday choices in relationships can have important implications for anthropological knowledge.[5] Thus the choices that are made when revealing shared moments between people are not arbitrary; they point us to other ways of knowing.

Though previous writers have challenged the ethical problems of intimate encounter in the field, they proceed from an assumption of the inherent power imbalance between the researcher and her "subjects." These assumptions do not allow for an adequate examination of the multidirectional power flows and mediations that occur in practice. "All relationships are agreements about distribution of power, agreements negotiated in varying degrees of intimacy."[6] The complexity of power distribution is articulated through these struggles. It is rare that one person "has" power, while power is exercised upon another. More often it is balanced by myriad factors, some of which are interpersonal, others of which are based upon social categories. In addition to these problems, the ethnographer's body must be understood as a marked space, and thus also be open to critical interrogation.

I contribute a perspective that represents the historical construction of African bodies but also interrogates the ethnographer's body within this discourse. I recognize how the black male body is both fetishized and pathologized while contributing an analysis of the construction and production of whiteness. In this context, whiteness perpetuates colonial ideology through continuous revalidation and legitimization. This occurs by a culturally specific prioritization of the inherent superiority and aesthetic value of whiteness as sexual power and beauty. This must be understood as a gendered experience, revealing the construction of the white female body as linked to the colonial endeavor.[7] It is clear, here, how the concept of ethnopornography generates the operative gaze around both black men and white women; both categories are inscribed through the circulations of imagery/ideology produced by systematized erotic racial imaginations.

As a white woman my body is subject to scrutiny in particular ways that both enable and impede field research. In addition to the experience of sexual objectification in the field, practices of intimacy remain taboo. Though female Africanists rarely discuss practices of desire, white male Africanists have discussed sexual encounters in field research as a means to verify their masculinity among male community members,[8] or quite commonly make no note of it at all, thus reinforcing the priority of their epistemic positions. White women's sexuality remains under greater scrutiny from the academic community and legitimized forums for knowledge production. This points to a continuing ideology of "otherness" regarding black men's sexualized bodies, which have been pathologized, and white women's bodies as the exclusive property of white men. What this configuration demonstrates is that while ethnopornographic accounts are generally understood to be produced and consumed in a unidirectional fashion by a group of people engaged in particular historical and cultural positions, they are actually produced and experienced in multidirectional and overlapping ways. This is significant because it acknowledges the more complicated power dynamics generated through ethnographic engagements that move us away from simplistic outsider/insider relations or flattened conceptions of power imbalance. In fact, a more complete analysis of the circulations of ethnopornographic narratives, images, and imaginations would incorporate an intersectional framework coupled with historical and cultural specificity.

From a disciplinary perspective, though much work has been done on erotic subjectivity both in terms of pleasure and violence,[9] I think there is still much to be done in terms of moving from interpersonal encounter to theoretical models of understanding these encounters as epistemically relevant to anthropological knowledge production. If we continue to receive these stories as personal accounts exclusively, we miss an opportunity to glean crucial points of knowledge about how human beings relate to each other and why they relate in those ways. My personal experience tells me that though the topic of erotic subjectivity is no longer taboo, it is quite possible to experience professional and personal retribution for disclosing these accounts. If we don't create space for these conversations either by (1) assuming that these relationships don't happen, or (2) acknowledging that they do happen but have nothing to do with what we know and how we learn it, then we immediately foreclose the possibility of greater insight. As a potentially corrective account, let us turn to two categories that demonstrate the complexities of race, sexuality, and ethnographic work.

Encounter: Violence/Subjugation

An important aspect to thinking through what constitutes violence/subjugation as distinct from that which is intimate/erotic has been the framework of the pornographic. Audre Lorde distinguishes between the two, writing, "The erotic has often been misnamed by men and used against women. It has been made into the confused, the trivial, the psychotic, the plasticized sensation. For this reason, we have often turned away from the exploration and consideration of the erotic as a source of power and information, confusing it with its opposite, the pornographic. But pornography is a direct denial of the power of the erotic, for it represents the suppression of true feeling. Pornography represents sensation without feeling."[10] She continues, "The erotic is a measure between the beginnings of our sense of self and the chaos of our strongest feelings."[11] Proceeding from her configuration of the erotic as a source of power that requires emotional, spiritual, and intellectual as well as physical connection, the pornographic becomes a harbor of that which is devoid of those connections—that which is objectifying and dehumanizing, that which can be consumed, that which emphasizes observation or surveillance over engaged and reciprocal viewing. It is crucial at this point to note that this configuration of the pornographic as apposite to the erotic is not absolute or universal. I use the dichotomy in order to both set up the dual encounters of violence and desire, and to theorize the possibilities for agency within ethnopornographic circulation.

This construction of the pornographic helps structure what I consider to be forms of ethnographic violence. Grappling with observation and surveillance, expectations of exchange, objectification, and physical and emotional fear are part of my ethnographic experiences. My body is subject to scrutiny during field research in particular ways that are determined by local discourses on race and sexuality. I work in a rural area on the northwestern border of Ghana and Burkina Faso, though these experiences include traveling and working in major cities in both countries as well. In this context, whiteness is considered a marker of high status and is aesthetically valued. My whiteness also increases my visibility, making me vulnerable to interrogation and regulation. Though people are subjected to various forms of violence during ethnographic work, there are four broad categories to which I want to draw attention:

1. Expectation of exchange

2. Institutional implications of revealing encounter

3. Physical violence

4. Surveillance

It is difficult for me to assess/describe these four categories because I continue to be regulated by a fear of naming and calling attention to these practices, particularly when my work is ongoing. This fear is produced partially by an anthropological discourse that suggests that when we encounter violence we have failed to adequately recognize the cultural cues, contexts, or circumstances that lead to those experiences. And that sense of failure has primarily to do with a gendered and racialized normativity in research accounts. Because white male bodies are governed differently (I'm going to leave aside issues of sexuality for the moment), these categories of violence affect them differently. Certainly men experience violence, and the ways that they are constrained from writing/speaking about that are real and meaningful, but they are also not subjected to the same systemic violence as women and people of color. Once you have to articulate difference, being made to feel violated, unsafe, or out of control as part of your research, you are making yourself vulnerable to the scrutiny of "white men's eyes." And that gaze is chilling because you didn't give consent to be watched.

Rather than articulate in detail many experiences that illustrate each of these categories, I am going to offer one that I hope will demonstrate the subtle ways that they become part of field research. This anecdote is drawn from a research trip in the borderland village of Ghana and Burkina Faso where I conduct much of my work:

> I was sitting outside at a drinking spot when he arrived.[12] My friend, Peter (a black Ghanaian), and I had already been there for a while by that time.[13] Though I had tried to avoid being near him, I felt that getting up and leaving would be more inappropriate, and so I decided to stay and behave casually, greeting him and his companions. After some time, he got up, came over, and began stroking my hair, which was pulled back into a ponytail. He started saying, "My wife, my wife," and then began touching my face, even leaning down to kiss my cheek. I recoiled, tried moving my face from his hands, and asked him to stop. He didn't react but went back to his conversation with his friends. I was seething, embarrassed, and angry. Touching a woman's hair or her face in public is unthinkable, especially if she is with another man. It presumes an enormous amount of intimacy. An intimacy that not only did we not share but that I would never want articulated in the way that he was doing it. The public display was intended more to posture towards his friends and Peter than for me, I thought. After he left, I asked Peter directly how he could sit quietly when I was visibly uncomfortable, even to the point of crying out for him to stop. I felt so violated; realizing that I had hoped my friend would protect me made me feel vulnerable and weak. After all these years I still needed a man to intervene on my behalf, to make me safe. It was a gesture of ownership to which I did not agree, that had nothing to do with how I knew him but only with the ways that he wanted other people to see him. Being able to hurt me, to insult me, and degrade me in public made him feel important, and there was no recourse available to me, no option but to say nothing. Who would I tell? What would the complaint be? The truth is that I let this person into my life not seeing clearly who he was or what I was agreeing to by being his friend. And I'll pay for that mistake as long as I remain unmarried—as long as I don't belong to another man. Peter, my friend, calmly explained that he had merely been seeking a

reaction from him; had he offered it to him, it would have provoked an extended dispute. By not reacting at all, Peter had sidestepped the conflict. Though I later saw his reaction as thoughtful and reasonable, I was still left with a sense of sadness and shame. Sadness for the loss of what once was an important friendship, sadness that he felt compelled to treat me as property, sadness that I felt he was more concerned with public perception than with anything else.

When I think about this, I cringe; I hate it. But it is not without analytical merit. There are questions that we would never ask, and if we did the responses to them would tell us nothing. But lived experience will reveal people's behavior and thought processes. The interaction here between this man and Peter is particularly revealing of how men engage and respond to each other, and what that says about local ideas of masculinity and status. My emotional response was countered by one that was more firmly grounded in a local model of conflict resolution between men. Just as cultural norms are important, deviation from them is informative; this man's behavior was well outside an appropriate cultural standard, but that tells me something about how men and women address each other and behave toward each other in public and why that is meaningful. It is a performance, even more so because the intention was to shock; it is a heightened example of how intimacy does or does not get performed in public in this community.

Encounter: Desire/Love

Is there a space to discuss intimacy in terms that provide insight into how white women and black men negotiate the historical constructions of their bodies? Can there be intimacy in these terms that circumvents these histories, that is comprised entirely of the subjectivity of two people? Probably not. What happens first in the mind of most readers when they hear a white woman tell a story of desire or love toward a black man during her research? What assumptions are made that inform the way the reader will process and understand that story? I believe that in the minds of most readers there is an assumption that racial difference has drawn you together and is a priority in your relationship, or that you are unaware of the implications of your racial difference and its history, and therefore are incapable of attaining a union on any kind of equal footing. The reader commits the same act of violence that subjects your body to scrutiny and his to pathology.

I opened this chapter with a quote from Nancy White, in which she elucidates the ways that both black and white women are regulated by white patriarchal dominance.[14] Patricia Hill Collins considers this quote at length, amid a discussion of controlling images.[15] She writes that even when negative images are replaced by positive ones (such as those of white women as desirable, beautiful, or valuable), they are not less damaging, nor will reliance upon them undo the system of domination and control that undergirds them.[16] In other words, there is no way to utilize the type of objectifying and dehumanizing images that are circulated through the ethnopornographic imagination in order to avert that gaze. When white women speak about desire and ethnographic encounter, the controlling images of white women and black men that were generated through the colonial order snap sharply into focus: what is happening is taboo, both of these bodies do not belong to their inhabitants, and arousal can be fueled only by either hatred or the desire to dominate white men's property. And the controlling image for white women is that desire is generated by a need to be transgressive. And those images and their circulation prevent the myriad possibilities of human connection that happen during ethnographic work from being fully discussed. In effect, these images and their attendant ideologies reinstate a colonial mindset—and neither black men nor white women can move away from that predetermined mold that assigns motivation and prevents subjective agency.

Audre Lorde suggests that the erotic requires an engagement with "our sense of self." Though she was referring to love between women, I think that we can equally apply her construction to desire and intimacy between men and women. In the context of ethnographic work, the terrain of desire is peppered with land mines.[17] And in the context of my work in West Africa, those land mines take many forms, but race is often primary because of the heightened visibility of difference and the particular history that it represents. So, as we seek to encounter another person fully, we may not be prioritizing their racial difference, but we are likely to step on a race mine because other people will call attention to and notice that difference. Essentially, race might not be the determining factor in the desire, but it exists whether or not we choose to acknowledge it.

But none of that prevents intimacy in its truest terms. In my personal experience, both love and desire are generative of many forms of intimacy, only some of which are sexual. In some cases, I have experienced a shared and heightened closeness with someone because people on the outside of the union are invested in seeing you a certain way that seems so different from your experience of each other. The desire backs up to violence, though, because it is easy to recognize that social expectation and interaction punctuates the interpersonal in ways that cannot be avoided. And in some ways, both people are placed under the ethnopornographic gaze as people assign desires and motivations to you. And then as a pair you are subject to the consistent mechanisms of regulation and surveillance. I think that the prominence of the violent encounters makes crossing the landscape of desire more difficult, because there is such a burden of institutional and disciplinary convention and regulation that it prevents people from "outing" these relationships or entering into them fully.[18]

Reflection

Both "encounters" offer portraits of possible ethnographic experiences. Taken together they demonstrate how interpersonal relationships are structured by context and informed by located understandings of race and sexuality. This chapter represents a taxonomy of limits: the ways that our bodies generate limitations on people's engagements and responses to us, and how we are limited/restricted by those responses and engagements. We exist within a context through which violence and desire take place, and sometimes within that context we learn interesting things that become difficult to report and effectively analyze because of institutional parameters. Those institutional parameters regulate men and women differently, and when women make claims that challenge those parameters and seek to clarify their experiences, they can be easily silenced by the same voices that uphold the institutional restrictions. Thus, the discipline is governed by invisible rules that come to bear when we try to talk about it. These systemic limitations uphold the white male normativity of the gaze that is being challenged. Ignoring erotic subjectivity is methodologically cynical because it suggests that there are ways that knowledge can be revealed and not revealed, and the idea that some means to knowledge are more legitimate than others ultimately sustains the limitations that are placed on people.

The idea of ethnopornography animates ethnographic encounters and the limitations that are placed on discussing those encounters. Observation has been so critical to anthropology—looking at, watching, scrutinizing, analyzing, studying, and charting. The mapping of another's world is the history of anthropology. Though we have addressed this unilinear model and seek more intersubjective methods of research and writing, the challenge remains how to represent multidirectional ways of looking and knowing, of charting each other, and exchanging and encountering and meeting partway and in between. Because there is no one model of power that exists between people, it is always renegotiated and reperformed. And the historical circumstances that inform how we see each other will come to bear differently at different times, and therefore have to be constantly considered. From this standpoint, ethnopornography as understood as multidirectional and historically and culturally specified opens up possibilities both for framing ethnographic encounters and for analyzing them. Disciplines that are grounded in ethnographic engagement, such as anthropology and ethnomusicology, require methodological and theoretical consideration of the production and consumption of racialized, gendered, and sexualized images and their attendant narratives that emerge in our work. This matters not only because the ethnopornographic informs knowledge production but also because it moves us toward more complex and varied portraits of human encounters, our vision of each other, and the stories that we tell and are told. Thus, while ethnopornographic circulations deserve critique, they also produce effective assessment tools through which to situate our work.

Many readers will recognize that the title of this chapter, "Under White Men's Eyes," refers obliquely to Chandra Talpade Mohanty's essay "Under Western Eyes," in which she so deftly critiques the representations of women in the Global South.[19] She effectively suggests that the eyes we look through, the perspective that is validated and understood as the priority, is skewing everything we see, and if we want to know more or know differently, we have to change the lens and the terms through which we evaluate other people's experiences. Though I began the chapter with reference to one white man and the way that he saw my experience, his vision is a stand-in for the institutional and disciplinary codes that consistently and effectively prevent dissent. As Nancy White points out, white women are rewarded for good behavior, but that reward will never be an admission to full subjecthood. And the punishment for deviance can be severe. And the fear of that punishment limits our anthropological engagements and the ways we are able to speak.

In ethnomusicology, a prominent example of the way that women's voices are edited is located in Kofi Agawu's *Representing African Music*, in which he criticizes Michelle Kisliuk for her account of a personal relationship in *Seize the Dance!*, an ethnographic account exploring the musical lives of the BaAka of the Central African rainforests in 1998.[20] Agawu's primary criticism was that Kisliuk did not fully account for the nature of her relationship with her field assistant, who is now her husband. Agawu claims that Kisliuk's failure to fully disclose the precise intimate nature of the relationship demonstrates that the author will always place the frame around the research agenda, what is written, and how it is represented, and thus attempts to research and write in ways that lay bare the procedure of knowledge production are not more ethical than more objective ways of writing. Agawu's choice to isolate Kisliuk's text speaks to a perception of reflective research accounts as "personal" when written by women and "introspective" when written by men.[21] The effect of such a critique is undermining because it (1) neglects the theoretical movements that Kisliuk was responding to, effectively portraying it as storytelling rather than a well-grounded research account, and (2) reinforces a gendered divide within the discipline, in which men might choose to share personal information or not, but women will be criticized if they do and paradoxically chastised for not sharing *enough* or the *right information*. Kisliuk responded to this critique with an essay coauthored with her husband in which she not only pushes back against Agawu but reveals a multilayered and rich account of the ways in which their relationship intersects with and is intertwined in both life and work.[22] The notion that one must reveal everything at all times in order to be both critical and reflective is untenable. Ethnography happens in the mind as much as in the physical field, and we process and understand moments and scenes of life in nonlinear and complex ways. No one can represent everything, and not everything is of critical importance at all moments of analysis. The point is not to share everything but to utilize reflexivity and positionality to add to our greater understanding of knowledge production, to situate one's stance, and to prioritize multiple ways of speaking and knowing. When someone suggests that my story is incomplete or that what I choose to tell is not the valuable information, they refuse to hear why I have chosen what I have said and what it might offer. And that refusal speaks to a disciplinary problem and a continued discomfort with erotic subjectivity, particularly when it is a white woman speaking about a relationship with a black man.

I think it is meaningful that I chose to respond to the white man's voice only to myself. That silent response, and the ethnographic details that I cannot include in this chapter, highlight the mechanisms of regulation, or what Adrienne Rich called the "cartographies of silence."[23] The structures of power that determine who has the authority to speak and when they speak and for whom they are making claims become critical in assessing the resultant dialogues. And in order to change how we are able to speak back to these regulations, we must call attention to them and consistently question how we hear some voices, what we assume, and how we read those stories. Because if a woman speaks and we criticize her truth, and how she knows, and we make it a personal story, we limit the impact of her knowledge. And if there is information that cannot be included, knowledge that cannot be shared, we must witness that silence as part of the story of anthropology and learn to hear those silences at the same volume as the loudest voices. I suggest that one reason for this continued silencing is that although we have begun to incorporate erotic subjectivity into anthropological accounts, we have not yet linked those accounts to ethnopornography in ways that allow for more profound theorization of the connections between ethnography, colonialism, and racialized erotics. By locating the myriad possibilities of human engagement within the frame of ethnopornography, we will deepen the analytical possibilities of the ethnographic encounter.

Notes

John Langston Gwaltney, *Drylongso: A Self-Portrait of Black America* (New York: Vintage, 1980), 148. The chapter opening quote comes from an interview with Ms. Nancy White. The quote can also be found in Patricia Hill Collins, "Learning from the Outsider Within: The Sociological Significance of Black Feminist Thought," *Social Problems* 33, no. 6 (Dec. 1986): S17. Patricia Hill Collins writes about this quote: "This passage suggests that while both groups are stereotyped, albeit in different ways, the function of the images is to dehumanize and control both groups" (ibid.). The same quote can be found in Patricia Hill Collins, *Black Feminist Thought: Knowledge, Consciousness, and the Politics of Empowerment* (New York: Routledge, 2000), 114.

1   Of course, as I'll show, this is a reductive statement, one intended to draw attention to the relationship established during colonialism that marks out the governance of the black male body by white patriarchal institutions. The man who made this remark did so in the context of trying to reduce interracial relationships to a preformatted mold of desire and violence.

2   Audre Lorde, "Uses of the Erotic: The Erotic as Power," in *Sister Outsider* (Freedom, CA: Crossing Press, 1984), 53–59.

3   On intimate encounter as a meaningful aspect of ethnography, see Don Kulick and Margaret Willson, eds., *Taboo, Sex, Identity and Erotic Subjectivity in Anthropological Fieldwork* (London: Routledge, 1995); Fran Markowitz and Michael Ashkenazi,

eds., *Sex, Sexuality, and the Anthropologist* (Chicago: University of Illinois Press, 1999); Gloria Wekker, *The Politics of Passion: Women's Sexual Culture in the Afro-Surinamese Diaspora* (New York: Columbia University Press, 2006). On intimate encounter as a subject position, see Ellen Lewin and William Leap, eds., *Out in the Field: Reflections of Gay and Lesbian Anthropologists* (Chicago: University of Illinois Press, 1996); Jafari Allen, *¡Venceremos? The Erotics of Black Self-Making in Cuba* (Durham, NC: Duke University Press, 2011); Jafari Allen, "One Way or Another: Erotic Subjectivity in Cuba," *American Ethnologist* 39, no. 2 (2012): 325–38; Lyndon Gill, "Transfiguring Trinidad and Tobago: Queer Cultural Production, Erotic Subjectivity and the Praxis of Black Queer Anthropology" (PhD diss., Harvard University, 2010); Lyndon Gill, "Chatting Back an Epidemic: Caribbean Gay Men, HIV/AIDS, and the Uses of Erotic Subjectivity," *GLQ: A Journal of Lesbian and Gay Studies* 18, no. 2–3, (2012): 277–95.

4   Lyndon Gill in particular has taken an expansive view on erotics and sexual encounter. See for example, his recent book, *Erotic Islands: Art and Activism in the Queer Caribbean* (Durham, NC: Duke University Press, 2018).

5   Esther Newton, "My Best Informant's Dress: The Erotic Equation in Fieldwork," *Cultural Anthropology* 8, no. 1 (1993): 3–23; Wekker, *Politics of Passion.*

6   Suzanne Cusick, "On a Lesbian Relationship with Music: A Serious Effort Not to Think Straight," in *Queering the Pitch: The New Gay and Lesbian Musicology*, ed. Philip Brett, Elizabeth Wood, and Gary C. Thomas (1994; repr., New York: Routledge, 2006), 71.

7   Anne McClintock, *Imperial Leather: Race, Gender, and Sexuality in the Colonial Contest* (New York: Routledge, 1995); Ann Laura Stoler, *Race and the Education of Desire: Foucault's History of Sexuality and the Colonial Order of Things* (Durham, NC: Duke University Press, 1995); Ann Laura Stoler, *Carnal Knowledge and Imperial Power: Race and the Intimate in Colonial Rule* (Berkeley: University of California Press, 2002).

8   Paul Rabinow, *Reflections on Fieldwork in Morocco* (1977; repr., Berkeley: University of California Press, 2007).

9   See Eva Moreno, "Rape in the Field: Reflections from a Survivor," in Kulick and Willson, *Taboo*, 166–89.

10 Lorde, "Uses of the Erotic," 54.

11 Lorde, "Uses of the Erotic," 54.

12 I have chosen to leave out the name of this man, but for clarification I will mention that he is a black Ghanaian who resides in the area where my work is conducted.

13 I have changed the name of my male companion to Peter for the purposes of this publication.

14 John Langston Gwaltney, *Drylongso: A Self-Portrait of Black America* (New York: Vintage, 1980), 148.

15 Patricia Hill Collins, *Black Feminist Thought: Knowledge, Consciousness, and the Politics of Empowerment* (New York: Routledge, 2000), 114.

16 Collins, *Black Feminist Thought*, 114.

17 This chapter owes much to many conversations with Chioke I'Anson. I am particularly grateful to him for helping me clarify my thought process and for offering constructive and thoughtful guidance. I thank him too for giving me the metaphor of "race mines," out of which much of this chapter emerged.

18 See also Patricia Tang, "*Ana sa jëkkër* (Where Is Your Husband?)": Writing Gender out of Ethnography," paper presented at the annual meeting for the Society for Ethnomusicology, Indianapolis, Indiana, November 15, 2013.

19 Chandra Talpade Mohanty, "Under Western Eyes: Feminist Scholarship and Colonial Discourses," *boundary 2* 12, no. 3 (1984): 333–58; Chandra Talpade Mohanty, "'Under Western Eyes' Revisited: Feminist Solidarity through Anticapitalist Struggles," *Signs* 28, no. 2 (2003): 499–535.

20 Kofi Agawu, *Representing African Music: Postcolonial Notes, Queries, Positions* (New York: Routledge, 2003); Michelle Kisliuk, *Seize the Dance!: BaAka Musical Life and the Ethnography of Performance* (1998; repr., Oxford: Oxford University Press, 2001).

21 For further discussion of how women's writing is portrayed as less serious when they employ unconventional research methods or narrative style, see Ruth Behar and Deborah A. Gordon, eds., *Women Writing Culture* (Berkeley: University of California Press, 1995).

22 Justin Serge Mongosso and Michelle Kisliuk, "Representing a Real Man: Music, Upheaval and Relationship in Centrafrique," *Emergences* 13, no. 1/2 (2003): 34–46.

23 Adrienne Rich, "Cartographies of Silence," in *The Dream of a Common Language: Poems, 1974–1977* (New York: W. W. Norton, 1978), 17.

PART II —
ETHNOPORNOGRAPHY AS COLONIAL HISTORY

Franciscan Voyeurism in Sixteenth-Century New Spain

They had a dirty and painful sacrifice, coming together in the temple and placed in order, each one pierced their virile members. They passed through the greatest quantity of cord as they could, and all of them became fastened and strung together. They anointed the demon with the blood of all of those parts. He who did this the most was taken as the most valiant.

—FRANCISCAN FRIAR DIEGO DE LANDA, describing a Maya ceremony, 1566 CE

With these words, Diego de Landa describes what he imagines as a violent ritual performed by Maya men in sixteenth-century Yucatán. In envisioning such a rite, Landa performs what in this volume we have termed "ethnopornography": he takes an indigenous ritual out of its context, imagines seeing the bodies—in particular, the penises—of the men, and provides enough titillation for his audience to get engrossed in the image that it both invokes an immediate visceral reaction and also becomes ingrained in the fantasies and fears of his readers—Landa intends to cause them nightmares.[1] Landa wants the ethnopornography to evoke an embodied reaction, and indeed this embodied reaction is key to ethnopornographic content in general: the author of the ethnopornographic text uses words and pictures that he or she thinks will cause the readers to have an immediate, even reflexive, response to the author's imagining of the body of the exotic other—the readers should be turned on or disgusted (hopefully both) by the image.

Landa uses the image of the penis-piercing rite, among many others, to sell his story to his readers, those individuals in Spain who would otherwise, in his view, persecute *him*.[2] This persecution would take place, in Landa's view, because he had appropriately punished the Maya, in many cases with torture, for engaging in traditional rituals that included this one, and many others yet more extreme in their violence.[3]

Landa fantasizes about Maya men's penises being pierced in a manner that causes both pleasure and pain and also seems perverse to the Franciscan and his readers. While Landa suggests that he tries to avert his gaze (as well as ours),[4] he instead draws our attention directly to the scene of the Maya penis piercing. Further, Landa emphasizes elsewhere the immense cruelty of the ancient Maya state—enforcing the power of an extremely violent warrior class.[5] By contextualizing this bloodletting ritual, we will see how Landa's gaze reimagined the ways that the Maya enacted rites that caused bodily pain.

Similarly, Bernardino de Sahagún, another Franciscan friar, provides us with images of Nahua sexual and sacrificial practices. He witnesses the connection between sex and violence, developing a gaze in which he and his aides promote/uncover a sexual universe that will show the readers of their texts the importance of the massive ethnographic project that Sahagún, under the auspices of the Franciscan order and the Spanish crown, had made his life calling. In doing so, Sahagún also emphasizes the perverse pleasures that Nahuas received from sexual acts he considered sinful. Through an analysis of the images that Sahagún's aides produced in preparation for the magisterial work, the *Historia general de las cosas de la Nueva España*, we will see that, like Landa, Sahagún was invested in viewing indigenous individuals as sexually perverse and many of the Nahua preconquest city-states as enhancing the power of a brutal warrior class.[6]

The sixteenth-century Franciscan ethnographers of the people of New Spain witness sex and violence and, in order to promote particular ethno-pornographic views of the indigenous populations, they use their voyeurism to recode the acts that they see. The Franciscans watched the Nahuas and Maya very closely, working to intermix with the indigenous populations, learning their languages and customs.[7] The Franciscans found it extremely important to gaze closely upon indigenous practices. While they were not unique in this regard, the Franciscans, more than the other religious orders and the secular authorities, prioritized direct and close contact with the natives, including the intimate movements of bodies and flesh. This is why, in all of their correspondence with the Spanish crown, the Franciscans insisted that they were the ones who worked most closely with the Indians: they needed to work so closely with them in order to engage in an act of witnessing, a voyeurism that would provide them access to the indigenous soul.[8]

Such acts of looking and observing are key to both ethnography and colonialism. This sentence may seem quite obscure to some: in the standard story, colonialism is an active process in which the colonizer defeats the colonized. Yet, as many studies of colonial processes have shown, observation is important.[9] Fifty-six years after the Spanish conquest of Tenochtitlán in 1521, Spain's King Philip ordered the preparation of vast descriptions of the New World. The responses, the *relaciones geográficas*, were to be extensive, intrusive observations of the conquered worlds. Despite the fact that the *relaciones* often were of limited use, the act of observation, the voyeurism directed at the indigenous populations and lands, was intended as a key colonial tool.[10]

Sahagún and, to a lesser extent, Landa argued that their writings were important to this process of observation and colonization. Further, the key writings that they produced were collaborative ventures with indigenous peoples. The authorship of Sahagún's *Historia general* involved four Nahua aides and many more informants, while Landa's *Relación* likely had several authors and should not even be considered a single coherent text.[11] This sense of collaboration, very familiar to some of the most recent and theoretically sophisticated ethnographies that have come out,[12] belies the fact that the two friars regularly inserted themselves—along with their own desires, fantasies, and fears—into their stories in extraordinarily opaque ways.

Throughout this chapter, I argue that we must understand the fantasies of Landa and Sahagún as both projection and abjection. They projected their own fears—of penetration and perversion—onto the Maya and the Nahuas. In doing so, they expressed their visceral disgust, creating an abject subject, one whose masculinity came into question through the fierce nature of sexual perversion and pain.

Franciscan Tradition

The Franciscans came to the New World with particular quirks in their own history: they condemned worldly pleasures of all kinds, often linked sex with violence, and engaged in extensive self-flagellation.[13] As they gazed upon the indigenous populations of New Spain, they witnessed ritual performances and daily activity, providing these events with meaning filtered through their preconceived notions of the world. Hence, Landa created the abject Maya man, with his penis strung together with other Maya men. And Sahagún created the Nahua sexual subject—a man proudly engaged in sacrifice linked with sex.[14] Landa and Sahagún both imagined the indigenous man gaining pleasure through violent ritual—only through the devil's embrace could such pleasure take place.

The Franciscans were not just any order of monks that came from the Catholic Church. In fact, they existed as a controversial order in a fraught relationship with both the social and the spiritual world.[15] If we look at the earliest attempts by the Franciscans to establish themselves in New Spain, we find the great lore of twelve friars who walked barefoot from Veracruz to Mexico City, where they greeted the conqueror, Hernando Cortés, who appeared before them on his knees.[16] This was a time of great Franciscan idealism, influenced heavily by the thought of the spiritual Franciscan reformers, those who believed that a corrupt church and society throughout Europe needed to move toward a state of nature, and a closeness with God, a position in line with an attempt to re-create what these reformers believed to be the simple lives of the early followers of Jesus.[17] The recently "discovered" Americas provided just that context for the Franciscans. This intellectual package led the twelve to believe that they could form, in the Nahuas, a kingdom of heaven on earth.[18]

More to the point, from the thirteenth century onward, the Franciscans had established a significant sect of millenarians who believed that the second coming of Christ was imminent.[19] They thus rejected the material trappings of society in favor of a bare existence that would allow them to focus their time and energy on the spiritual world rather than the material one. The appearance of this pious and impoverished order caused significant controversy both within the Church hierarchy and among European political leaders.[20] Individuals within the Franciscan order were often seen by members of high society (and likely by commoners as well) as always unusual and sometimes threatening in their efforts at asserting significant piety at the expense of material betterment.[21]

Further, their adherence to self-flagellation in an effort to both rid the body of unwanted desires and become more intimate with the experience of Christ during the Passion, seemed to many, both inside and outside of the Church, as problematic.[22] In fact, this link with the suffering Christ allowed the Franciscans to use the mortification of their own bodies to transcend the boundaries between the material and spiritual realms—flagellation, in other words, allowed Franciscans to experience physical pain and spiritual pleasure at the same time.[23] These spiritual concepts seemed to many outside of the order as potentially dangerous, leading to the persecution of some Franciscans by the Inquisition and other authorities.[24]

Still, by the sixteenth century, the Franciscans had received more mainstream acceptance—partially as a result of Catholic response to early rumblings of the Protestant Reformation.[25] The Franciscans received permission from the Spanish Crown to set up parishes in the New World, and particularly to establish control over the education of the indigenous populations in much of New Spain. They thus became intricately linked with the conquest—developing a complex relationship with the conquerors, many of whom had more concern for material wealth than the spiritual health of the people.[26] The Franciscans, the conquerors knew, could help acculturate the indigenous peoples. But at the same time, the conquerors did not trust the Franciscans, and they continually lodged complaints about friars who interfered with their efforts at exploiting the indigenous populations for material gain.[27]

Almost immediately after the conquest the Franciscans began their efforts at understanding the indigenous populations with the express purpose of instructing them in Christian religion and ritual. The Franciscans engaged in a great effort to learn indigenous languages (particularly Nahuatl, but also Maya and other languages) in order to penetrate the true beings of their indigenous parishioners in what many have termed a form of early colonial ethnographic practice of native bodies, practices, customs, and beliefs.[28] They further worked to establish the various sacraments, including confession, designed to get the indigenous populations to bare their souls to their priests.[29] Finally, the Franciscans established a genre that in some manner resembles ethnography in order to gain an understanding of indigenous lives, ritual practices, and gods.[30] However, while some have argued that these practices are related to the founding of modern ethnography, this is too simplistic: these Franciscan ethnographies are didactic, polemical, and have the purpose of religious instruction. This ethnographic genre, in other words, developed through the concept of the Franciscan gaze. Franciscans needed to attend carefully to their spiritual duties, and they could do so only by remaining vigilant as they watched the indigenous populations very closely.

This form of ethnography reached its most mature stage with Bernardino de Sahagún's work. By the time Sahagún and his four Nahua aides began their ethnographic research in the 1550s, the Franciscan days of idealism had ended, even as their linguistic skills increased. Sahagún, who had arrived in New Spain in 1529, turned out to be an excellent philologist who learned the intricacies of Nahuatl very quickly. He further provided a critique of conversion and instruction in Christianity.[31] In doing so, he portrayed himself as a doctor diagnosing his patient. Like a good doctor, he asserted, the cleric must understand the history of the individual before him.[32] In this case, that meant a careful, painstaking dissection of Nahua religion and society. By closely surveying the lives of the people that the priest desires to change, he would discover the real problems that the parishioners sought to solve through their spiritual frameworks.[33] This required close and detailed observation, which demanded a careful gaze placed upon the Nahuas. Through decades of working very closely with Nahua aides, living in Nahua communities, talking to many Nahuas, searching through preconquest Nahua manuscripts, and educating himself and others in Nahua traditions, Sahagún believed that he knew the Nahuas as well as any Spaniard could possibly know them.

Diego de Landa was perhaps more of an accidental ethnographer. He came to Yucatán in 1549 with a small group of Franciscans. He became enmeshed in the Maya population, learning a great deal about their language, history, and culture. By 1561 he had become the leader of the Franciscans in Yucatán.[34] In 1562, however, something went awry as Landa found evidence of idolatrous activities and human sacrifice in one region of Yucatán. At this point, Landa established an inquest into the practices in which priests throughout the province questioned four thousand Maya individuals under the threat of torture in order to get them to confess to committing idolatrous acts. Hundreds died through torture, while others committed suicide.[35] When Yucatán's first bishop, Francisco de Toral, arrived, he halted Landa's extirpation campaign.[36] By 1563 Landa had returned to Spain in order to defend himself. During that time, Landa wrote parts of what we now know of as the *Relación de las cosas de Yucatán*. Vindicated in Spain, Landa returned to Yucatán, as the bishop to replace Toral, in 1573.[37]

Diego de Landa and Maya Sacrifice

It is in this context that we must understand Landa's *Relación* and his portrayal of the Maya sacrificial activity described at the beginning of this chapter. Landa had become deeply disappointed in the Maya, who, according to his view, continued to engage in idolatry and human sacrifice. He thus developed an extensive account of these practices. We need to note as well that the text suggests a direct witnessing of a wide variety of Maya ceremonies, including the one with which I began this chapter. Landa's gaze, despite the absence of any discussion of his place in the text, is central to his ethnographic project.

But, while reading the *Relación*, one quickly notices that the text is quite disjointed. As historians Matthew Restall and John Chuchiak have noted, we cannot view this text as a singular piece of writing authored by Landa, but rather must see it as a series of related texts and notes compiled by Landa over as many as three decades.[38] There is no evidence that he intended this as a single text, or even that he wrote all of it himself. It seems likely that parts of the text were written by at least one of his key Maya informants, Gaspar Antonio Chi. Further, the text may incorporate other unmentioned authors (both Franciscans and Maya), and some of the text may simply reconstruct Landa's research notes. Finally, the compilers of the *Relación* (who compiled the text after Landa's death) may have left things out that Landa intended to include. This all suggests that the enterprise to produce the *Relación* incorporated many authors and influences: it was a collaborative project.[39] However, in this collaboration, it is clear that Landa's imagination and passionate interest in Maya spiritual and cultural life greatly influenced the final text that would come to be known as the *Relación*.

Landa's interests focused on Maya ritual, including the ethnopornographic portrayal that serves as an epigraph to this chapter. Here I use this ceremony as a prototypical example of Landa's ethnopornography. In doing so, I do not mean to suggest that here Landa portrays a sexual act for the purpose of prurient pleasures. Indeed, one would be correct in assuming that the Maya did not consider such an act "sexual." As I have noted elsewhere, the Maya did not delineate a category of sexuality in the same way that modern Westerners would come to understand the term, or even a category of "carnal sin" as Europeans of the time understood it.[40] For the purpose of this chapter, moreover, the important point is how Landa and his fellow Franciscans conceived of this rite. Landa was perplexed both by the pain and the drive of the Maya men to engage in such activity. He maintains that he saw the pierced penis as something "dirty" (*sucio*) and "painful" (*penoso*). He uses these terms to express his visceral sense of disgust at witnessing such a ceremony. For, how could the Maya man consider the penetration of his penis by a stingray spine to be a test of masculine "valor"? Landa wants to focus our gaze upon this pierced virile member;

he wants us to experience with him the visceral reaction to the Maya male body, and to the person with the desire to pierce his own penis.

I argue that Landa engages in a particular type of ethnopornography by asserting strategic difference between himself, as a Franciscan persecuted by the Church hierarchy (Bishop Toral) and secular authorities, and the Maya men, who in this text escape persecution, but who outside of the text face Landa's wrath. In asserting such a distinction between himself and the Maya man as Other, I argue that Landa in essence queers the Maya man. What could be more queer than a bunch of men with their penises strung together, offering their genital blood to a demon? In asserting the presence of the Maya men engaging in blood sacrifice, Landa says much about himself as a member of an unusual order of Christian men, a man both disappointed by Maya men and persecuted by Spanish men. By engaging in this act of queering the Maya men, Landa wishes to evoke the visceral: as he witnesses the queer act, he wants his readers to imagine the friar's body convulsing with disgust.[41]

Landa goes on to portray his reaction to this rite: "It is horrifying how enthusiastic they were."[42] In other words, from Landa's perspective, it is not just that the individuals involved engaged in an idolatrous act, the ostensible rationale for his extirpation campaign, but more to the point, the men were extremely enthusiastic about this practice—they got something out of the ritual. One wonders how Landa's own frightful reaction compared to his understanding of the corporeal reactions of the flagellant groups that existed among the Franciscans in late medieval Europe.[43] Indeed, Landa's imagination would have certainly gone there, allowing him to think about the demonic influences that provide individuals with ecstatic pleasure as they approach their gods—Landa certainly understood, as his Maya informants would have portrayed it, that these rites allowed Maya men to become closer to the gods. Hearing this, Landa would wonder about the immense pleasures of his own predecessors (and himself) as they mortified their bodies for Christ. And he would conclude that the Maya had a mistaken notion regarding the presence of the true god, but a correct notion that one needed to engage in bodily sacrifice in order to approach that god. Still, Landa's visceral reaction would have been disgust, a position that shows his belief that the Maya men had a warped sense of masculinity and spirituality.

In order to understand the position of this rite within the thought of the Franciscan friar, one must work through the meanings of the comparisons that Landa wished to emphasize, the context of his existence in a Catholic order that had recently gone through a reevaluation of its own humanistic idealism, and his presence in the midst of a colonial enterprise in which a relative handful of Spaniards and Africans lived among several hundred thousand Maya people.[44]

Most centrally here, we can envision Landa's notion of a flawed Maya masculinity in which his gaze appeared to condemn Maya men while elevating Maya women to a state of perpetual quasi-innocence.[45] By engaging in such a description, Landa means to focus our attention on an ethnopornography of Maya men.

To understand the form of Landa's ethnopornography, we must briefly review the place of blood sacrifice in the Maya ritual universe. For the Maya population before the Spanish conquest, the sacrifice of one's own blood and the blood of others was an important element of a broader set of religious performances.[46]

The blood rituals signified much about how Maya elites concerned themselves with the sexed body and notions of fertility. According to a variety of sources, the shedding of blood from the penis mimicked the menstruation of women.[47] By shedding this blood, male leaders envisioned themselves as both communicating with the gods and "giving birth" to the entire social body: this blood ensured the fertility of the world. The kings and priests, through their sacrificial acts, gave birth to crops on the earth, animals throughout the world, humans in their communities, and deities in the cosmos.

Unlike Landa's depiction, however, these rites did not just involve men, but rather could include both male and female nobles and commoners. So, in figure 5.1, we witness a woman piercing her tongue, with a man about to pierce his penis. The woman has pulled a rope through her tongue, and the hieroglyphic text tells us that the man will engage in similar blood sacrifice. We note that the bone between his spread legs is well positioned to begin to pierce the penis. The text says that the bloodletting was occasioned by the birth of a future king in 752 CE. Here, the child's parents, the current king and queen, sacrifice their own blood to ensure that the world will survive to see the child's rise to power.[48]

The importance of the queen's tongue in such a rite cannot be overstated. In almost all of these types of images, we see the woman's tongue, but not the man's penis. And it is not that the Maya were shy about showing the penis: Rosemary Joyce notes the prevalence of phallic images in Maya statues and within caves.[49] Yet, it appears that the types of rites discussed here mandated *both* a cloaked phallus and an exposed tongue. In a similar bloodletting rite that took place in 709 CE, the queen kneels before

FIGURE 5.1 King and queen shedding their own blood, 752 CE. After Linda Schele and David Freidel, *A Forest of Kings*, 287. Copyright 1990 by Linda Schele and David Freidel. Reprinted by Permission of HarperCollins Publishers.

the king, who holds a lighted torch. She pulls rope through her tongue, and has blood spotted on her cheek. Below her the blood collects in a basket, which also holds the stingray spine that had pierced her tongue. The king, Shield Jaguar, according to the text, will also sacrifice his own blood. The woman's tongue appears to assure the reader that the invisible penis was also pierced, that the noble man also engaged in a sacrificial act to ensure the future of the earth.[50]

The phallic sign asserts not a clear gendered division but rather a communicative practice to assure fertility.[51] The blank stares of the individuals engaged in blood sacrifice in Maya images assure the viewer that their gaze is not of this world but rather ensures that the participants have visions of and communications with the gods. In fact, these images may be read as

FIGURE 5.2 Queen shedding blood from her tongue, 709 CE. After Linda Schele and David Freidel, *A Forest of Kings*, 267. Copyright 1990 by Linda Schele and David Freidel. Reprinted by Permission of HarperCollins Publishers.

FIGURE 5.3 Men shedding blood from the penis, 766 CE. After Linda Schele and David Freidel, *A Forest of Kings*, 302. Copyright 1990 by Linda Schele and David Freidel. Reprinted by Permission of HarperCollins Publishers.

texts that show where the nobles go once they have shed their blood—they see the serpents that lead them to the world of the gods.[52]

In other rites that involved only men, we witness the importance of penis piercing to the maintenance of the community, both in agricultural rituals and in more cosmically oriented events that men held with each other. In figure 5.3, we see the king in 766 CE across from one of his governors. The king pierces his penis, and his blood collects in a container on the ground. Even here, while his blood flows, an image of a perforator god hides the penis.[53]

Maya nobles and commoners viewed blood sacrifice as an event central to the community in that it signified the future of the world. Without such sacrifice, both from men's genitals and from women's tongues, the crops would not grow, and animals and humans would not survive. In all these rites the Maya participants intended to shed their blood, cause their pain, in order to assure fertility and futurity.

So, how did Landa, an expert on Maya culture and religion, miss this context? I argue that this had to do with the purpose and meaning behind ethnopornography. As the historian Inga Clendinnen says of Landa and the Franciscans, "There was a worse betrayal with the realisation that the Indians they had so tenderly protected, whose sufferings had so aroused their pity, whose trust they thought they had won, remained strangers: their faces closed, averted, masked, concealing depthless duplicity."[54] Bishop Toral believed that Landa was "enslaved by the passions of anger, pride, and cruelty."[55] Feeling betrayed and deeply disappointed, even depressed, according to his contemporaries, Landa returned to Spain.[56] In his return, he gathered his thoughts (and notes), and developed a vigorous and, as we have noted, ultimately successful, defense.

In his writings, by portraying Maya men as out of control, Landa showed that they engaged in orgies, abused women, and, most importantly, performed idolatrous acts in which they did unspeakable things to the bodies of themselves and others.[57] Maya women and children were innocent, chaste, and good Christians. Maya women came to Landa and to other priests and friars to find out about Christianity and to resist the sexual and idolatrous advances of Maya men.[58] Those men, however, with some exceptions, resisted Christianity and engaged in idolatrous and sacrificial practices. These men, participating in all male communal rites, could be seduced by the devil into performing such sacrifice, into lining up with each other and stringing their penises together: into, in other words, an inverted queer relationship with their gods. And they went even further than this as Maya men developed a cult of warriors that engaged in extreme torture, human sacrifice that began with the warrior using his arrow to "wound the individual, whether a man or a woman, in the private parts."[59] Landa thus misappropriates Maya ceremonial practice by producing ethnopornography to express his visceral disgust directed toward Maya men.

Bernardino de Sahagún and Aztec Pornography

When I first studied Landa, I assumed that he was an exceptional—and exceptionally cruel—figure. But I soon discovered that, while he did indeed torture the indigenous' population, his writing and particularly his research emanated from the same type of rhetoric that occupied the rest of the Franciscan order (and, to a certain extent, Catholic clerics more generally). Even Bernardino de Sahagún, the famed Franciscan who produced the encyclopedic *Florentine Codex* (the aforementioned *Historia general de las cosas de Nueva España*), an extensive ethnographic study of Nahua society, produced a certain type of ethnopornography to support his ideas.[60]

Consider this scenario: Bernardino de Sahagún, the sixty-year-old Franciscan friar, walks into the room in the sweltering heat of summer in Tepepulco. He and his entourage had arrived in the Nahuatl-speaking community a year earlier, and now his Nahua aides had begun to engage in extensive research: their job was to study the culture and society as it had existed at the time of the Spanish conquest. Sahagún and his fellow friars had trained these four aides, and they were fluent in Spanish and Latin (as well as Nahuatl). Sahagún, also fluent in these languages, oversaw the project and provided an outline for the research. Today, the aides sit across the table from five old men, the leaders of Tepepulco. The aides have been asking the old men about the terms for different types of people, men and women, in the community, and have asked them to describe the different categories. After each category is placed on paper, they discuss the characteristics of the individual described. Now that the friar has entered the room, the discussion has stopped. Sahagún asks one of his aides to see the paper on which they have been writing. He takes his time reading the Nahuatl (there is no Spanish text), and he notes that his aides have described men and women by age and marital status; they have established certain metaphorical representations for many of them. He asks for a clarification about one category (a very old stooped woman), but the friar has something else on his mind. He is thinking about sin, and particularly about *el pecado nefando*, the "abominable sin" of sodomy. So

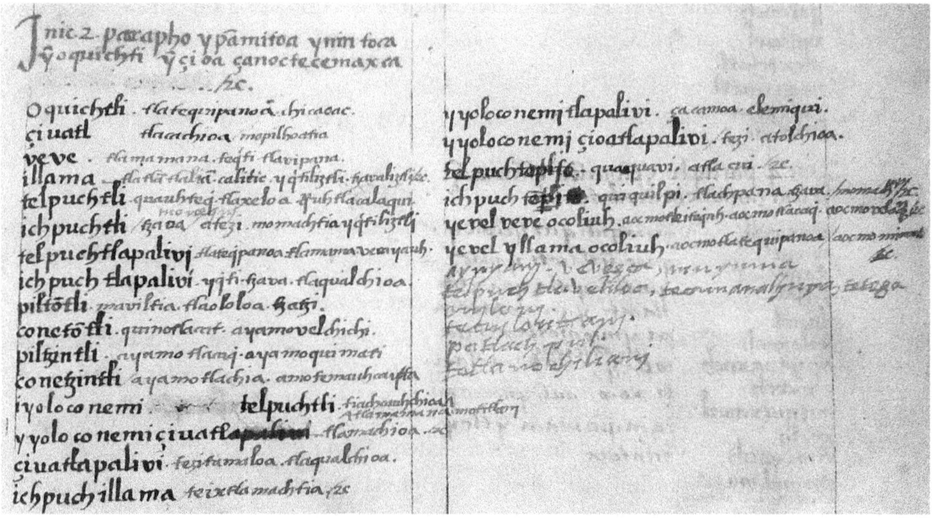

FIGURE 5.4 Sexual identities according to Bernardino de Sahagún, *Primeros memoriales* (facsimile) (Norman: University of Oklahoma Press, 1993), f. 82r.

he asks the elderly men about sinners, and Sahagún himself, having taken the quill from one of his aides, writes down what they say: *tepuchtlaveliloc, tecamanalhuya, tetaza* ("wicked [male] youth; one who makes fun of people; one who knocks people down"). Dissatisfied with this answer, the friar turns to his aides and says that he wants to ask about the pecado nefando. His aides explain to the elderly men, who simply provide a few words: *cuilonj, tecuilontianj, patlachpul, tetlanochilianj.* While Sahagún asks for further description, the elders give none.[61]

In figure 5.4 we read the results of this scenario: toward the end of the folio we read *in Sahagún's own hand* the terms mentioned above.[62] This is from the *Primeros memoriales*, the text derived from the early research of Sahagún's team. The terms *cuiloni* (the correct spelling, once such spelling is standardized, of Sahagún's *cuilonj), tecuilontiani,* and *patlachpul* are complex terms related in some manner to homosexual activity, while the final term, *tetlanochiliani,* is a term used for those who procure prostitutes.[63] This is the only place in the entire manuscript that discusses quotidian sexual activity of any kind.

Here we have laid before us the process in which early modern Franciscans produced ethnopornography. The Nahua men had discussed what they thought to be an effective set of categories for the women and men of their society. But the Franciscan thought this insufficient as, in accordance with Christian doctrine of the time,[64] he wanted to challenge the carnal sins of the population. Thus, in order to train Franciscan friars, in order for him to show them how they need to observe the indigenous population, he wanted to find categories for those sins. In our scenario, here, however, I have just suggested that the friar used the term "pecado nefando," without any further explication. But did he use such a term? The Spanish terms are somewhat unclear: would he have used "pecado nefando," *sodomía*, or some other term to elicit the responses? And what Spanish phrase would he have used to get the Nahuas to respond with *patlache*, a term apparently related to some individual with a female or gender-indeterminate body engaging in sexual activity with women? Perhaps he used the obscure terminology utilized by his Franciscan colleague, Alonso de Molina, in his definition *hazerlo vna muger a otra* ("for one woman to do it with another")?[65]

The ethnopornographer creates a taxonomy of subjects, in this case queer subjects, over whom the Spaniards would rule. Of course, from Sahagún's perspective, he was simply trying to understand the realities of the Nahua population in order to combat non-Christian beliefs and instruct the population in proper Christianity. In doing so, he needs to gaze closely upon Nahua sexual activity, and he requires Catholic confessors to follow up by peering even more closely at Nahua bodies.

I argue that the power of ethnography, a term I use as a conscious anachronism, links with the ability to represent observation as objective fact when it instead creates for us the fiction of the desiring indigenous individual, a fiction promulgated by the need for the colonizer to produce a stable subject over whom to rule. This ethnographic observation was in full force in the early sixteenth century, when both Spanish and indigenous ethnographers engaged in a taxonomic revolution that changed indigenous concepts of sacrifice to sin and, eventually, to sex, and it remains in full force today.

The Ethnopornographic Images of the *Florentine Codex*

In order to more fully comprehend the place of the Franciscans in the creation of ethnopornography, we must analyze the pornographic imaginary in the most sophisticated version of Franciscan ethnography, Sahagún's *Historia general*. Here I use five images from the text, images produced by Nahua scribes/artists, known in Nahuatl as *tlacuilos*. The tlacuilos were traditionally trained to paint images that told extensive stories of history, ritual, and religion. Trained readers/priests would interpret these images and tell the stories to the communities.[66]

I argue that the images here become pornographic when the *Historia general* refers to a body engaged in sexual activity or with an identity that presumes such activity. That body becomes intelligible as a sexed individual only through its colonization and archivization.[67] Thus the writers and artists producing the *Historia general*, and particularly the authorizing voice of Sahagún, want the readers to imagine the individual body engaged in sexual activity. This process of mistranslating the indigenous individual into the colonized sexed subject forms a pornographic imaginary universe connecting the Franciscan friar to his desired European readers.

In the case of the *Historia general*, Sahagún sought out individuals trained in traditional painting and writing, but he of course wanted a different type of story told.[68] For him the images would be illustrative additions to the text, and the topics presented by the images would be different from the topics traditionally addressed by tlacuilos. So, for example, while tlacuilos before the conquest never painted anything about quotidian activities of individual people, the first three images presented here signify quotidian sexual behavior.[69] This very fact tells us much about the ethnopornographic process at work: it is not just the fact that these images present sexual activity but also the very nature of the documentation: quotidian, individual subject formation is taking place in this text.

Figure 5.5 is the image that appears alongside a text for the *cuiloni*. The text connects "cuiloni" with excrement, corruption, filth, mockery, and cross-dressing. As I have noted elsewhere, "cuiloni" appears to be an approximate equivalent for the passive partner in sodomy. The term *tecuilontiani*, mentioned above, appears to be a term for the active partner in sodomy.[70] While we can recognize the English terms as outdated and referencing activities with biblical connotations that Nahuas could not have understood before the conquest, this is in fact the point: through the placement of the image and the above text promulgated by Sahagún's intervention, we have Spaniards peering at Nahuas and envisioning sexual acts and identities that have little to do with the original framework in which these acts and identities may have been situated. We have access here only to Spanish ethnopornography, in which we imagine the cuiloni as the sodomite.

The image in figure 5.5 appears intended to make such an identification perfectly clear but does little to help us understand Nahua frameworks. On the left side, we witness two individuals speaking with each other, one dressed as a man, the other dressed as a woman. Between them, we have two

FIGURE 5.5 "Cuiloni." From the *Historia general de las cosas de Nueva España*. Bernardino de Sahagún, *Códice florentino*, book 10 (Florence, Italy: Biblioteca Medicea Laurenziana / Mexico City: Archivo General de la Nación, 1979), f. 25v.

speech scrolls and a flower. The Nahuas did not likely view the seemingly phallic speech scrolls as phalluses, but they did envision the flower as a sign of sexual activity. Still, the figures are fully dressed, and we do not have any portrayal of sex. On the right side of the image, we witness more ethnopornography through violence. The text tells us that the cuiloni was burned by fire, and here we see the individual's body burned. The connection between sex and violence was of course a familiar one for the Franciscan friar, and the presence of such an image in the text could have assured him of similar moral values asserted by the Nahuas. We recall of course that Sahagún himself inserted the concept of cuiloni into the research project, and here has gotten his aides and tlacuilos to define the concept in terms familiar to the friar. This ethnopornography creates the colonial sexual subject.

Figure 5.6 references the patlache. The standing figure appears to be a woman with exposed breasts and a hand covering her genitals. She also wears a cape, typically worn by a man. She points at another individual, who is seated and wears women's clothes. The text that accompanies this image says that the patlache has a penis and the various body parts of a man. In other words, the patlache, according to this text, seems to reference a woman who passes as a man (and who may, it appears, have sex with women). The image suggests Sahagún, his aides, and the painter as ethnopornographers trying, unsuccessfully, to translate from one signifying system of sex/body/gender to another. Here the erotic component of the two individuals seems lost and the ethnopornography has failed.[71]

In figure 5.7, we find the *alhuiani*, the Nahua "pleasure woman" or "prostitute." We can note that Nahuatl does not reference gender here, and "alhuiani" simply translates approximately as "one who provides pleasure."

FIGURE 5.6 "Patlache." From the *Historia general de las cosas de Nueva España*. Bernardino de Sahagún, *Códice florentino*, book 10 (Florence, Italy: Biblioteca Medicea Laurenziana / Mexico City: Archivo General de la Nación, 1979), f. 40v.

FIGURE 5.7 "Alhuiani." From the *Historia general de las cosas de Nueva España*. Bernardino de Sahagún, *Códice florentino*, book 10 (Florence, Italy: Biblioteca Medicea Laurenziana / Mexico City: Archivo General de la Nación, 1979), f. 39v.

Further, the individual painting the image does not show us anything that we would deem lascivious or representative of prostitutes either in early modern Europe or today. We have a woman in an outfit with flowers on it—and we know from the text that the flowers signify her role as a prostitute. Hence we also find her holding flowers and stepping on other flowers. So the flowered garment becomes her signifier. In this case, as in figures 5.5 and 5.6, we are left without an obvious referent to sexual activity, but instead we have a sign that serves as an identifying marker of sexual subjectivity.

So, how do these three images link with the topic of this chapter and this volume? I argue that the very presence of such images in the *Historia general* is a form of ethnopornography. Sahagún placed his system of categorization in the imaginations of his aides, tlacuilos, and informants in the 1550s, the time when they engaged in the production of the *Primeros memoriales*. Twenty years later, as they were completing the *Historia general*, the Nahuas working with Sahagún had developed some understanding of sexual subjectivity, and this understanding led to the production of images of the cuiloni, patlache, and alhuiani. While those images do not seem particularly salacious to us, the very placement of sexual subjectivity where there had been none represents a particularly pernicious form of ethnopornographic production. The very process of *mistranslation* of the body and its sexed acts—sexed, that is, in a European frame—is an effective form of ethnopornography. The European audience becomes aware of the sexed indigenous body through a power relationship in which the friar invents this particular body, taking it out of its indigenous context and thereby helping to form a subjugated, colonized individual.

This ethnopornography is further developed in the *Historia general*'s descriptions of ritual ceremonies. The focus here on violence, sacrifice, and fertility, I maintain, is evocative not of a reproduction of Nahua rites but rather of the violent gaze of ethnopornography. In particular, the description of the ceremony of Toxcatl, a ceremony celebrating warriors, allows us a greater understanding of the imagined sexual activity and gendered aesthetic of a particularly powerful Nahua god, the trickster Tezcatlipoca.[72]

Here the images present a somewhat different story than the accompanying text in the *Historia general*. In the text, the priests select one man at the beginning of the year to become the Tezcatlipoca *ixiptla* (the ixiptla, commonly translated as "impersonator," obtains Tezcatlipoca's name and becomes destined for sacrifice).[73] We see this individual in the center of figure 5.8, with his headdress, shield, and mirror. The text says that the

FIGURE 5.8 "Tezcatlipoca Ixiptla." From the *Historia general de las cosas de Nueva España*. Bernardino de Sahagún, *Códice florentino*, book 2 (Florence, Italy: Biblioteca Medicea Laurenziana / Mexico City: Archivo General de la Nación, 1979), f. 30v.

high priests choose the Tezcatlipoca ixiptla from among the noble captives. He should be a high-level noble, and his physical attributes should signify the perfect masculine individual in the Nahua universe. Furthermore, he should play the flute well and be an excellent warrior. The narrative tells us that the individual goes around the community for an entire year, being worshipped as Tezcatlipoca, and at the end of the year, he is sacrificed.

In figure 5.8 we see this ixiptla standing between the men and women of the community, and I argue that the image presents him without a clear gender. He wears a body suit that covers his genitalia in such a manner that we do not know if the individual even has genitals, while the men to his left wear loincloths and capes. The loincloth draws our attention to the cloaked phallus, but for the ixiptla our attention is focused elsewhere. Further, his position between the men and the women suggests an indeterminate gender, though of course the men and women are prostrating themselves before him because they worship him as a god.

Tezcatlipoca was a trickster god, one who could appear on earth as man or woman, animal or human. This ambiguous position enhanced the power of this particular god, who could signify the female and the male at the same time. More to the point, here in this image, he brings the community together for the Toxcatl ceremony.

As the narrative moves along, the ixiptla asserts masculine sexuality in a polygamous frame as he is married off to four goddesses signifying various elements of the earth: he will make the earth fertile through his sexual activity, something not shown in the images. He also will arguably engage in bisexual sexual activity, as the narrative mentions an obscure sexual connection with another ixiptla, a representative of the supreme Mexica war god, Huitzilopochtli.[74]

In one final image (figure 5.9), we see the ixiptla sacrificed. Here, let us begin our analysis at the bottom of the pyramid, where we see broken flutes. The flute was key to Tezcatlipoca's ixiptla. He had to play a flute well.[75] For, "with [the flute] he held his flowers and his smoking cane, and [he would] blow and suck on [the flute], and smell [the flowers]."[76] The acts of blowing on the flute and smelling the flowers signify Tezcatlipoca's sexual nature. The flower, for the Nahuas, connected the earth with sexual activity and specifically signified sexual desire.[77] The ixiptla smelling his flower suggests he gives birth to sexual elements in society.

The flute, a phallic signifier, becomes a central element in Toxcatl as the ixiptla goes about the community blowing and sucking on the flute. As he ascends the pyramid, he "shatters his flute [*itlapitzal*], his whistle [*jvilacapitz*]."[78] As art historian Cecelia Klein notes, one should not underestimate the significance of the shattered flute.[79] The flute signifies the phallus, and its root, *pitz*, has sexual significance. The term relates to huffing and puffing on something, blowing something, and playing an instrument. At the same time, *pitz* relates closely to *pitzahtzi*, "to speak in a high voice," presented elsewhere as "to sing in falsetto," or to "speak like a woman."[80]

The broken flutes on the temple appear to come tumbling down. The ixiptla and the priests had likely trampled on the two at the bottom while they made their way to the pyramid. This act—trampling upon the flutes—suggests a phallic divestiture in which the priests literally stamp out a key element of Tezcatlipoca's existence. In the image, the broken flutes parallel the blood running down the temple. Just as the flutes come tumbling

FIGURE 5.9 "Tezcatlipoca sacrificed." From the *Historia general de las cosas de Nueva España*. Bernardino de Sahagún, *Códice Florentino*, book 2 (Florence, Italy: Biblioteca Medicea Laurenziana / Mexico City: Archivo General de la Nación, 1979), f. 30v.

down, so will the blood. Further, the story continues, as we can see, at the top of the pyramid, as three priests stretch out the ixiptla while a fourth excises this individual's heart. The priests wear loincloths and capes, while the ixiptla appears naked, though his genitals are blocked by the priest kneeling down as he removes the heart. In other words, here at the very end, we witness the priests' signified phalluses (the loincloths) while the ixiptla's phallus (signified by the flutes) has been destroyed.[81] In the end, the priests will fling the ixiptla's body off the temple, so this body, like the flutes, will come down, thrown away like trash.[82]

The Toxcatl ceremony signified fertility, sexual activity, and warrior status. Here the *Historia general* has used the ceremony to evoke particular reactions among readers: disgust and intrigue. The tlacuilos who painted the images did not focus on sexual activity per se but rather worked to promote some understanding of the violent nature of the ritual. By evoking the connection between violence and fertility in Nahua thought, Sahagún promotes a particularly partial view of Nahua religion, one in which the masculine cult of warriors appears bloodthirsty. The positions of the bodies of these warriors and the ixiptla signify early attempts at developing and theorizing an ethnopornographic approach to the Other by promoting the bloody nightmare of the sacrificed Tezcatlipoca.

In creating sexual subjects on the one hand while witnessing extraordinary acts of ritual violence on the other, Sahagún wants us to think of him as an objective observer, describing what he understands to be the sexual and ritual components of Nahua life. However, like later ethnographers, Sahagún hides his position in the creation of the ethnography. We see some sleights of hand as he plays an active role in the creation of the Nahua sexual subject, seeking to fit this individual into a developing and constantly changing European taxonomic universe. Similarly, when portraying rituals of violence, Sahagún and his painters create a fearsome rite for European readers, and Sahagún warns elsewhere that his Franciscan contemporaries need to exercise caution and vigilance in seeking out idolatrous activities that have the potential to destroy the veneer of Nahua civilization and Christianization.

Desire and the Archive

> The life of civilized peoples in pre-Columbian America is a source of wonder to us, not only in its discovery and instantaneous disappearance, but also because of its bloody eccentricity, surely the most extreme ever conceived by an aberrant mind. Continuous crime committed in broad daylight for the mere satisfaction of deified nightmares, terrifying phantasms, priests' cannibalistic meals, ceremonial corpses, and streams of blood evoke not so much the historical adventure, but rather the blinding debauches described by the illustrious Marquis de Sade. This observation applies, it is true, mostly to Mexico.
> —GEORGES BATAILLE, "Extinct America," *October* 36 (1986): 3.

Over three centuries after Landa and Sahagún wrote their tracts, Georges Bataille, the French modernist and cultural theorist, augurs in further nightmares, fantasies about a bloodthirsty Mexico (he primarily means to reference the Nahuas but also includes the Maya in his description) beyond even the historical dramas that one may find in medieval Europe, invoking the specter of the Marquis de Sade. One may ask why Bataille would reference Sade—an individual connected with torturous sexual acts—rather than barbarous conquerors from the Crusades, Roman emperors engaged in acts of sacrifice, Muslim or Chinese rulers famous for their brutality, or even the Spanish conquerors. Bataille would have known of all of these possibilities for comparison but instead used Sade to make a particular point—the Aztecs and Maya engaged in torturous activity beyond the historical imagination, activity that a European mind could only conceive as excessive; Bataille wanted his readers to imagine bodies going through tortures that would cause them nightmares, that would disrupt their sensibilities. And this disruption could only lead his readers to think through the extreme pleasures and desires sought by Sade, equally performed by the ancient Mexicans he summons. Bataille performs a modernist version of Landa and Sahagún's ethnopornography. He takes the indigenous rite out of its context and suggests the most sexually depraved Western author imaginable to him as a point of comparison—and from there he forecloses the Nahuas and Maya from history itself.

Landa, Sahagún, and Bataille share similar fantasies and fears. They all fantasize about the debauched indigenous sexual subject, one who does not adhere to the rules of the civilized world but rather pierces penises and engages in orgies. The Franciscans, along with Bataille, feign shock at the practices of these people—but they cannot stop looking at them. They witness strange sexual practices, disgusting violence, and degrading bodily mortifications. But they keep staring; and they make us look.

As we invest our time in the archive, we often encounter significant boredom, going through many texts that archivists placed in the building simply because somebody notarized a particular document, making it worthy of archivization. Then we come across texts in Seville like the one written by Landa, or in Florence like the one authored by Sahagún, and we become excited, exhilarated even, to find that the original authors had become extremely dedicated to their projects for various reasons: they wanted to wipe out idolatry, respond to charges against themselves, understand indigenous lore, and control an unruly population. In doing so, they developed portrayals that emphasized the perverse nature of indigenous bodies: malformed, penetrated, and engaged in disgusting sexual and ritual activity. The Franciscan authors, feeling persecuted for their own actions, projected such feelings onto the bodies of the indigenous peoples. As they engage in such projection, the friars force us to look at the Franciscan magic. Suddenly they create a sexual subject. Suddenly they deform an indigenous body through (viewing) violent acts. And—poof—they produce an ethnography and make us think of it as objective when it in fact develops a pornographic version of truth.

Notes

1 For a discussion of the visceral and its relationship with the colonial Latin American archive, see Zeb Tortorici, "Visceral Archives of the Body: Consuming the Dead, Digesting the Divine," GLQ: A Journal of Lesbian and Gay Studies 20, no. 4 (2013): 407–37.

2 Inga Clendinnen, Ambivalent Conquests: Maya and Spaniard in Yucatan, 1517–1570 (Cambridge: Cambridge University Press, 1987), 93–111.

3 Diego de Landa, Relación de las cosas de Yucatán (Mexico City: Consejo Nacional para la Cultura y las Artes, 1994), 126–30.

4 Landa, Relación, 125.

5 Landa, Relación, 129–31.

6 On the Nahua city-state, the altepetl, see James Lockhart, The Nahuas after the Conquest: A Social and Cultural History of the Indians of Central Mexico, Sixteenth through Eighteenth Centuries (Stanford, CA: Stanford University Press, 1992).

7 See Lockhart, Nahuas after the Conquest.

8 Note that for the preconquest Nahuas and the Maya, such an act of witnessing was also key. For it was the gaze of the commoners and the nobles of neighboring polities upon the participants in massive sacrificial ceremonies that led to the maintenance of spiritual and earthly authority for the leaders of the central powers.

9 See particularly Zahid R. Chaudhary, Afterimage of Empire: Photography in Nineteenth-Century India (Minneapolis: University of Minnesota Press, 2012).

10 For a discussion of the relaciones, see Barbara E. Mundy, The Mapping of New Spain: Indigenous Cartography and the Maps of the Relaciones Geográficas (Chicago, IL: University of Chicago Press, 1996).

11 Matthew Restall and John F. Chuchiak, "A Reevaluation of the Authenticity of Fray Diego de Landa's Relación de las cosas de Yucatán," Ethnohistory 48, no. 3 (2002): 651–69.

12 See, for one recent example, Leslie A. Robertson and the Kwagu'l Gixsam Clan, Standing Up with Ga'axsta'las: Jane Constance Cook and the Politics of Memory, Church, and Custom (Vancouver: University of British Columbia Press, 2012). Robertson and the Gixsam Clan collectively wrote the book. The nonlinear narrative, with the focus on an interaction between the anthropologist, the indigenous community (Cook's descendants), and the memory of Cook, provides a way of dealing with memory and history through the presentation of multiple voices.

13 See David Burr, *The Spiritual Franciscans: From Protest to Persecution in the Century after Saint Francis* (University Park: Pennsylvania State University Press, 2001). See also the classic history of the Franciscans: John Moorman, *A History of the Franciscan Order from Its Origins to the Year 1517* (Oxford: Clarendon Press, 1968).

14 See Pete Sigal, *The Flower and the Scorpion: Sexuality and Ritual in Early Nahua Culture* (Durham, NC: Duke University Press, 2011), 79–84, 92–102.

15 See Moorman, *History of the Franciscan Order*, 339–49, 479–500.

16 Robert Ricard, *The Spiritual Conquest of Mexico: An Essay on the Apostolate and the Evangelizing Methods of the Mendicant Orders in New Spain, 1523–1572*, trans. Lesley Bird Simpson (Berkeley: University of California Press, 1966), 15–38.

17 D. A. Brading, *The First America: The Spanish Monarchy, Creole Patriots, and the Liberal State, 1492–1867* (Cambridge: Cambridge University Press, 1991), 104–6. On the thought of the spiritual Franciscans, see Burr, *The Spiritual Franciscans*.

18 Brading, *First America*, 108–9; Ricard, *Spiritual Conquest of Mexico*, 128–32.

19 Brading, *First America*, 108–9; Moorman, *History of the Franciscan Order*, 256–93.

20 See Moorman, *History of the Franciscan Order*, 302–19. On the Mexican context, see Amos Megged, *Exporting the Catholic Reformation: Local Religion in Early-Colonial Mexico* (Leiden, Netherlands: Brill, 1996); Osvaldo Pardo, *The Origins of Mexican Catholicism: Nahua Rituals and Christian Sacraments in Sixteenth-Century Mexico* (Ann Arbor: University of Michigan Press, 2004).

21 See Moorman, *History of the Franciscan Order*, 337–49; Burr, *Spiritual Franciscans*; Bert Roest, *Franciscan Learning, Preaching, and Mission c. 1220–1650: Cum scientia sit donum Dei, armatura ad defendendam sanctam Fidem catholicam . . .* (Leiden, Netherlands: Brill, 2014).

22 Burr, *Spiritual Franciscans*, 191–212. See also Gary Dickson, "Encounters in Medieval Revivalism: Monks, Friars, and Popular Enthusiasts," *Church History* 68, no. 2 (1999): 265–93.

23 Burr, *Spiritual Franciscans*, 151–59. For a salacious take on this theme, see William M. Cooper, *Flagellation and the Flagellants: A History of the Rod* (Amsterdam: Fredonia Books, 2001), 70–74.

24 Burr, *Spiritual Franciscans*.

25 Megged, *Exporting the Catholic Reformation*; Pardo, *Origins of Mexican Catholicism*.

26 See Nancy Farriss, *Maya Society under Colonial Rule: The Collective Enterprise of Survival* (Princeton, NJ: Princeton University Press, 1984); Lockhart, *Nahuas after the Conquest*; Matthew Restall, *The Maya World* (Stanford, CA: Stanford University Press, 1997).

27 For some examples, see Matthew Restall, Lisa Sousa, and Kevin Terraciano, eds., *Mesoamerican Voices: Native-Language Writings from Colonial Mexico, Oaxaca, Yucatan, and Guatemala* (Cambridge: Cambridge University Press, 2005).

28 See Ricard, *Spiritual Conquest of Mexico*.

29 On confession in Mexico, see Pardo, *Origins of Mexican Catholicism*.

30 On Sahagún as the first ethnographer, see J. Jorge Klor de Alva, H. B. Nicholson, and Eloise Quiñones Keber, eds., *The Works of Bernardino de Sahagún: Pioneer Ethnographer of Sixteenth-Century Aztec Mexico* (Austin: University of Texas Press, 1988); Miguel León Portilla, *Bernardino de Sahagún: First Anthropologist*, trans. Mauricio J. Mixco (Norman: University of Oklahoma Press, 2002).

31 Luis Nicolau D'Olwer, *Fray Bernardino de Sahagún*, trans. Mauricio J. Mixco (Salt Lake City: University of Utah Press, 1987), 4–12; León Portilla, *Bernardino de Sahagún*, 92–95.

32 Bernardino de Sahagún, *Códice florentino* (Florence, Italy: Biblioteca Medicea Laurenziana / Mexico City: Archivo General de la Nación, 1979) [hereafter CF], book 1, prologo, f. 1r; Arthur J. O. Anderson and Charles Dibble, *Florentine Codex, General History of the Things of New Spain*, by Bernardino de Sahagún, 13 vols. (Santa Fe, NM: School of American Research / Salt Lake City: University of Utah, 1950–82), *Introduction and Indices*, 45.

33 León Portilla, *Bernardino de Sahagún*, 37–43.

34 Clendinnen, *Ambivalent Conquests*, 70–71.

35 Clendinnen, *Ambivalent Conquests*.

36 Clendinnen, *Ambivalent Conquests*, 97–100.

37 Clendinnen, *Ambivalent Conquests*, 108.

38 Restall and Chuchiak, "Reevaluation."

39 Restall and Chuchiak, "Reevaluation."

40 See Pete Sigal, *From Moon Goddesses to Virgins: The Colonization of Yucatecan Maya Sexual Desire* (Austin: University of Texas Press, 2000), 39–62.

41 The sense of "queer" that I evoke here comes from an analysis of the epistemology related to the assertion of radical difference from the other based on one's disgust at the other's embodied actions, particularly as those actions relate to same-sex attachments, which are then viewed as promoting destruction. See Eve Kosofsky Sedgwick, *Epistemology of the Closet* (Berkeley: University of California Press, 1990); Lee Edelman, *No Future: Queer Theory and the Death Drive* (Durham, NC: Duke University Press, 2004); Jasbir Puar, *Terrorist Assemblages: Homonationalism in Queer Times* (Durham, NC: Duke University Press, 2007); and Mel Y. Chen, *Animacies: Biopolitics, Racial Mattering, and Queer Affect* (Durham, NC: Duke University Press, 2012).

42 Landa, *Relación*, 127.

43 Niklaus Largier, *In Praise of the Whip: A Cultural History of Arousal* (Brooklyn, NY: Zone Books, 2007), 125–26, 169–72.

44 See Matthew Restall, *The Black Middle: Africans, Mayas, and Spaniards in Colonial Yucatan.* (Stanford, CA: Stanford University Press, 2009).

45 Sigal, *From Moon Goddesses to Virgins*, 83–84.

46 Linda Schele and David Freidel, *A Forest of Kings: The Untold Story of the Ancient Maya* (New York: Morrow, 1990); Sigal, *From Moon Goddesses to Virgins*.

47 Sigal, *From Moon Goddesses to Virgins*, 150–82.

48 Schele and Freidel, *Forest of Kings,* 285–90.

49 Rosemary A. Joyce, "A Precolumbian Gaze: Male Sexuality Among the Ancient Maya," in *Archaeologies of Sexuality,* ed. Barbara Voss and Rob Schmidt (New York: Routledge, 2000), 263–83. See also Lynn M. Meskell and Rosemary A. Joyce, *Embodied Lives: Figuring Ancient Maya and Egyption Experience* (New York: Routledge, 2003), 95–127.

50 Schele and Freidel, *Forest of Kings,* 265–72.

51 Here we do not see phallic divergence and power in the same way we do in the Western world. While the phallus has some significant importance to the Maya, the gendered divisions are not as clear. See Sigal, *From Moon Goddesses to Virgins;* Joyce, "A Precolumbian Gaze." See also Chelsea Blackmore, "Ancient States and Ordinary People: A Feminist Re-imagining of Ancient Maya Power and the Everyday," *Critique of Anthropology* 36, no. 2 (2016): 103–21.

52 Schele and Freidel, *Forest of Kings,* 254–56, 287.

53 Schele and Freidel, *Forest of Kings,* 301–4.

54 Clendinnen, *Ambivalent Conquests,* 128.

55 Clendinnen, *Ambivalent Conquests,* 127–28.

56 Clendinnen, *Ambivalent Conquests,* 102.

57 Landa, *Relación,* 116–17.

58 Landa, *Relación,* 110–11, 133–35.

59 Landa, *Relación,* 128.

60 See also Sigal, *Flower and Scorpion,* 177–205.

61 Here I use some imagination in a process of overreading the archive. While we cannot know for certain how this exchange took place, the situation I have imagined is significantly more likely than the ways we often read our notarial sources for transparent realities. The point here is that the source is highly mediated. See Kathryn Burns, *Into the Archive: Writing and Power in Colonial Peru* (Durham, NC: Duke University Press, 2010).

62 The entire text that is in Sahagún's hand reads as follows:

"aynyanj. Vevezca, muyuma
telpuchtlaveliloc, tecamanalhuya, tetaza
cuilonj.
tecuilontianj.
patlachpul.
tetlanochilianj"

For more information on translation and interpretation, see Pete Sigal, "The *Cuiloni,* the *Patlache,* and the Abominable Sin: Homosexualities in Early Colonial Nahua Society," *Hispanic American Historical Review* 85, no. 4 (2005): 555–94.

63 Sigal, *Flower and Scorpion,* 82–83.

64 Sigal, *Flower and Scorpion,* 92.

65 See Alonso de Molina, *Vocabulario en lengua castellana y mexicana y mexicana y castellana,* 2 vols. (Mexico City: Editorial Porrua, 1992), 2:f. 80r. Also see Alonso

PETE SIGAL

de Molina, *Confessionario breue, en lengua mexicana y castellana* (Mexico City: Antonio de Espinosa, 1565), f. 12 v, in which he asks, "Cuix aca occe ciuatl, amoneuan ammopatlachuique?"

66 See, for example, the description of *tlacuilos* in Eloise Quiñones Keber, *Codex Telleriano Remensis: Ritual, Divination, and History in a Pictorial Aztec Manuscript* (Austin: University of Texas Press, 1995).

67 See Tim Dean, "Introduction: Pornography, Technology, Archive," in Tim Dean, Steven Ruszczycky, and David Squires, eds., *Porn Archives* (Durham, NC: Duke University Press, 2014).

68 See Eloise Quiñones Keber, ed., *Representing Aztec Ritual: Performance, Text and Image in the Work of Sahagún* (Boulder: University Press of Colorado, 2002).

69 On the practices of the *tlacuilos* before and after the conquest, see Elizabeth Hill Boone, *Stories in Red and Black: Pictorial Histories of the Aztecs and Mixtecs* (Austin: University of Texas Press, 2000).

70 See Sigal, "*Cuiloni.*"

71 *CF*, book 10, f. 40v: "Patlache: In patlache: ca tlahelcioatl, cioatl xipine tepule, choneoa, mioa, ateoa, mocioapotiani, mocioaicniuhtiani, mocicioapiltiani, cicioapile, oquichnacaio, oquichtlaque, ôoquichtlatoa, ôoquichnenemi, tetentzone, tomio, tzôtzoio, tepatlachuia, mocioaicniuhtia, aic monamictiznequi, cenca quincocolia aiel quimittaz in oquichti, tlatetzauia."

72 See Davíd Carrasco, "The Sacrifice of Tezcatlipoca," in *To Change Place: Aztec Ceremonial Landscapes*, ed. Davíd Carrasco (Niwot: University Press of Colorado, 1991); Cecelia Klein, "The Aztec Sacrifice of Tezcatlipoca and Its Implications for Christ Crucified," in *Power, Gender, and Ritual in Europe and the Americas: Essays in Memory of Richard C. Trexler*, ed. Peter Arnade and Michael Rocke (Toronto, Canada: Centre for Reformation and Renaissance Studies, 2008); Sigal, "The Perfumed Man," in Arnade and Rocke, *Power, Gender, and Ritual in Europe and the Americas.*

73 "Ixiptla" is a complex term used to refer to the position in between a human and a god, the person who becomes the god in sacrificial rituals. The ixiptla is most commonly translated as "impersonator." But this individual's position is quite complex, a liminal identity between the human and the divine. The two scholars who have studied this extensively both agree that the ixiptla was more than an impersonator. This person has an extensive amount of power, as s/he becomes a god. Yet, in another manner this person is among the least powerful in Nahua society, for s/he is destined for human sacrifice, and there is no way s/he can avoid that fate. See Alfredo López Austin, *Hombre-dios: Religión y política en el mundo náhuatl* (Mexico City: Universidad Nacional Autónoma de México, 1973); Serge Gruzinski, *Man-Gods in the Mexican Highlands: Indian Power and Colonial Society, 1520–1800* (Stanford, CA: Stanford University Press, 1989).

74 See Klein, "Aztec Sacrifice of Tezcatlipoca."

75 See also Samuel Marti, "Flautilla de la penitencia: Fiesta grande de Tezcatlipoca," *Cuadernos Americanos* 72, no. 6 (1953): 147–57; Guilhem Olivier, "The Hidden

King and the Broken Flutes: Mythical and Royal Dimensions of the Feast of Tezcatlipoca in Toxcatl," in Keber, *Representing Aztec Ritual.*

76 CF, book 2, chap. 24, f. 33r; Anderson and Dibble, *Florentine Codex*, 2:68.

77 See Sigal, *Flower and Scorpion.*

78 CF, book 2, chap. 24, f. 33r; Anderson and Dibble, *Florentine Codex*, 2:68.

79 Klein asks, "What did these broken flutes signify to the viewers of and participants in this ritual? Ethnographic reports from Melanesia, as well as South America, have noted the association of flutes with the male sex, and in some places specifically with the phallus. This raises the possibility that a similar connotation existed in preconquest Central Mexico. There is, it turns out, evidence that this was the case. The Nahuatl root of the word for flute, *tlapitzalli,* also appears in an adjective used by Sahagún's informants to describe the penis." Klein, "Aztec Sacrifice of Tezcatlipoca," 280–81.

80 CF, book 2, chap. 30, f. 72r; Anderson and Dibble, *Florentine Codex*, 115.

81 CF, book 2, chap. 30, f. 72r; Anderson and Dibble, *Florentine Codex*, 115.

82 CF, book 2, chap. 30, f. 72r; Anderson and Dibble, *Florentine Codex*, 115. On trash and its relationship to Nahua ritual, see Sigal, *Flower and Scorpion.*

European Travelogues and Ottoman Sexuality

Sodomitical Crossings Abroad, 1550–1850

Ethnopornography thrives in the intersection formed by the sexual cultures of Europe and the Middle East, as the history of Orientalist discourse has taught us and as Orientalist painting has made so graphically explicit. One of the most potent yet underestimated forms that such expressions take, I argue in this chapter, involves aspersions about and covert expressions of male homosexuality. This homoerotic dimension of Orientalism primarily finds expression in centuries of European hyperbole fomenting visions of the sodomitical proclivities of men in the vast terrains once encompassed by the Ottoman Empire. But it also often involves the complex, sometimes unexpected ways in which these European fantasies and projections have been shaped by already existing, widely disseminated Middle East erotic and literary cultures. When these dimensions are read in contiguity to each other, the ethnopornographic propensities fueling much Orientalist discourse about male-male sexuality can take surprising forms of expression, ones that necessitate a more subtle, and supple, revaluation of the intertwined sexual as well as political histories of the West and the Middle East than the binary oppositions common to popular imagination allow.

Hence I share with Sidra Lawrence, in her contribution to this volume, the desire to move beyond one-sided "assumptions do not allow for an adequate examination of the multidirectional power flows and mediations that occur in practice." Rather we need to embrace the challenge—which is a simultaneously ethical and interdisciplinary one—of creating methods that allow us to "represent multidirectional ways of looking and knowing, of . . . exchanging and encountering and meeting partway and in between." Because ethnopornography as an approach collapses method and object, it in a sense already inhabits this "in between," making the concept an especially fertile terrain for attending to these entanglements and for developing, as the editors of this volume propose, an alternative reading practice and "a redemptive analytical position from which Western intellectuals might contribute to the rehabilitation of intercultural knowledge."

In terms of my focus on the cross-cultural complexities both dividing and uniting the West and the Middle East, the charges lobbed between Grecian and Turkish soccer rivals in 2007 form an instructive example of what happens when homosexuality becomes the source of ethnopornographic rhetoric and rage. Trading insults is a typical component of this sports rivalry, but name-calling assumed a new level when a YouTube video posted by Greek enthusiasts gleefully intimated that the Turkish Republic's founding father, Mustafa Kemal Atatürk was homosexual. Outraged Turks responded by reminding their western neighbor of *its* reputation as the birthplace of pederasty, while the Turkish judiciary took the dramatic step of banning YouTube broadcasts within the nation.[1] History, inevitably, fuels this dispute. Greece was part of the Ottoman East from the fall of Athens in the mid-fifteenth century to its declaration of independence in 1821, and this period of Turkish rule (known in Greece as Tourkokratia) underlies the animosity that exists between the two countries to this day. In light of this history, the YouTube incident represents a fascinating return of the repressed, in which ethnopornographic constructions of "West" (in this case Greece, despite its incorporation into the Ottoman Empire) and "East" (in this case Turkey, despite its efforts to join the European union) pugilistically reassert their categorical integrity in the name of reaffirming twenty-first-century national identities. Even more revealing is the way in which charges of male homosexuality—who has "it," and who doesn't—became the trigger for this display of mutual xenophobia, laying bare an ethnopornographic logic that has been in play between the so-called Middle East and Western Europe for centuries.

As this chapter's survey of European travelogues commenting on Ottoman sexuality demonstrates, male homoerotic desire and its counterpart, homophobic dread, have for centuries provided the battleground upon which the ideological division of Islamicate and Judeo-Christian cultures has been staged. For four hundred years it was the uptight Christian "West" that accused the debauched Islamic "East"—most often identified, in Europe, with the Ottoman Empire—of harboring the contaminating germs of the sexual perversion euphemistically known as the male "vice." Pete Sigal shows how this same demonization was deployed in the queering of indigenous subjects in the Yucatán as part of the colonial project in his contribution to this volume. Yet, as Nabil Matar has demonstrated, this use of the language of sexual perversion to support the conquest of "New Spain" in the Americas was, in fact, borrowed directly from European accusations of sodomy directed against Ottomans and implemented to incite Europe's resistance to the latter's increasingly alarming imperial ambitions.[2] It is instructive to note how the twentieth and early twenty-first centuries have witnessed an ironic reversal of such charges, as Islamic conservatives across the Middle East have increasingly leveled the same charge of sexual deviancy at the "decadent" West in the name of nation building and cultural authenticity. Ethnopornographic derision, it seems, is not the property of one culture or civilization; it is transnational in its incitements and uses.[3]

This chapter attempts to illuminate the deep history of this phenomenon by tracing the rhetorics of male sodomy and pederasty that recur in European travel narratives about the Ottoman Empire throughout the early modern period and the long eighteenth century. The ideological work performed by such accounts, as a generation of postcolonial critics has shown, lies in the projection of desires deemed unacceptable at home onto a foreign terrain, in order to reencounter those desires "at a safe distance[,] in stories, gossip, and even the respectable garb of social science."[4] As Pernille Ibsen notes in her essay on the ethnopornographic aspects of European travel accounts of West Africa in this volume, these travel narratives served "two very different, but not mutually exclusive, interests": the economic (furthering European "trading and colonial expansion" through the presentation of helpful facts and demography) and the erotic (titillating readers with salacious accounts of exoticized difference). This fetishization of foreign otherness constitutes a discursive mode that Irvin Cemil Schick in *The Erotic Margin* labels "ethnopornography," in which the pretense of scientific objectivity barely disguises prurient desires that border, at times, on the pornographic (1–15).

In the analysis of travel narratives written from the sixteenth to nineteenth centuries that follows, my primary aim is that of unpacking the aesthetic, sociocultural, and psychosexual implications of Europeans' projections of male homoeroticism onto the Middle East in general and the Ottoman world in particular. At the same time, I hope to move beyond orthodox postcolonial critiques of Orientalism, which tend to view such projections unidirectionally, by also attending to those articulations of male homoeroticism arising within Ottoman culture, articulations that intersect with, and often frame, European eyewitness testimony and discursive expressions. As the work of any number of recent historians of Middle Eastern sexuality has demonstrated, European references to and depictions of Middle Eastern homoeroticism cannot exclusively be seen as exotic fictions or fantasies of a wishfully dominant culture.[5] Those representations are in dialogue with representations emanating from, and practices rooted in, regions of the Ottoman Empire that were themselves potent spaces of cross-cultural exchange within which circuits of knowledge and desire flowed for centuries in multiple directions.[6]

To put these cross-cultural resonances into dialogue, I employ what Edward Said in *Culture and Imperialism* calls a contrapuntal mode of analysis. Such a mode of reading allows one to attend, as in music, to "various themes play[ing] off one another with no privileging of the one over the other" in order to grasp a "composite" built of atonalities.[7] On the micro level of narrative, such reading practice allows the critic to imagine the interpretive possibilities that exist between the lines; on the macro level, it contributes to the larger epistemological project of undoing the binaries that for centuries have defined the Middle East and the West, as well as heterosexuality and homosexuality, in deceptively oppositional terms. These reading methods, in turn, are intricately intertwined with the perspective I bring to this archive as a literary scholar trained in close reading and narrative theory. All the disparate artifacts that make up this body of work—be they English travel narratives or epic Ottoman poems—are forms of cultural storytelling, and attending to the complex, often contradictory, structures of meaning that exist within and between these myriad stories—asking *how* they are told as well as *why* they are told—begins to suggest the myriad, rather than singular, forms of sexuality and eroticism that have always traveled across these politically freighted divides.

What is sometimes forgotten in limning the ethnopornographic cor-relatives of the Orientalist will to power is a simple fact that Said sidesteps in *Orientalism*: the specter of male homoerotic possibility that generations of Occidental male writers, artists, travelers, and thinkers, ever since the opening of the Islamic Middle East and North Africa to European diplo-macy and trade in the mid-1500s, have written into their narratives and their fantasies of Oriental libidinal excess.[8] This homoerotic undercur-rent stands to reconfigure the very premises of ethnopornography, in-sofar as the male traveler/observer—occupying the position of amateur ethnographer—sees reflected in the homoerotically signifying indigenous subject the very desires and fears that call into question Western assump-tions about masculinity, heterosexual primacy, and the sexual aim itself. As such, an altered ethnopornographic praxis—to paraphrase this vol-ume's editors—has the potential to contribute to theoretical critiques of the transformation of the liberal subject.

What story ensues when we read side by side two seemingly disparate seventeenth-century texts that just happen to situate sexuality between men at the juncture where myths of East and West collide? One English, the other Ottoman; one a didactic religious tract less than ten pages long, the other a flowery narrative poem of nearly three hundred couplets: the first is an anonymous pamphlet published in London in 1676 (never reissued) and titled *The True Narrative of a Wonderful Accident, Which Occur'd upon the Execution of a Christian Slave at Aleppo in Turky*; the second is the seventh tale, or *mesnevi*, of a book-length verse narrative by Ottoman poet Nev'izade 'Atayi completed in 1627.[9] Despite their overt differences, the ideological objectives and sexual resonances of these two contemporary narratives illuminate each other—and in the process illuminate the history of sexuality—in ways that demonstrate what may be gleaned by ventur-ing outside disciplinary constraints and reading representations of the past contrapuntally.

The shorter, seemingly less complex English text, *The True Narrative of a Wonderful Accident*, is an unabashed example of Christian propaganda that illustrates the degree to which religion and pornography may work hand in hand. Written in a sensationalist idiom that aims to titillate and hor-rify its readers,[10] this cheaply produced pamphlet recounts the horrific fate that a "handsome young French slave" suffers when subjected to brute Turk-ish male lust, figured as "that horrid and unnatural sin (too frequent with the *Mahumetans*), *Sodomy*" (2). While the trajectory that follows is typical of Christian martyrdom narratives, replete with a miraculous apotheosis as its climax, the tale is encased in a frame calculated to place the "unnatural" lusts of the Turk at as far a remove from English mores as possible: constructed as a letter addressed to an anonymous "Sir," the unnamed English narrator doesn't recount his own experience but retells a history that has been told to him by merchants returning from Aleppo who themselves have heard this story. This framing device effectively situates the reader at four levels of remove from the narrated events, establishing a moral as well as ethnogeographical gulf between its English audience and those vicious desires to which Turks are too often "addicted." Likewise, the fact that the victim is French, rather than English, brings the horror home to Europe but strategically stops it short of leaping the English Channel.[11]

The "handsome" eighteen-year-old Christian slave (presumably the victim of a raid on a merchant vessel by Turkish privateers[12]) has been left alone at his wealthy master's home with the master's steward. The latter Turk is one of the many men of his nationality "much addicted" to the despicable sin of sodomy and, having had his "lustful Eyes" on the good-looking youth for some time, finds the moment propitious for executing his "Villa[i]nous design." Failing to persuade the youth to "consent to his (more than Brutish) Devillish desires," the steward leaves off wooing and resorts to violence, attempting to rape him. However, the slave, good Christian that he is, refuses to yield his virtue to such "Devillish" ploys; during the ensuing struggle the Turk dies, and the beset youth, anticipating the "Cruel and Tyrannical nature of the Turks" (3) upon discovery of this mishap, runs away in hopes of finding sanctuary in the city's European enclave.

His attempt to escape, however, is stymied when he bumps into his master returning home, and sure enough, he's charged with murder of the steward. But in a reversal that momentarily dissolves the opposition between Europe and Other, the magistrate hearing the charges deems the slave's story to be true and upholds his innocence. Why? Because the magistrate has an agenda up his sleeve: his hope is that the case will serve as an object lesson helping "deter the Turks from the base sin of *Sodomy*" (4), a social problem he no less than the pamphlet's author feels to be all too pervasive among his countrymen. Ironically, however, his Turkish cohorts pressure the *bashaw* to reverse his decision. They do so not because they dispute the charge of rape or because they're especially concerned about sodomy one way or the other but because they are worried that freeing a slave who has killed a superior will set a bad example among other slaves, thereby upsetting the socioeconomic order. As such, the pamphlet's overt intention—to use the horror of male sodomy to demonize the infidel Other—momentarily rubs up against a strand of social realism that complicates a simplistic interpretation of Ottoman mores and morals. Nothing is as clear-cut as it seems.

Social realism is left behind in the execution scene that follows, an allegory of Christian martyrdom set into motion by the pious youth's prayer that God grant some "bodily sign" of his "innocence" (5). God's "sign" will soon follow, but not before the pamphlet's narrator delivers a voyeuristic peek at the handsome prisoner's naked physique. For as our "Chast[e] Martyr" (6) is stripped of his clothes, his nudity reveals to his onlookers a most "lovely body"—the same physical charms, one presumes, firing the steward's rapist desires. This narrative striptease, ironically, no less than the steward's "lustful" (2) gaze, eroticizes the Christian youth as an object of desire. Here, however, the ethnopornographic impulse underlying the lurid description ironically undermines its own intention: the English (and purportedly Christian) readers not only become intimate onlookers to this display but also find themselves occupying the position of the gazing, sodomitical infidel.[13]

This *erotic* display of the nude male body becomes, moreover, part of the Christian hero's *spiritual* apotheosis. For in the same sentence that "discover[s]" and thus uncovers his "lovely *body*," the reader is informed that this flesh is inhabited by a yet "more lovely *soul*" (5). The miracle toward which the entire arc of the narrative has been building, the wonder-filled "accident" announced by the pamphlet's title, comes to fruition after the youth's execution by decapitation: the dogs that tear at the bodies of a group of Turkish prisoners executed on the same day won't touch the Christian youth's body; nor does the corpse putrefy for the ten days it lies unattended. His lovely flesh, that is, remains "chaste," its intact beauty serving as God's outward "sign" of the victim's inner purity. In resisting the sexual advances of the heathen Turk and maintaining the "Virtue of a devout and Chast[e] Christian" (6), the martyred slave becomes an example to the reader of the spiritual rewards awaiting those faithful who follow the path of the righteous.

Not unlike *A Wonderful Accident*, the seventh tale of 'Atayi's *Heft han* also traces a religious allegory, one that is just as proselytizing despite its poetic form. In it, too, capture at sea by the infidel Other, homoerotic tensions, imprisonment, legal judgments, escape attempts, and reversals of fortune play prominent roles. Moreover, its conclusion also celebrates "lovely souls" in "lovely bodies" attaining a heavenly reward. At the same time, for Western readers, this poem may seem to issue from another world altogether.[14] For the final tale in this verse narrative is nothing less than a love story between men that ends happily.

The story begins with a folkloric staple: two prosperous merchants of Istanbul who are "each other's [best] comrade and companion" sire two wonderful sons, Tayyib and Tahir. Given that Tayyib means "beautiful" and Tahir means "pure," the two boys thus share between them the enslaved French youth's two distinguishing marks: purity and beauty. As they reach "the springtime of life"—seventeen or eighteen years of age—these friends turn to those archetypal pleasures that tend toward youthful folly: sex, wine, and music. The deaths of their parents leave them with inheritances that allow them to indulge these sensual pleasures. Relishing the pangs of love, they chase after the "heart-throbbing beauties" of both genders of Galata and Goksu, and they frequent Pera's all-male wine establishments (see an equivalent in figure 6.2). Here their "unreserved lovers," in 'Atayi's metaphor, flirtingly "count the threads of their beards" (these newly sprouted beards are the signature of Tayyib and Tahir's recently developed manhood).[15] That this takes place in a tavern named "Köse" is an inside joke, since the word *köse* also means "beardless lads," those very objects of desire who are counting the two heroes' whiskers. Of course, all these polymorphous pleasures— concubines, boys, wine—prove as fleeting as youth itself: Tayyib and Tahir spend their inheritances, suffer rejection by their fair-weather comrades, and in desperation set off across the Mediterranean to join a popular order of Sufi dervishes based in Egypt. As 'Atayi puts it, with delicious under-statement, "They smelled the mortal rose and hit the road."[16]

Hitting the road, however, cannot reverse the wheel of fortune when it's on a downward spin: the ubiquitous storm-at-sea and shipwreck-of-romance narrative follows; next the two survivors are plucked from the sea by a warship as "full of infidels as hell"—"blood-thirsty Franks" (the ubiq-uitous Ottoman term for European Christians) who put Tayyib and Tahir in chains. An even worse fate looms when the vessel reaches shore: they are separated from each other for the first time in their lives. Numbering among their infidel captors are two valiant noblemen "resembling the sun and the moon," Sir John (Can) and Janno (Cano), and these nearly identi-cal men ("Cano" being a derivative of "Can") claim the equally mirror-ing Tayyib and Tahir as their respective slaves, carrying them off to their separate estates in an unspecified European country. At this point, 'Atayi's poem becomes a kind of captivity narrative, but one that *reverses* the open-ing proposition of *A Wonderful Accident*: here virtuous *Ottoman* youths are at the mercy of Christian unbelievers, instead of a virtuous European at the mercy of Muslim infidels. But this is an inversion with a difference, for Tayyib and Tahir's masters, unlike the villainous steward of the English text, are elegant, good-hearted gentlemen who are "heart-stopping beauties" in their own right. Forthwith, each youth not only "falls captive" *to* his master, but secretly "falls captive *for*" him; in 'Atayi 's metaphor, their adoration transforms what would otherwise be "beheading" grief (recall the fate of the French martyr of the English pamphlet) into rapture that lifts their heads up "to the mountain of love."

At this juncture, the perspective narrows to the plight of Tayyib, wasting away in a dungeon. Fortuitously his master Sir John happens to visit, feels sorry for the lad, and sends him to work on his estate's grounds, a "rose garden of love" that cannot but lift Tayyib's spirits and mend his health. Thus begins an ascending pattern of improving fortune. One day Sir John holds a party in his garden attended by "several beautiful boys with faces like the moon" and their male admirers, and the company takes appreciative notice of Tayyib as the wine flows freely and kisses are bestowed all around like roses. Here 'Atayi represents the widespread and well-documented Ottoman cultural institution known as the *sohbet*, a garden party at which Lovers and Beloveds, elite men and beautiful boys, indulged in poetry, wine, mannered discourse, and flirtation.[17] Tayyib tells his woeful story, moving everyone to tears, and within couplets Sir John has fallen "deeper and deeper" in love with his slave. Empowered by his benefactor's compassion, Tayyib confesses his grief at being separated from his soul mate, Tahir. This leads Sir John to send for Sir Janno and Tahir, who too have fallen in love like "moon and sun uniting in the same sign of the zodiac." Both couples now reunite in bonds of amorous intoxication and paradisiacal bliss (see figure 6.1).

This private Eden, however, must undergo a series of public trials that suggest that homoerotic love occupies a precarious place in its world—which is set in Europe, even though it manifests the trappings of elite Ottoman male culture. These tests are set into motion when a meddling "busybody" spies on the lovers in their private garden, and then reports what he sees to the head of the local police, a Christian zealot who "believ[es] the love of beauties a crime." Fueled by puritanism, sexual repression, and spiteful jealousy that burns inside him "like a wrathful fire," this foe of the flame of true passion throws the two noblemen into prison and readies to behead Tayyib and Tahir. Comparable to the Turkish judge in the English pamphlet, this prosecutor also uses the situation to serve a moral agenda: to "make [the

FIGURE 6.1 An illustrated copy of 'Atayi Nev'izade's romantic tale illustrating Tahir and Tayyib's reunion. Tahir is entering the European pleasure garden—styled on the tradition of an Ottoman sohbet—with Sir Janno (*upper left*), while Tayyib sits at the table with his beloved, Sir Jan (*to the right*). Khamsa (1721). W. 666, fol. 138a. Courtesy of the Walters Art Gallery, Baltimore, MD.

two youths] an example for others to dread." However, the crowd of onlookers, playing a role similar to that of the Aleppo citizens, are moved to pity for the two young men, and *again* for reasons that are pragmatic and political: "Is it meet . . . to foul our names in eyes of friend and foe?," they ask. "If we start killing prisoners this way / What's to keep Muslim swords from coming into play? / If captives on both sides are caused to die / Who on Judgment day will answer why?"[18] 'Atayi's clever word plays in these couplets serve two purposes. First, they deflect the "foulness" that the policeman attributes to homoerotic love onto the fate that their *own* reputations will suffer ("Is it meet . . . *to foul our names* in eyes of friend and foe?" they ask [emphasis mine]). Second, the police commander's harsh verdict is implicitly weighed against the far more important "Judgment day" to come. Forced to yield to this argument, the policeman unhappily commutes the death sentences of Tayyib and Tahir to enslavement on a Christian galley.

With this return to the sea, the narrative is ripe for an instance of rep-etition, which indeed occurs when the boat is beset by Muslim ships that overcome it in battle. As narrative theory teaches, repetition (which inevi-tably involves difference) is almost always laden with significance, which is true in this case as well. Tayyib and Tahir are freed by their fellow Muslims and, in an ironic turn of fate, are given command of the European craft on which they were previously enchained: "The pirates of love became the captains of the sea." Meanwhile, in a neat chiasmus, their former masters, Sir John and Janno, languish in prison chains, occupying the place formerly filled by their beloveds. This nadir, however, proves to be the path to true freedom. Thrown into the company of Muslim prisoners, the two noblemen become interested in Islam, share a dream vision in which a figure in green (the Prophet's color) tells them "the gates of their wishes have been opened," awaken to find their chains miraculously sundered, and make good their escape in a rowboat. Simultaneously Tayyib and Tahir have a premonition that impels them to sail in the direction of this drifting craft. They prepare to attack it as an enemy vessel, only to discover that it has delivered their hearts' beloveds to them: "They met friends instead of foes, they saw two beauties coming . . . each met his lover, became friends with each other's lover." Discord yields to concord both in the small instance (mistaken en-emies who turn out to be allies) and on the larger metaphysical plane as the last obstacle to happy union—religious difference—is removed by the Europeans' conversion, allowing all four reunited lovers to return "joyful and happy" to Constantinople, at which point "their pleasure reached the heavens." Narrative coincidence thus becomes an emblem of miraculous providence. Sir John is henceforth known as Mahmud (meaning "praise-worthy") and Janno as Mes'ud (meaning "fortunate"). When at the end of their lives the two couples pass from this world into "the holy garden" of the next, they do so filled with "pure love," and the "magical legend" of their story becomes a lesson and inspiration for all who open their ears.

So 'Atayi's verse romance ends, as does *A Wonderful Accident*, on an allegorical note, illustrating the heavenly rewards that await those whose love remains "pure." But there is a difference, since homoerotic love is the *very* agent of conversion and hence salvation in the tale of Tayyib and Tahir, whereas homosexual sodomy is the "unnatural" sin that precipitates the French youth's martyrdom in the English pamphlet. In a brilliant addition to the history of sexuality titled *The Age of Beloveds: Love and the Beloved in Early-Modern Ottoman and European Culture and Society*, Walter G.

Andrews and Mehmet Kalpakli argue that the sexual scripts represented in literary works such as *Heft han* reflected a very real dimension of love that existed on many tiers of Ottoman society. Tayyib and Tahir move through a man's typical life stages from youthful folly (chasing *any* beautiful boy or girl) to mature appreciation of true love based on the model of male lover and male beloved. On one level, then, reading these two seventeenth-century texts in tandem reveals a striking *disjunction* between European and Middle Eastern attitudes toward homoeroticism; passions that are vilified in the former are celebrated in the latter, and what is deemed natural in one is deemed unnatural in the other. On another level, however, viewing these texts contrapuntally warns against an overly binaristic reading of *either* of these cultures. For instance, while the English *A Wonderful Accident* forms a textbook example of Orientalist projection in the name of religion, in which the home culture's taboos and fears are read onto a literally demonized Other, the Ottoman text engages in its own level of fantasy and wish fulfillment, namely through the fictional creation, by text's end, of a hyperidealized world in which its happy male foursome never has to face the social pressures of marriage and progeny, a component of the adult Ottoman male's social and sexual script normally *coexisting* with the culture of male beloveds.

Moreover, if the Turkish steward in the former narrative is a projection of European fantasies of brutish heathen lust, the creation of his Occidental counterpart in *Heft han*, the repressed police official who "believes love a crime," strategically allows 'Atayi to displace onto a foreign other, Europe, what was in fact a threatening reality within the Ottoman world itself: namely, the success of increasingly powerful conservative religious elements (such as the Kadizadeli and followers of Birgili Mehmet) in demanding that the sultan crack down on an array of immoral activities, ranging from homoerotic activity and wine drinking to coffeehouses. Projecting this social reality *onto* a Christian infidel allows 'Atayi to critique a threat looming on *his* home front, but to critique it obliquely and at a distance.[19] Likewise, if reading these texts in tandem discloses a latent similarity between homophobic English culture and the repressive zealotry that 'Atayi fears threatens the Ottoman heritage of homoerotic bonding, the unabashed homophobia of *A Wonderful Accident* doesn't preclude a degree of homoerotic voyeurism when it comes to displaying the naked charms of the handsome Christian martyr. The linkages and disconnections between "West" and "East" over the terrain of male homoerotic desire begin to reveal, in examples such as these, a complexly imbricated history whose actualities and representations—literary as well as ethnopornographic—cannot be reduced to the oppositions that the popular imagination so often summons forth when using homosexuality to categorize and castigate the other.

Ethnopornography and Homoerotic Spectacle in European Travel Narrative

With these complexities in mind, the following pages explore a range of European perceptions of male homoerotic activity in the Middle East that were recorded in an exponentially increasing number of texts that followed the explosion of diplomatic and trade relationships between Christian and Ottoman worlds in the early modern period. While the degree of empirical truth these commentaries reflect will always be open to debate, they nonetheless serve as invaluable repositories of narrative patterns, themes, and tropes whose cumulative record speaks to specific material realities and moments of cultural interexchange while revealing the range and depth of the constructions, fears, and fantasies that their writers bring to the "forbidden" forms of eroticism to which their travels expose them. As I also attempt to show, these patterns and desires also exist in contrapuntal dialogue with Islamicate sources on similar subjects. To be sure, the sexual curiosities that fascinated most European writer-observers were heterosexual in orientation—foremost the Muslim practices of polygamy and the imagined delights of the harem. But a surprising number of accounts turn their narrative eye, at least for an instant and at equally surprising moments in texts otherwise often laden with mind-numbing trivia, to those homoerotic forms of sexual expression among men that, in contrast to the unseen mysteries of the female harem, appeared—to Western sensibilities—all too visible, too public, and too discomfiting, staring the observer right in the eye.[20] If the pornographic depends on the interplay between concealment (the forbidden) and exposure (the taboo made visible), these accounts of Ottoman customs and culture make for an unexpected ethnopornographic frisson, in which voyeuristic pleasure is displaced by the shock of the spectacle (men's desire for men) that such commentators feel themselves compelled to report to their readers.

One much-remarked-upon space of public homoerotic exchange is the Ottoman coffeehouse (see figure 6.2). An instructive example occurs in

George Manwaring's account of his travels as an attendant accompanying the British ambassador to Persia in 1599. Particularly interesting is the way he begins his comments on the sexual practices encouraged by Ottoman coffeehouse culture by noting a *commonality* between East and West that evolves into a contrast: "As in England we ... go to the tavern, to pass away the time in friendly meeting, so [the Turks] have very fair houses, where this kaffwey is sold; thither gentlemen and gallants resort daily." This commonality, however, quickly evolves into a contrast as Manwaring explains how the café owners attract clientele by "keep[ing] young boys: in some houses they have a dozen, some more, some less; they keep them very gallant in apparel. These boys are called Bardashes, which [the patrons] do use ... instead of women."[21] Likewise, in a volume of travels written a decade later, George Sandys mentions in an aside that "many of the Coffa-Men" keep "beautiful Boys, who serve as Stales [lures] to procure their customers," and Pedro Teixeira similarly notes the "pretty boys, richly dressed," serving up coffee in Aleppo (the setting of *A Wonderful Accident*).[22] Notable is the focus on the rich apparel of these kept boys, making them not only the visual focus of the customers they serve but also the textual focus of the gaze of the European observer and his readers.

These European representations of sexual difference intersect, intriguingly, with a variety of Ottoman texts commenting on coffeehouse and wine-tavern culture. In the mid-seventeenth century, Ottoman historian Ibrāhīm Peçevi in *Tarih-i Peçevi* (c. 1640–50) explains that coffee establishments sprang into vogue the century before, their rise in popularity dovetailing with Süleyman the Magnificent's reluctant banning, under pressure from conservative religious revivalists, of Istanbul's popular wine taverns in 1554.[23] Primarily Greek and Portuguese establishments located in Galata, the European quarter of the city north of the Golden Horn, these taverns had hitherto served as favored meeting places of Turkish pleasure seekers and their male minions (recall Tayyib's and Tahir's youthful frolics in Galata in 'Atayi 's *Heft han*; in the miniature reproduced in figure 6.3, the youthful rake's appreciative gaze at the sumptuously dressed dancing boy who performs for him hints at the sensual pleasures proffered by the all-male wine tavern). The author of the Ottoman manuscript *Risalu fi ahkam al-gahwa* also mentions the "youths earmarked for the gratification of one's lusts" to be found in coffeehouses, and Ottoman courtier Mustafa Âli, in his deliciously nasty *Tables of Delicacies Concerning the Rules of Social Gatherings* (*Mevā'idü'n-Nefā'is fi Kavā'idi'l-Mecālis*, c. 1587), sketches a colorful portrait of these wine taverns. Their patrons, he writes, include "hot-blooded young

FIGURE 6.2 Peak hours in the Ottoman coffee shop. Multiple forms of male camaraderie are on display in this miniature. Ottoman Album CBL 439, fol. 96. Courtesy and © of the Trustees of the Chester Beatty Library, Dublin, Ireland.

men [and] . . . potent youths fond of drinking and fornicating with women and boys." Female beloveds being prohibited by definition from such gathering places, these establishments became spaces of socialization where men openly brought their male beloveds, with whom, Âli writes,

> they eat and drink, and when evening falls they make their way over to the tavern's private room. According to the demands of their lust, they extract milk from the sugar cane [that is, achieve orgasm]. . . . Friday night is reserved for approaching, with the abandonment of all decorum, young men, and every Friday afternoon for servant boys and beardless lads whom they have tucked up their sleeves. And so, according to the code of wine worshippers, on Fridays [the Islamic Sabbath] after prayers they head for the taverns. They clink their drink bowls together and say, "It's the lucky day for giving a purgative!" [e.g., having anal intercourse] because men of the craft trades, being free of work that day, and government officials, who are connoisseurs in these matters, both wander about "on the path of aspiration" [e.g., hoping for a successful pickup]. One may be certain that when the sun goes down and they go home, they spread out the pillow, mattress, and sheets and take young beauties and beardless servant boys into their arms.[24]

Once the wine taverns so evocatively described by Âli were banned and replaced by coffeehouses, the homoerotic antics associated with the former quickly shifted to the latter. In turn, the religious revivalist factions that had advocated the closing of the wine taverns now increasingly inveighed against the coffeeshops as threats to social order. Hence in an edict written at the same time that Manwaring is touring Turkey, one jurist condemns coffeeshops that "take on beardless apprentice boys" in order to attract "those . . . addicted to [such] love," and, almost as bad, those addicted to "coffee"![25] Within a century, the "problem" of this double addiction— boys and coffee—appears ubiquitous throughout the empire, evidence of which includes the guild complaints registered against neighborhood cafes where the hiring of "beardless youths to wait on . . . morally corrupt" customers is said to have led to a slacking of religious duty, because customers are too busy fornicating to remember to attend to their religious duties. "They openly boast of doing all these reprehensible acts even during times of prayer," the guild laments (such "open" boasts and behavior providing evidence of the public displays that many European observers find so shocking).[26]

FIGURE 6.3 Levand and entertainer in an Ottoman wine tavern. Fazil Bey, *Huban-name* (Book of Beautiful Youth). T 5502, fol. 0041. Courtesy of Istanbul University Library.

A more complex picture thus emerges, when European and Ottoman texts such as these are considered in conjunction, than that of a sexual economy in which Turks indulged in sodomy with impunity. Taken together, these sources convey the sense of a thriving but not always welcome homoerotic subculture that—as scholars such as Dror Zeʾevi, Khaled El-Rouayheb, and Andrews and Kalpakli incisively detail—coexisted with *other* subcultures in a multilayered social order whose constituencies often included overlapping members. Note that in most of the European accounts, the basic tenor is carnal—coffeehouse boys are seen as "kept," sexually available to customers at a price. In contrast, Ottoman sources such as Âli's *Table of Delicacies* depict a *range* of subjects and objects of desire inhabiting this environment: idealized beloveds accompanied by their lover-patrons, willing young beauties ripe for the picking, apprentices who are off work on Fridays, and servant boys. Likewise, patrons range across classes, professions, and ages; they include connoisseurs of pleasure who may equally desire girls and boys, randy young hotbloods, wealthy masters who probably aren't so young, married men, members of the artisan and working classes, elite government administrators, soldiers from the janissary ranks, and (as Âli also notes) the usual number of aging lechers and debauchees. Indeed, it is not always clear *who* among the café's patrons is the pursuer and *who* the pursued—the "hot-blooded young men" that Âli says are fond of fornicating with boys or girls aren't rhetorically distinguishable from 'Ali's subsequent reference to those "young men" who are the *objects* being pursued on Friday nights, nor are the "men of the craft trades" depicted as being on the prowl necessarily distinct from "apprentice-boys" who succumb to their advances.

Even more to the point, while these sources attest to a widespread institutionalization of homoerotic behavior, its existence is not unproblematic, as the crackdowns (initially on wine taverns and then on coffeehouses) attest. At such moments, what has hitherto been the mutual coexistence of social groups espousing different value systems reaches a pressure point when the religious proponents and guardians of morality gain the upper hand; but, simultaneously, it appears that attempts to suppress any given venue for homoerotic gatherings merely creates another. As complex and sometimes contradictory as such formations may be, it is not hard to see why their very existence—as well as persistence and relative visibility—aroused the shocked amazement of European visitors for whom such sights were, indeed, "foreign."

The oscillation of voyeuristic titillation and moral indignation common to most ethnopornographic accounts is also obvious in the contrasting use of tropes of excess—particularly sexual excess—in early modern European and Ottoman texts, but with a telling difference in viewpoints. Scot traveler William Lithgow, an opinionated and deeply conservative Protestant, begins *The Totall Discourse, of the Rare Adventures, and Painful Peregrinations of Nineteen Long Years* (1632) by railing against his hell-bent age, focusing first on Rome, which his rabid anti-Catholicism leads him to label a "second Sodom."[27] Traveling eastward, he uses increasingly lurid language to describe the heathen Turks, whom he accuses of being "extreamly inclined to all sorts of lascivious luxury; and generally addicted, besides all their sensual and incestuous lusts, unto Sodomy" (163). (In counterpoint, it is instructive to note that Lithgow's Turkish stay occurred within seven years of 'Atayi's composition of the romantic tale of Tayyib and Tahir). By the time he's reached Fez, all hell has broken loose: "Worst of all, in the Summer time, they openly Lycenciate three-thousand common Stewes of Sodomiticall boyes. Nay, I have seene at mid-day, in the very Market places, the Moores buggering these filthy Carrion and without shame or punishment go freely away" (367). As the chapters in this volume by Helen Pringle and Mireille Miller-Young in particular stress, it is once again the visual spectacle of what should be hidden ("they *openly* Lycenciate," "I *have seene* at mid-day") that so rivets, and thus paradoxically justifies, such ethnopornographic voyeurism. The reader might assume that this exponentially increasing outrage diminishes upon Lithgow's return to Europe. Instead, ironically, the "damnable libidinous" excess (266) that has haunted him abroad only multiplies as he crosses from North Africa to Italy. For now, ranting at how the Papists have rendered Rome one great "Stewe" (406; note the echo of page 367), he expends four pages detailing the depraved sodomitical practices of a roster of Popes and cardinals. It's as if the lip-licking Lithgow can't get too much of what he detests most, particularly when it helps him defame foes nearer to home, those anti-Protestant Catholics.

If Lithgow's text illustrates the danger of the plentitude of foreign vice overrunning one's narrative and deconstructing its claim to moral superiority, Mustafa Âli's chapter in *Table of Delicacies* on "Beardless Boys" evinces an equally copious overflow of the homoerotic and it does so in ethnopornographic language—but in this account erotic excess is deployed to quite different ends. For sexual plentitude is part of the ironic fun, evinced in the figuratively as well as literally racy catalogue Âli provides of the ethnic and national differences in appearance, compliance, and desirability of the farflung empire's youth available for sex and companionship. Among these "delectable morsels," the dancing boys from the East European provinces are "gentle"; the "fierce-looking lads" from Bosnia-Herzegovina turn out to be the most "obedient" and longest-lasting beauties (whereas the "agile lads of Arabia" lose their looks by twenty years of age); and the "narrowwaisted" boys of the inner provinces are ingenuous flirts whose "outward gentleness" is matched, Âli warns, by "inward contrariness." Kurdish roués, in contrast, are "dedicated to submission," and "fall over themselves in obeying" their master's requests—never a bad quality in a sexual companion. While some Albanians "are worthy of taking as a lover," most "are terribly contentious and obstinate"—potential lovers take warning! Likewise, the wise man will avoid Russians and Georgians, who betray their masters at the drop of a hat; much better to procure a Hungarian lad, who can be counted on to be "charming and pleasant."[28]

In a similar vein, Ottoman courtier, administrator, and poet Gazali makes libidinal excess the foundation of the panoply of sexual behaviors he divides into multiplying categories and subcategories in *The Book That Repels Sorrows and Removes Anxieties* (*Dāfi'ü'gumūm ve rāfi'ü'humüm*, written between 1483 and 1511), a popular and innovatively styled work steadily recopied over the centuries.[29] What makes this pornographic send-up of the traditional erotic treatise of special interest to this discussion is the degree to which the volume's cataloguing of the range of sexual proclivities not only celebrates (and cunningly privileges) same-sex relations among men but willfully embraces the "excesse" and diversity of Ottoman erotic behaviors that most European travelers saw as threatening the boundaries of the normative and the permissible. The degree to which Gazali intends his erotic taxonomy to give play to desire's polymorphous plentitude and its often laughable practice is obvious in his third chapter, which creates a detailed inventory of modes of homoerotic love, with racy anecdotes and poems illustrating each category. First Gazali illustrates *four* kinds of love—from the unrequited and successful to the loyal and deluded. Next he presents an alternative classification of boy-lovers into *three* types. This he follows with a dissection of the *five* predispositions creating sexual attraction among males; next, *nine* ways of seducing a youth (the anecdotes grow longer and more colorful); and, finally, a list of *eight* favored sexual positions. What's clear, as my italicizing of the numerals above indicates, is the degree to which these ever-unfolding categories—instead of imposing limits to desire—encourage the imagining of *infinite* erotic pleasures. Erotic plentitude is a desirable quality in Gazali's textual world, not the fearsome destroyer of boundaries that sexual excess represents in many Europeans' visions of an Ottoman world in which sodomy, to cite Lithgow's culinary metaphor, is treated as a mere "dainty to digest [with] all their other libidinous pleasures" (*Totall Discourse*, 163).

Michael Baudier's *Histoire generalle du Serrail, et de la cour du Grand Seigneur* (1626) exemplifies another narrative tendency shared by several European travel writers: promised glimpses of the Orient's feminine mysteries that are derailed by mentions of male homoeroticism. The penetrative image of "enter[ing]" an Ottoman East is the governing trope of Baudier's preface, which with a prototypically ethnopornographic flourish solemnly pledges to usher its readers across the threshold of the forbidden and invisible female "quarters" of the sultan's seraglio, where "the secret of all things is carefully shut up."[30] The heteroerotic voyeurism implicit in these simultaneously scopic and phallic metaphors of entering female space appears ready to deliver its soft-core equivalent of "the money shot" in a chapter titled "Of the Grand Seigneurs Loves." Here Baudier takes the reader "inside" the hidden world of the harem by *imaginatively* tracking the footsteps of the sultan as he traverses the women's quarters—which is to say that, at this narrative juncture, Baudier's history becomes *purely novelistic* in its use of narrative omniscience, creating the illusion that the author is spying on an actual occurrence. First he visualizes the scene of the sultan's selection of his female companion for the evening. Next he pictures the sultan joining his concubines in their private outdoors retreat: "*let us . . . follow him into his garden, where he is in the midst of his lascivious imbracements*," Baudier tantalizes his readers, adding, "It is dangerous *to see* him: but no fears of danger should deter us from serving of the publique" (55; emphasis mine) by revealing the truths that his spying eyes reveal.

Having thus promised the reader scenes of "riots of love," Baudier's narrative makes two abrupt turns. First, in a classic statement of castration anxiety, he demurs that the violence that the sultan "observes against those who should see him, forbids [Baudier] to reveal the secret" scene of these "imbracements" after all! Second, he announces that the sultan's dalliances with these women are "not the most blameable of his affections." Without a pause, he breathlessly launches into a disquisition on "the detestable excess of an unnatural passion"—the sultan's "love of men"—that continues right up to the chapter's conclusion. The ironic effect is that the narrative climax of a chapter promising to showcase the sultan's harem beauties in their unveiled glory reveals, instead, nubile boys: "He burnes many times for the love of men; and the youngest Boyes which are in the *Levant*, the floure of beautie and the allurement of graces, are destinated to the filthiness of his abominable pleasures. . . . This *disorder* is so inveterate . . . [that] of [the] twenty Emperours which have carried the Turkish scepter, you shall hardly find two that were free from this vice" (156).

Baudier proceeds to name names, which in turn leads him to meditate philosophically on the obligations of rulers: what matters all the grand conquests of the Ottoman princes if they themselves are captive to this addictive vice? "The Prince is the Physician of the State; but how can he cure it if he himself bee sick?" (57).

Having strayed this far from his original subject matter, Baudier picks up the subject of women in the following chapter, although nothing contained therein equals in shock value the representation of "unnatural passions" to which the reader has just been made privy. To which topic Baudier finds himself returning, as if compelled to tell more—or as if he knows the greater the inequities he brings to light, the greater the ethnopornographic thrill of the incensed reader. Chapter 14's account "Of the filthy & unnaturall lust of the [Pashas] and of the great men of the Court" exposes not just the sultan's perversions but also the sodomitical "myre of filthy pleasures" into which the governmental courtiers and administrators surrounding the sultan "plung[e] themselves": "They abandon their affections to young Boyes, and desperately follow the allurements of their beauties. . . . This abominable vice is so ordinary in the *Turks* Court, as you shall hardly find one [pasha] that is not miserably inclined toward it: It serves for an ordinary subject of entertainment among the greatest when they are together; they speak not but of the perfections of their *Ganimedes*" (162).

Now Baudier truly provides the "to-the-moment" reporting as his novelistic imagination again takes over, visualizing, complete with dialogue, such a gathering of men: "One sayes, they have brought me from *Hungarie* the most beautiful and accomplished Minion. . . . Another saith, I have lately bought *a young Infant of Russia . . . ,*" and the reported "conversation" goes on. Finally, creating a level of diegetic scopophilia mirroring the voyeurism being incited on the narrative plane, Baudier depicts one pasha asking another to put his newly acquired "Angell" on display—"[He] entreat[ed] him earnestly *to have a sight . . .* that he may be satisfied *by his eyes*" (162; emphasis mine), at which point the narrator inserts a lavish description of the arts used to "beautify" these boys. One is uncannily reminded, with a difference, of Mustafa Âli's cataloguing of the youths of multiple ethnicities available throughout the empire in *Table of Delicacies*. Where Âli aims to amuse, Baudier means to scandalize, but the effect implicates Baudier all the more in the "vices" that his own ethnopornographic imagination is making visible in the readers' minds. For instead of penetrating the female harem, the reader's mind is penetrated by the sodomitical images that Baudier's prose summons forth. "By semiotically stimulating desire," Silke Falkner writes of the rhetorical use of sodomy in early modern European accounts of Turkey, "texts may facilitate the vice as much as they attempt to combat it."[31]

A similar tension between an excess of titillating homoerotic detail and moralistic outrage characterizes English diplomat Aaron Hill's virulent response to a pederastic tryst he unintentionally witnesses, yet nonetheless proceeds to narrate at great length, in *Account of the Present State of the*

Ottoman Empire (1709). Hill has gathered a party of fellow countrymen at an open kiosk in a park overlooking a nearby river to welcome the new ambassador. Enjoying the vista, the group spies, on the opposite bank, a well-dressed, middle-aged Turk leading an adolescent boy to a secluded area, where "he began, *to our surprise*, and *inexpressible confusion*, to prepare himself and his *consenting Catamite*, for acting a Design so hateful to our sight, and such a stranger to our Customs, that we scarce believ'd our Eyes."[32] Despite the dismayed ballyhoos and catcalls of the English party, the "lustful Wretch" (81) persists until Hill breaks up the encounter by firing his fowling piece at the man.

In this defamiliarizing world of visible and invisible sexualities, however, Hill's high-minded intentions are turned on their head. Several chapters later, he announces (like Baudier) that the time has come to give the reader egress into the voyeuristic delights of the seraglio, "not only trac[ing] the *Sultan* to his amorous Pastimes . . . with the *Virgines* of his *Pleasure*, but admit[ting] the Reader to the close Apartments of the fair SERAGLIO LADIES, nay . . . into the retir'd Magnificence of their *Bedchambers*" (149). But before Hill gets around to penetrating the "immodest and indecent Pastimes" of these ladies, he suddenly abjures the task, claiming he doesn't want to embarrass his female readers. Failing to deliver on his original narrative promise means, ironically, that Hill's description of the sodomitical sighting in the park remains the text's most graphic example of the "amorous Pastimes" of the Turks.

There is, moreover, another reading of the sexual tryst in the park that Hill and company miss altogether. As noted in the tale of Tayyib and Tahir, Ottoman male elites of the sixteenth and seventeenth century perfected the art of the sohbet or outdoor garden party. At these refined gatherings, elite lovers and favored youths came together to share wine and delicacies, poetry, mannered discourse, and the unspoken language of "signs" in a sophisticated atmosphere of flirtation, admiration, and seduction. These sohbets were often held out of doors, in wooded parks and gardens with open kiosks very much like the venue described in Hill's text (see the representation of one such pleasure party in figure 6.4). The Ottoman travel writer (and amateur ethnographer in his own right) Evliya Çelibi, writing four decades before Hill, praises the "Loggia Pavilion" of one such pleasure grove where "every afternoon [male] lovers gather behind the tall trees and shady spots and flirt with their beloveds. It is a delightful gathering-place for men of culture." Rhapsodizing about the bountiful amenities—flowing water, pleasure domes, trellises, bowers, kitchens, pantries—of another

FIGURE 6.4 The refined male garden party. Ibrahim Mirza, *Haft Awrang of Jami* (1556–65), fol. 179b. Courtesy of the Freer Gallery of Art, Smithsonian, Washington, DC. Purchase F1946.12.179.

park in one of the empire's far-flung provinces, he adds, "Here countless love-striken young men come to sing love songs to the handsome boys they adore. . . . They pour out their emotions so sweetly and sadly that the nightingales get tongue-tied with admiration. In every corner [of the park] there is flirtation and fun and drinking and carousing."[33] Given the popularity of such pleasure spots, it is highly unlikely that Hill's was the only group frequenting the river park on the occasion of the party for the ambassador. And it is entirely possible, following this train of logic, that the "pornographic" scene that Hill's group witnesses is *not* the furtive, crude maneuvering of a wretched scoundrel out to have his way with a minor (the man, after all, is well-dressed—to Hill's surprise—and the boy is compliant). Rather, this encounter might well be the culmination of a flirtation between two attendees at an offstage sohbet occurring in the same park.

Tactfully having wandered out of the viewing range of their own party into one of those shady nooks described by Evliya, these two gentlemen have inadvertently strayed into the sight lines of a more easily shocked and less forgiving English audience. Had this gathering been composed of Ottoman gentlemen, its participants would no doubt have exercised their good manners by discreetly turning their gaze to another aspect of the natural view, respecting the private intentions of the two lovers.

The European Traveler as Participant Observer

Literally dozens of similar commentaries on Middle Eastern homoeroticism appear in European travel narratives and histories published throughout the eighteenth and nineteenth centuries, repeating with slight variations the attitudes, strategies of representation, and rhetorical expressions surveyed thus far. Among these texts, one early nineteenth-century traveler's comments stand out for the highly personal nature of the encounter of cultural viewpoints it records and for the unusual degree of empathy that ensues. James Silk Buckingham wrote several books about his travels throughout Asia Minor, and nothing is more instructive than comparing his initial reaction to the male "vice" he first witnessed in Baghdad in 1827 to his revised view of love between men in a volume appearing in 1829.[34] Casting Buckingham's writing as a form of ethnographic fieldwork, one might venture that his performative engagement in, rather than evaluative observation of, Ottoman homoeroticism models an ethics of cross-cultural encounter that allows for "multi-directional ways of look and knowing, of . . . encountering and meeting part way and inbetween."[35]

In the account of Ottoman Baghdad from 1827, Buckingham assumes a censorious tone as he announces his unhappy "duty, as an observer of human nature," to speak "in the least objectionable manner" of objectionable depravities: to wit, the practice he's witnessed of "boys publicly exhibited and set apart for purposes of depravity not to be named" (*Travels in Mesopotamia*, 166). The volume from 1829, however, sings a surprisingly different tune for one shocked to learn that "the vice" of which he had previously only heard rumors "was not merely imaginary" (*Travels in Assyria*, 168). This change of heart is due to personal circumstances that figuratively and literally open the writer's eyes to the possibility of an *honorable* passion existing between man and youth, where before he has only imagined debased, brute lust.

The narrative structure Buckingham creates to set forth this revelation is optimally designed to draw readers in and win their sympathies; and the tenor of its language, compared to the severity of the volume from 1827, assumes the vocabulary of literary romanticism, as experiences of natural feeling, intuition, and benevolence replace moral outrage. The chapter opens with Buckingham's glowing account of the "favorable impressions" (77) that his hired guide, the Afghan dervish Ismael, has made on him. The depth of Ismael's intellect and metaphysical studies, his lofty soul and independent spirit, his charity to others—all these characteristics incite Buckingham's curiosity to learn why a man of such "overflowing benevolence" (77) has given up worldly possessions to become a wandering dervish. The arc of Ismael's experiences, it turns out, is not unlike the life pattern of Ottoman males glossed in the story of Tayyib and Tahir: Ismael devotes his early years to serious study till he comes to feel all knowledge is vanity; gives himself over for a period to sensual enjoyments and "forbidden gratifications" (78); reforms and enters a trade (as engraver and jeweler) that allows him enough income to wander the world and satisfy the romantic restlessness of his "vivid and ardent mind" (79), for which the stimulant of spontaneous feeling is the one thing that makes life worth preserving.

Such spontaneous overflow, indeed, explains Ismael's instantaneous decision to become Buckingham's companion and guide. Upon meeting the narrator in Baghdad, Ismael—following the spontaneous promptings of his heart—declares, "I will follow you." He refuses any compensation, explaining, "It was my destiny to follow you wherever you might go" since from "the moment I saw you and heard your voice, I felt that your soul contained what I had all my life been searching for in vain" (80). As proof of the depth of his commitment to fulfill this call of destiny, Ismael explains that he will be leaving behind the "one tender object of [his] affections" (80), a beloved he values more than his own existence. Of course, this hint of romance only piques Buckingham's "strong desire to know more of my companion"—who a few pages before was reported to have courted a "pretty damsel of [the] Aphrodinian race" (67) in Kurdistan. This mystery in turn fosters the reader's narrative desire to press onward—who doesn't enjoy a love story?—and Buckingham is even more moved at Ismael's sacrifice when he witnesses his guide tearfully parting with his beloved's father, a Christian merchant named Elias. The journey commences, and the two men become soul mates, discoursing long into each night on various subjects. One evening, Buckingham comments how much Ismael must miss Elias's daughter. Ismael corrects him; the object of his life's passion is not a girl but Elias's *son*. "I shrunk back from the confession as a man who recoils from a serpent," Buckingham states, but lest his readers take too much of a thrill in assuming the worst, Buckingham makes a proleptic leap forward in the very next sentence, where he informs us that he was soon "delighted" to learn that Ismael's love is "a pure and honorable passion," one characterized by "a genuine infusion of *nature*, and in no way the symptoms of a *depraved* feeling" (85; emphasis mine).

With these words, Buckingham turns on its head two hundred years of European travel commentary, in which "nature," aligned with procreative heterosexuality, is counterpoised to those unnatural "depravities" such as sex between men said to flourish in the Levant. At this point Buckingham launches into a six-page digression on the classical tradition of the "honorable" (86) love of boys reaching from Crete to Athens. First Buckingham argues that because Greek love—and its echo in Muslim culture—was rooted in the desire to inspire youth to noble deeds and noble thoughts, these pederastic relationships were by definition "virtuous" and without "corrupt effects" (85–86), regardless of the "flame" (88) of erotic passion and sexual consummation he attributes to these relationships. Yet when Buckingham says his "severe and minute" (90) interrogation of Ismael has convinced him that his guide harbors no "impure desires" or "unchaste thoughts" (91) for his beloved, it might seem that Buckingham is now interpreting "platonic" love in the Victorian sense, as in a nonsexual friendship.[36] Buckingham is in fact making a more nuanced distinction. For when the narrator finally declares, "I could no longer doubt the existence in the East of an affection for male youths, *of as pure and honorable a kind as that which is felt in Europe for those of the other sex*" (93; emphasis mine), he is in effect suggesting that purity resides in the *quality* of the passionate eros felt for the love object, not in whether or not it is physically consummated.

Indeed, on the emotive and sensate level, such romantic "affection" *is* erotic, as Ismael makes clear when he argues that *if* a man can love a woman and desire "enjoyment" of her "person" without acting upon that desire until it is appropriate to do so, so too can a man passionately desire another male (and desire "enjoyment" of his "person") without giving offense to propriety. In effect, Ismael's argument leads Buckingham to conclude there is no qualitative difference between Ismael's feelings for Elias's son and the erotic desires drawing together the love interests of any nineteenth-century romantic novel in which the heroine, if not the hero, remains chaste until novel's end. The fact that Ismael's love is for a Christian boy not only adds a note of cross-cultural desire but also implicitly demonstrates to Buckingham and his reader that such higher homoerotic feelings are not exclusive to the Orient and parallel those "felt in Europe."

The catch, of course, is that there is no socially sanctioned "happy ending" (such as novelistic marriage) for Ismael's love, and both he and Buckingham remain silent on how one acts upon one's erotic feelings in the absence of an approved outlet. On the public level, Ismael's love for the boy is doomed to exquisite frustration, which may illuminate why Ismael chooses to become Buckingham's dedicated companion, even if it means separating himself from his beloved: such an act of sublimation and triangulation only heightens the as-yet-unfulfilled desire for the original object. In terms of narrative structure, it may also explain part of Ismael's autobiography that Buckingham inserts at this juncture. Six years previous, Ismael tells Buckingham, on a bridge over the Tigris he happened to observe a beautiful Turkish boy "whose eyes met his, as if by destiny" (91). The boy blushes with all the signs of love at first sight, Ismael's head swirls, the two declare their mutual love to the approval of their friends, and they continue meeting for months as they grow into "one soul" (92)—at which point the boy falls fatally ill and Ismael abandons himself completely to the youth's care till the latter's death. If the tragic ending of this love story is ennobling, it is also—to say the least—erotically frustrating, since death imposes the ultimate separation between lovers, erasing the possibility of physical consummation in the process.

It is this second tale that ultimately convinces Buckingham of "the existence in the East of an affection" (93) between males every bit as passionate *and* virtuous as any European male's romantic feelings for the female object of his desire. Convinced that such love exists—love that transcends the carnality associated with the male prostitutes in Baghdad from whose approaches he recoiled in the earlier volume—Buckingham narrates a radical conversion experience, one that may be influenced by social developments in England (including the publicity surrounding the increased persecution of men engaged in sexual acts) and by romantic literary sensibilities, but one that he would never have reached without his travels abroad.[37] Buckingham's affirmation of passionate homoerotic love, furthermore, circles us back to the idealized world of ennobling male-male love allegorized in 'Atayi's story of Tayyib and Tahir, and this moment of convergence between European and Ottoman perspectives serves as a healthy riposte to the voyeuristic ethnopornography and titillated homophobia that characterize travelers such as Hill and Baudier.

Buckingham isn't alone, however, in his more generous observations; traveling by its very nature is not always, or simply, voyeuristic, imperialistic, or unidirectional. The very act of crossing borders into realms of the foreign or unknown not only facilitates domination over or penetration into some monolithic "Other"; it also tacitly signifies the vulnerability of the voyager in the face of unsuspected multiplicities in cultural ways of being and renders the traveler-ethnographer an engaged participant as well as a distanced spectator.[38] In the opening of *A Voyage into the Levant* (1636), published just one year after Baudier's salacious account of the sodomitical perversities practiced by the sultan and his court, the English traveler Henry Blount writes that the true goal of travel is that of witnessing the unknown precisely in order to *undo* common stereotypes and prejudices, and throughout his text he reminds his readers he is reporting "what I found" rather than "censuring [those institutions] by any [preconceived] rule."[39] Criticizing travelers who "catechize the world by their own home" (3), Blount censures those who arrive in foreign lands with preconceived opinions, and he presciently advocates an ethos of cultural relativity when he explains that Turkish customs assumed to be "absolutely barbarous" to European eyes may in fact conform to "another kind of civilitie, different from ours" (2). Likewise, his nonjudgmental observations about sodomy when confronted with the friendly hospitality of a catamite accompanying his Ottoman master remind us of a truth that certain travelers, Eastern and Western, have always intuited: that desperately attempting to enforce the boundaries of self and other diminishes rather than expands one's notion of self.[40]

In the same vein, Horatio Southgate, an American Episcopal priest serving as a missionary in "the dominions and dependencies of the Sultan," admonishes the readers of his *Travels* (1840) "not to judge" Muslim culture by European standards. Although his narrative makes it clear that he laments the "vice" of same-sex love that has "deeply stained" the "eastern character," he maintains that while such customs may seem "unpleasing to us, because they belong to a different order of society," they "yet are not more unpleasing than are some of our own peculiarities" in the eyes of the Oriental subject.[41]

These examples of the open-mindedness regarding sexual matters that may ensue from travel are not unique to Europeans. One finds their counterpoint in an observation made by Evliya, traveling in Eastern Europe just a few decades after Blount's sojourn in Turkey. Passing through an Albanian town on a festival day, he reports having witnessed male "lovers go[ing] hand in hand with their pretty boys," adding that "this . . . quite shameful behavior" is "characteristic of the infidels." But, he adds, "it is their custom, so we cannot censure it." In a fascinating reversal of the modern reader's expectations, however, it turns out that Evliya is not censuring, as may first appear, male homoerotic display. What he judges to be "quite shameful," rather, is the fact that these tipsy "infidel" couples are "danc[ing] about in the manner of the Christians" on what is likely a saint's festival day. But, tolerant Muslim that he is, Evliya wisely chooses, like the Reverend Southgate, not to censure those religious "custom[s]" and "manner[s]" not one's own.[42]

While this chapter has presented only a mere fraction of the attitudes and representations contained in European narratives about the Ottoman East and those of their Ottoman counterparts, it is my hope that the archive it has tapped conveys a sense of the richly cross-cultural dialogue that exists waiting to be discovered by further work in the field, as well as a sense of the sometimes unexpected interpretative possibilities that emerge when putting such texts into dialogue. This latter method of contrapuntal reading allows us to begin to recover a much more complex story of Orientalist ethnopornography, its homoerotic dimensions, and its homophobic discontents, a story in which the destabilizations that confront the European male traveler forced to deal with the social and psychological constructions that other cultures bring to sexual attraction are echoed in the instabilities and mutually coexisting contradictions that are part and parcel of the sexual scripts of the Ottoman world itself. In such accounts of sodomitical crossings, the Middle East is not "just" a blank screen onto which European men have historically projected their repressed fears and transgressive yearnings, especially those welling up around the taboo of homosexual desire. That same screen is also alive with the words and worlds of responsive, competing, flickering images that, once we know how to look, and how to read, we can begin to perceive, palimpsest-like, inhabiting our own discursive self-reflections.

Notes

1   Nico Hines, "YouTube Banned in Turkey after Video Insults," *Times (London) Online*, March 7, 2007. The offending video, according to Claire Berlinski, "Turkey's YouTube Ban Is Cause for Concern," *Radio Free Europe Online*, July 08, 2009, (https://www.rferl.org/a/Turkeys_YouTube_Ban_Is_Cause_For_Concern/1772003 .html) showed Atatürk weeping lavender-colored tears to the music of the Village

People. In Turkey it is illegal to defame Atatürk or the republic. Most US coverage of the banning of YouTube in Turkey omitted the fact that the originating cause lay in homosexual and homophobic slurs, only mentioning that the Greek videos were perceived by Turk authorities as an "insult" to the republic's founder. Ironically, omitting the nature of the "insult" continues to repress the discussion of homosexuality enacted by the Turkish judiciary.

2   Nabil Matar, *Turks, Moors, and Englishmen in the Age of Discovery* (Chicago: University of Chicago Press, 1999).

3   On the history of Western tendency to view the East as the source of homoerotic vice, see Irvin Cemil Schick, *The Erotic Margin: Sexuality and Spatiality in Alterist Discourse* (London: Verso, 1999). The inverse phenomenon, whereby homoerotic perversions are said to flow from the West to the East, was graphically illustrated in the Egyptian media reports surrounding the 2001 police raid in Cairo on the Queen Boat, a gay nightclub, in which over fifty men were arrested and accused of being homosexual perverts and Satanists. The headline in *Al-Ahram al-Arabi* on August 25, 2001, declared "Be a pervert, and Uncle Sam will approve," and *Al-Masa'* ran a story on May 15, 2001, titled "Confessions of the 'Satinists' in 10 Hours: We Imported the Perverse Ideas from a European Group." See Scott Long's analysis of this controversy in "The Trials of Culture: Sex and Security in Egypt," *Middle East Report* 230 (spring 2004): 12–20; as well as Brian Whitaker, *Unspeakable Love: Gay and Lesbian Life in the Middle East* (London: Saki, 2006).

4   Walter K. Andrews and Mehmet Kalpaklı, *The Age of Beloveds: Love and the Beloved in Early-Modern Ottoman and European Culture and Society* (Durham, NC: Duke University Press, 2005), 19.

5   For groundbreaking studies of the Ottoman heritage of same-sex sex, love, and patronage, see Andrews and Kalpaklı, *Age of Beloveds*; Dror Ze'evi, *Producing Desire: Changing Sexual Discourse in the Ottoman Middle East, 1500–1900* (Berkeley: University of California Press, 2006); and Khaled El-Rouayheb, *Before Homosexuality in the Arab-Islamic World, 1500–1800* (Chicago, IL: University of Chicago Press, 2005). On parallel developments in the Persian-Iranian heritage, see Afsaneh Najmabadi, *Women with Moustaches and Men without Beards: Gender and Sexual Anxieties of Iranian Modernity* (Berkeley: University of California Press, 2005); and Janet Afary, *Sexual Politics in Modern Iran* (Cambridge: Cambridge University Press, 2009). On the Arab heritage of male same-sex relations, see Joseph Massad, *Desiring Arabs* (Chicago, IL: University of Chicago Press, 2007). The essays gathered together in Kathryn Babaryn and Afsaneh Najmabadi, eds., *Islamicate Sexualities: Translations across Temporal Geographies of Desire* (Cambridge, MA: Center for Middle Eastern Studies / Harvard University Press, 2008), take up the challenge of forging intersections between the study of the history of sexuality across these Middle Eastern domains and queer theory. Comparable work on medieval formations of Middle Eastern homoeroticism can be found in Sahar Amer, *Crossing Borders: Love between Women in Medieval French and Arabic Literatures* (Philadelphia: University of Pennsylvania Press, 2008); and J. W. Wright Jr. and

Everett K. Rowson, eds., *Homoeroticism in Classical Arabic Literature* (New York: Columbia University Press, 1997). Rowson has produced a series of essays combining a historian's understanding, deep knowledge of medieval Arabic traditions and literatures, and developing trends in queer theory.

6   For a sense of how the history of shifting political alliances within as well as between European and Ottoman states deconstructs facile constructions of an East/West binary and demonstrates the fluidity of contact across Christianity and Islamic cultures, see Joseph Allen Boone, *The Homoerotics of Orientalism* (New York: Columbia University Press, 2014), 26.

7   Edward Said, *Culture and Imperialism* (New York: Random/Vintage, 1993), 32; see also 49, 66, 259, 521.

8   Edward Said, *Orientalism* (New York: Vintage, 1978).

9   *The True Narrative of a Wonderful Accident, Which Occur'd upon the Execution of a Christian Slave at Aleppo in Turky* (London, 1676). Subsequent page numbers are included in parentheses in the text. My quotations from the seventh tale of the *Heft han* are adapted from a word-for-word translation I commissioned from N. Evra Günhan, from the Old Ottoman text in the Bogacizi University library collection. I occasionally enhance our translation with word choices used in the prose paraphrase and partial poetic translation provided in Andrews and Kalpakli, *Age of Beloveds*, 59–62. I am indebted to Andrews and Kalpakli for bringing this evocative text, which they use as a touchstone of their discussion in *Age of Beloveds*, to my attention.

10   At the time of the pamphlet's dissemination, Turkish imperial ambitions were at their zenith: in 1676 the Ottoman army had seized part of Poland, and seven years later, in 1683, laid siege to Vienna in its most audacious (and ultimately failed attempt) to see all Europe submit to Ottoman control. This palpable threat increased the degree of hysterical demonization that one finds in documents such as *The True Narrative*.

11   While Ottoman texts uniformly refer to all Europeans as "Franks," it appears this English writer is using the designation "French" literally.

12   Typically seamen from mercantile vessels taken prisoner by Turkish corsairs were sold into slavery or ransomed to the home country. Multiple accounts exist of Englishmen and other Europeans seized in the Mediterranean. Barbary piracy seems to have been particularly pronounced in the 1670s and 1680s, as evinced in C. R. Pennell, *Piracy and Diplomacy in Seventeenth-Century North Africa: The Journal of Thomas Baker, English Consul in Tripoli, 1677–1685* (Rutherford, NJ: Farleigh Dickinson University Press, 1989). One of the fears of being enslaved by Turkish corsairs was being converted not only to Islam but also to homosexuality, as noted by Robert C. Davis in *Christian Slaves, Muslim Masters: White Slavery in the Mediterranean, the Barbary Coast, and Italy, 1500–1800* (New York: Palgrave, 2003), 125–27.

13   Such effects are linked, as Silke Falkner notes, to the frequent use of rhetorical trope of *hypotyposis*—the deployment of especially vivid imagery and linguistic codes to help readers "see" the described scenario as if unfolding before their eyes—in travel narratives about the Middle East. Falkner, whose focus is on the

frequent references to sodomy in early modern German *turcica*, provocatively asks what it means when a nude male Christian body is textually displayed as the object of a specifically Muslim gaze (as is also the case regarding the martyred French slave in *Wonderful Accident*). See Silke Falkner, "'Having It Off' with Fish, Camels, and Lads: Sodomitic Pleasures in German-Language *Turcica*," *Journal of the History of Sexuality* 13, no. 4 (2007): 402, 405, 425, 427.

14 The "Seven Stories" was the fourth of a series of five mesnevi poems (making up a *hamse*, or pentad) composed by Nev'izade 'Atayi in emulation of the hamse masterpiece of his famous Persian predecessor, Nizami. Andrews and Kalpakli (*Age of Beloveds*, 59) note that most of the poem-narratives of "Seven Stories" use the pretense of inspiring the reader to moral behavior in order to relate bawdy, immoral goings-on; the seventh tale is an exception, in that it takes up the story of lovers who are not evildoers and are eventually rewarded for loving rightly.

15 Pera is the European sector of Istanbul in Galata, north of the Bosporus and the old city; here the sultans allowed Christians—mostly Greeks and Portuguese—to operate wine establishments, making Galata the de facto pleasure center of the city; Gosku was a famous excursion spot on the Bosporus where lovers often met clandestinely.

16 The particular sect, the Gulseni, a branch of the religious order Halvetiye, was founded by Ibrahim Gulseni, who was born in 1422, and was particularly popular among Ottoman elites, so joining this sect would, paradoxically, represent an elevation in class status for the boys despite their loss of portable income. Sufi conclaves are uniformly associated with male homosexual practices in the Ottoman past, since part of the ritual to reach transcendent ecstasy involved gazing upon (and touching) beauty, epitomized in male youths. Ze'evi analyzes the war in religious literature between the Sufi-based dervish societies, strongly patronized by the elite Janissary guards, and more conservative religious movements in *Producing Desire*, "Morality Wars: Orthodoxy, Sufism, and Beardless Youths," 48–77.

17 See Andrews and Kalpakli, *Age of Beloveds*, 77–79. See also chap. 54, "Wine Gatherings," in Mustafa Âli, *Tables of Delicacies Concerning the Rules of Social Gatherings*, annotated English trans. by Douglas S. Brookes (Cambridge, MA: Harvard University Department of Near Eastern Languages and Civilization, 2003), 111–13. This account gives a detailed description of the accoutrements expected of the properly refined wine party, from the presence of "much-desired rosy-cheeked" beauties, lovers, singers, and reciters to no less than "forty or fifty" appetizer trays, flowers in vases, and, "if roses are in season," sprinklings of rose petals all around.

18 Here I use Andrews and Kalpakli's (*Age of Beloveds*) rhymed translation for its poetic effect; the words are quite close to the literal translation.

19 This threat from repressive religious revivalists lies behind Mustafa Âli's warning, in *Counsel for Sultans* (1581), that it is the sultan's duty to shut up "the insolvent and slanderous preachers" whose repressive measures are seen as a direct strike against the privileges of the ruling elite. See *Counsel for Sultans*, trans. and ed. Andreas Tietze, 2 vols. (Vienna: Akademie der Wissenschaften, 1979), 1:55.

20 Ironically, what Europeans find all too visible in the Middle East is precisely what some Middle Eastern travelers to Europe in the same period find startlingly *absent*. Visiting Paris between 1826 and 1831, the Egyptian scholar Rifa'ah al-Tahtawi remarked on the Franks's "lack of [a] predilection for the love of male juveniles," which for these Europeans "would be one of the worst abominations [*fawahish*], so much that they have rarely mentioned it openly in their books but rather eschew it as much as possible." Quoted in Matar, *Turks, Moors, and Englishmen*, 32. At the same time, Europeans' preexisting conceptions about the prevalence of the eastern "vice" sometimes led to Middle Easterners in Europe finding themselves propositioned by the same Europeans who "eschew[ed]" such practices "as much as possible"; so Temesvarli Osman Aga reports in his memoirs, *Gavurlarin Esiri* ("Prisoner of the Infidels," 1724; rpt., Istanbul: Milliyet Yayangbri, 1971), that when he fell captive to the Austrians in 1688 (the year of the Ottoman siege of Vienna), he was approached one night by an Austrian boy for sex who tells him, "I know all Turks are pederasts."

21 Manwaring's account is included in E. Denison Rong, ed., *Sir Anthony Sherley and His Persian Adventure* (London: Routledge, 1933), 186–87. Aside from one use of the epithet "beastly" to describe male-male sexual practice in Turkey, Manwaring's account is relatively objective and nonsensationalizing in tone.

22 George Sandys, *Travels, Containing an History of the Original and Present State of the Turkish Empire*, 7th ed. (1615; London, 1673), 32; Pedro Peixeira, *The Travels of Pedro Teixeira*, trans. and annot. William F. Sinclair (London: Hakluyt Society, Series 2, no. 9, 1902), 62.

23 Peçevi, *Tarih-i Peçevi*, 2 vols. (Istanbul, 1864–67), 1:363. Quoted in Bernard Lewis, *Istanbul and the Civilization of the Ottoman Empire* (Norman: University of Oklahoma Press, 1963), 132–33. For a history of the coffeehouse, see Ralph S. Hattox, *Coffee and Coffeehouses: The Origins of a Social Beverage in the Medieval Near East* (Seattle: University of Washington Press, 1985), 78–109. Hattox mentions the reputation of coffeehouses as sites of homosexual debauchery on page 109.

24 The Ottoman manuscript (Ms. Berlin) is quoted in Hattox, *Coffee and Coffeehouses*, 62. See Âli, *Tables of Delicacies*, chap. 73, "Wine Taverns," 131–32. ("Meva'idu'n-Nefa'is fi Kava'idi'l-Mecalis," circa 1587). I have altered a few words of Brookes's translation to accord with that provided in Andrews and Kalpakli, *Age of Beloveds*, 140–42.

25 Quoted in Andrews and Kalpakli, *Age of Beloveds*, 283.

26 From a collection of documents dealing with guild relationships in the seventeenth century, later published by Mahmūd 'Ali 'Ailah, *Watha'iq al-tawa'if al-hirafiyya fi'l-quds fi'l-qam al-sabi ashar* (Nablus, 1992), 2:146–47. Quoted in Ammon Cohen, *The Guilds of Ottoman Jerusalem* (Leiden, Netherlands: Brill, 2001), 55. Yaron Ben-Naeh gives an illuminating example of a similar incident in Ottoman Damascus of the eighteenth century, where a coffeehouse known as a site of homosexual trysts was ordered to shut its doors, not for being a hangout for homoerotic exchange but because people of the neighborhood complained that it had turned into a center

for crime. See Ben-Naeh, "Moshko the Jew and His Gay Friends: Same-Sex Sexual Relations in Ottoman Jewish Society," *Journal of Early Modern History* 9 (2005): 84.

27 William Lithgow, *The Totall Discourse, of the Rare Adventures, and Painful Peregrinations of Nineteen Long Years* (1632; London, 1640), 14. All further references to this work are cited in the text.

28 Âli, *Table of Delicacies*, chap. 8, "Beardless Boys," 29–30.

29 Gazali was the pen name of Mehmed of Bursa, also known as Deli Birader ("Crazy Brother"). I use the translation Selim S. Kuru provides in his well-annotated and informative PhD thesis, "A Sixteenth Century Scholar Deli Birader and His *Dāfiü 'lgumūm ve rāfi'ü'l-humūm*" (Cambridge, MA: Harvard Department of Near Eastern Languages and Civilizations, 2000).

30 Michel Baudier, *Histoire generalle du Serrail, et de la cour du Grand Seigneur*, trans. E. G. S. A. [Edward Grimeston, Sargent at Arms] (1626; London, 1636), 1. All further references to this work are cited in the text.

31 Falkner, "Having It Off," 25.

32 Aaron Hill, *A Full Account of the Present State of the Ottoman Empire in All Its Branches* (1709), 81; emphasis mine. All further references to this work are cited in the text.

33 Evliya Çelebi, *Seyahatname* ("Book of Travels"), books 5–8, trans. and ed. Robert Dankoff and Robert Elsie as *Evliya Çelebi in Albania and Adjacent Regions* (Leiden, Netherlands: Brill, 2006), 182–83, 213.

34 James Silk Buckingham, *Travels in Mesopotamia* (London: Colburn, 1827), and *Travels in Assyria, Media, and Persia* (London: Colburn, 1829). All further references to these works are cited in the text.

35 See Lawrence, "Under White Men's Eyes," chapter 4 in this volume.

36 This is the reading that Stephen O. Murray gives the passage. Although I disagree with Murray's ultimate assessment, I am grateful to his essay "Some Nineteenth-Century Reports of Islamic Homosexualities," in *Islamic Homosexualities: Culture, History, Literature*, ed. Will Roscoe and Steven O. Murray (New York: New York University Press, 1999), 204–8, for bringing Buckingham's narrative to my attention.

37 Buckingham's political radicalization as the result of his travels began with his sojourn in India in the mid-1820s. His denunciation of the practices of the East India Company led to his expulsion by the colonial authorities, whereupon he undertook the Middle Eastern travels that resulted in these volumes. Thanks to Mary Ellis Gibson for this insight.

38 Steve Clark, "Introduction," *Travel Writing and Empire: Postcolonial Theory in Transit*, ed. Steve Clark (London: Zed Books, 1999), 4–5, 7.

39 Henry Blount, *A Voyage into the Levant* (1636; London: Theatrum Orbis Terrarum, 1977), 61. All further references to these works are cited in the text.

40 In his chapter on Blount in *The Rise of Oriental Travel: English Visitors to the Ottoman Empire, 1580–1720* (New York: Palgrave, 2004), Gerald M. MacLean also notes

the occasions on which Blount uses homosexuality to turn a question of moral "vice" into one of cultural difference (150); he also speculates on Blount's possible homosexuality (151)—he is a bachelor at the time of his travels—but Blount's exchange with Murat Basha's favorite boy seems based on genuine curiosity and politeness, untouched by covert sexual desires.

41 Horatio Southgate, *Narrative of a Tour through Armenia, Kurdistan, Persia, and Mesopotamia: With Observations upon the Condition of Muhammadanism and Christianity in Those Countries*, 2 vols. (London, Tilt and Bogue, 1840), 2:200.

42 Çelebi, *Seyahatname*, in Dankoff and Elsie, *Evliya Çelibi in Albania*, 85.

Sexualizing the Other

From Ethnopornography to Interracial
Pornography in European Travel Writing about
West African Women

Wherever they traded, settled, and colonized during the European expansion, European men had sex with indigenous women, and indigenous
women's sexuality and interracial sex became ongoing themes in contemporary travel accounts. On the Gold Coast during the era of the slave
trade, interracial sexual relations were at least as common as they were in
other parts of the world, and European travel accounts supplied direct and
practical information on how to get a West African woman and what to pay
for her. Pieter de Marees's Dutch account from 1602, for example, included
a Fante phrasebook in the back that advised the newly arrived European
on how to demand a woman. The literal English translation reads, "I won't
listen. You talk a lot. Shut your mouth. Give me a woman who is very sweet.
Woman, your vagina inside eat."[1] In 1662, the German Wilhelm Johan Mül-
ler described how West African women would offer themselves to European men for a small present or for as little as a bottle of brandy, and stay
with the men as long as they lived on the coast.[2] Though the descriptions

vary in length and content, most European travel accounts about West Africa from the seventeenth, eighteenth, and nineteenth centuries describe West African women's sexual behavior and their sexual relations with African and/or European men.

Many such descriptions of sexual behaviors and acts of West African women in European travel accounts could certainly be described as a kind of ethnopornography, in a broad sense of the word, as sexualized depictions of ethnically "other" women meant to arouse sexual excitement in their readers. As noted by Irvin C. Schick, ethnographic descriptions have often been a "good source of erotica," and, in fact, ethnography and pornography share many common themes and representational practices.[3] In this chapter I will discuss and compare a few European ethnopornographic depictions of West African women in a Dutch, an English, and a French travel account from the eighteenth and nineteenth centuries in an attempt to complicate the concept of ethnopornography and to relate it to the modern genre of American pornography known as "interracial" pornography.

Linda Williams has argued that the genre of interracial pornography is powerful because it plays on specific historical structures of and expectations about race: "all depictions of interracial lust develop out of the relations of inequality that have prevailed between the races. They grow out of a history that has covertly permitted the white man's sexual access to black women and violently forbidden the black man's access to white women."[4]

What makes interracial pornography work, according to Williams, is that the genre plays on modern American hierarchies of race, and it is particularly exciting when it transgresses the line between black and white "that has been most firmly erected by America's history of chattel slavery."[5] In other words, the genre depends on a collective memory of a racial hierarchy in which black women are inherently subordinate to white men and white men have full power over black women's bodies.

Yet, as Schick and others have noted, white men's fantasies about having easy sexual access to and control over black women's bodies are not necessarily limited to American plantation slavery or its aftermath.[6] European expectations of white superiority have a long and complicated history in addition to the lived practice on North American plantations. In fact, as I argue in this chapter, eighteenth-century European travel accounts have a lot in common with modern interracial pornography—particularly in the ways the pornographic descriptions are organized around white men's easy and uninhibited access to black women's bodies. In addition to being early modern forerunners to interracial pornography, though, these depictions are also, I argue in the following, "classic" eighteenth-century European pornography, which was exported to the liberating realms of the *porno-tropics*.[7]

However, the interracial hierarchy that Linda William refers to in her definition of interracial pornography implies more than white men's easy access to black women's bodies: it also cites a powerful history of racial degradation. Unlike the eighteenth-century travel accounts that I discuss in this chapter, interracial pornography comes after a century of colonization, scientific racism, and racial segregation in the Western world, but particularly and specifically so in the United States. This era of "full-fledged" scientific racism, I suggest, changed the nature and style of ethnopornography in a direction that helps explain why the transgression of lines between black and white is so particularly powerful in modern American pornography. In the last section of the chapter, I look at one example of an ethnopornographic description of West African women that is informed by a more "modern" scientific/biological concept of race to discuss how this might be read as a more direct historic precursor to American interracial pornography.

Pornography is a contested concept in our contemporary world. The cultural wars over whether pornography is harmful and should be illegal have caused academics and activists to choose sides for or against explicit sexual images and movies, with perhaps the most extreme standpoint being represented by the arguments of Andrea Dworkin and Catharine MacKinnon that pornography not only can lead to but *is* sexual abuse.[8] The following chapter is not a contribution to this ongoing debate about the value and/or dangers of pornography. Nor am I, in this chapter, making an effort to present anything close to an exhaustive history of ethnopornography in travel accounts from West Africa. More modestly, I attempt to raise questions about the genre of ethnopornography. My hope is that a closer look at how European travel accounts sexualized West African women can historicize the concept of ethnopornography, open a discussion of ethnopornography's relationship with the modern genre of interracial pornography, and help promote what Linda Williams has called a more substantive critique of pornography.[9]

Leaving aside broader claims about implicit power relations in contemporary pornography, ethnopornographic depictions in European travel accounts can therefore not be separated from their colonial contexts of travel writing. Both the earlier eighteenth-century pornographic depictions of West African women and the later nineteenth-century example of ethnopornography discussed here were, in different ways, structured by European colonial expectations of cultural supremacy. Though the slave trade in

West Africa was not specifically colonial in purpose, the travel accounts about West Africa represented a much larger Atlantic system of colonization and plantation slavery in which white men's encounters with black women were structured by both gender and race. As Felicity Nussbaum has argued, any "consumption of the Other woman" was fundamentally embedded in a colonial power relationship.[10]

Exotic Witches

Travel writing was a popular genre in the early modern era. Accounts from all over the world were printed, reprinted, and translated at a fast pace, and—like early modern pamphlets about witches or murderers on trial—

owed much of their popularity to their shock and excitement value. Yet travel accounts were also crucially important for European trading and colonial expansion. Investors, captains, and merchants needed precise and trustworthy information to follow the development of the trade and plan future expeditions, and trading companies served their interests by supporting both the writing and printing of travel accounts, which also helps explain the genre's explosive growth in the early modern era.[11] European travel accounts therefore served two very different, but not mutually exclusive, interests, and trade facts and exotic tales were often placed side by side in the texts. These different interests invested in travel accounts from the early modern era makes them some of the most important historical documents we have on the history of West Africa in the precolonial period, but in this chapter I am not going to read them as sources of a history of West African women. In this chapter they are solely sources of European male perceptions of West African women.

Some subjects were more likely than others to play the part of exotic and exciting sales elements in travel accounts, though, and at least some descriptions of West African women's sexuality and interracial intimacy appear to have functioned as such. As in early modern European travel accounts from other parts of the world, descriptions of indigenous African women's sexuality appeared in the texts, along with descriptions of witches, cannibals, and monstrous animals and peoples. In fact, in earlier accounts from the seventeenth and eighteenth centuries, West African women were often compared to or described as contemporary European witches. In an account from 1603 describing West African women dancing at the full moon, the German Andreas Josua Ulsheimer wrote, "These women are very lascivious and very lustful for men of foreign nations. Each year they hold two dances—one when they sow, the other when they reap. They do this for four weeks and always begin when it is full moon. At night they dance most."[12]

In general, in the early accounts West African women were depicted as simultaneously inviting and dangerous, as when the German Samuel Brun, who traveled along the coast of West Africa from 1611 to 1620, described how the European group he was traveling with had once lost six men who had slept with African women "on account of the black wenches; for the men's sperm or genitals decayed, till blood and finally death itself followed."[13]

These simultaneously dangerous and inviting witchlike women were physically different from European women. In some accounts, West African women could give birth without pain and had breasts so long they could throw them over their shoulder to feed their babies on their backs.[14] They were part of a largely unfamiliar and dangerous foreign world, in which all the lands beyond Europe's borders were described as otherworldly places. As Anne McClintock has powerfully shown, this fundamentally "other" world represented a "porno-tropics for European imagination"—a figurative space onto which Europeans could project fantasies and desires.[15] Since this space had not yet been conquered in the early modern era, it was still very openly a dangerous space, and not one where white men had easy access to black women's bodies through an intrinsic colonial order or racial hierarchy. In these early accounts of West African women's sexuality, a larger European colonial ambition was entangled with ambivalence and fear. Not a fear of losing control of what had been conquered—that would come later—but a fear of being engulfed, lost, and swallowed, accompanied by an acute paranoia and a profound sense of male anxiety and boundary loss.

Whether these descriptions of otherworldly physically different women functioned as pornography in Europe depends on their reception. Today's definitions of pornography, though they vary on other aspects of the concept, agree that an important element that makes a text or an image pornographic is that a description of sexual behavior is intended to cause sexual excitement in the reader or viewer.[16] To decide whether these texts were pornographic, we would therefore need to know about their reception in Europe, which is not a topic for this present chapter. What is more important for the present purpose is the void that was left in this porno-tropic space of travel writing when the witches disappeared.

As the witches and the monsters all but disappeared from the travel accounts in the later seventeenth century, European travel accounts from

West Africa began describing West African women as physically more similar to European women. In fact, in some accounts African women are described as so similar to European women that European men could choose to ignore their skin color in the dark. In Jean Barbot's French-English account from 1679, the women he met in Accra were, for instance, ingeniously dressed, good-humored, and skillful in the art of seducing European men: "I saw several of them richly adorned . . . in such manner as might prove sufficiently tempting to many lewd Europeans; who not regarding complexions, say *All cats are grey in the dark*."[17] Other accounts correct earlier descriptions of monstrous African women, as did that of the Danish Johannes Rask, writing early in the eighteenth century: "Nowhere on the Gold Coast have I seen the exceedingly sagging breasts that Dapper described. In general they have well-shaped decently hanging breasts."[18]

However, the comparatively high level of similarity between African and European women in late seventeenth- and eighteenth-century accounts should not mislead us to think their writers found no difference. In these accounts the difference is cultural rather than physical; West African women were no longer witches or monstrous, and their "otherness" came to be defined more specifically as sexual availability. European male travel writers found that, in comparison with European women, the primary difference was that West African women were extremely sexually available, interested in and willing to have sex with European men. Several travel writers even suggested that African women preferred European to African men and regarded it as an honor to have Euro-African children.[19]

As the witches disappeared, West African women seem to have stopped being dangerous; their sexual availability is not ambivalent or destructive, as in the earlier accounts. Instead, I want to suggest, the porno-tropic space of the travel accounts was now a space that was perfectly fitted for the export of pornography, as if the disappearance of seventeenth-century monstrous bodies and witches had left a textual void that some travel writers opted to fill with pornography (another genre of exotic writing). In the following I will focus on two specific examples of such an "export" of eighteenth-century European pornography to the realm of travel writing, and suggest that to understand how these specific sexualizations of West African women worked in their texts, we need to relate them to contemporary European pornography as well as place them in the context of other examples of ethnopornography in this anthology.

The two examples that I will discuss here, the Dutch William Bosman and the English William Smith, are both remarkably similar to contemporary eighteenth-century European pornography. In both cases the implicit reception by European male readers is unmistakable, which suggests that the explicit intention of arousing sexual excitement is central in making a text pornographic. The first text was written as personal letters directly to an uncle in Amsterdam; the other was presented as a conversation between two European men on a European ship leaving Africa. As I will discuss, both authors make a number of hints and suggestions to the readers that suggest that the material is meant to be titillating. Equally important, the subject matter discussed in the two travel accounts are classic themes in eighteenth-century European pornography; in both cases the author delves at length into the subject of prostitution and the habits and practices of prostitutes and courtesans, which was the defining theme of pornography in the eighteenth century. As the Greek word suggests, "porno-graphy" had developed specifically as the genre of writing about prostitutes.[20]

The first example of European pornography being exported to the realms of travel writing is William Bosman's account of an institution of "public whores" in West Africa in his 1704 account *A New and Accurate Description of the Coast of Guinea*.[21] Bosman's account was one of the most widely read and cited northern European travel accounts about West Africa in the centuries that followed.[22] His description of prostitution on the Gold Coast is set in a fantasyland in which European men had very easy access to African women's bodies. In his universe, both class and age are suspended in the encounter between European men and West African women; all West African women are sexually available to European men.

Bosman describes prostitution in general but also, more specifically, relates a longer description of an institution of "public whores" that I think is of particular interest for this present discussion. Bosman was one of three travel writers who mentioned this institution of public prostitutes, the other two being the Dutch Olfert Dapper (1668) and the French Jean Godot (1704), and, as historians Adam Jones and Emmanuel Akyeampong have both remarked, there are some differences among the three accounts.[23] The three travel writers agreed that it was the practice for a West African community to buy an enslaved woman and make her a public prostitute through an initiation ceremony. They also agreed that she was paid very little or nothing for sexual relations with male members of the community. However, the accounts did not agree whether only bachelors or also married men were allowed to visit the public prostitutes, and they differed on how the initiation rite took place. Bosman was the only one of the three travel writers who included the information that during the initiation rite the enslaved woman had to simulate sexual intercourse with a young boy in public in the marketplace: "The Novice is smeared all over with Earth, and several Offerings offered for her success in her future Occupation. This over, a little Boy, yet immature for Love Affairs, makes a feint or representation of lying with her before all the People; by which 'tis hinted to her that from this time forwards, she is obliged to receive all Persons indistinguishable who offer themselves to her, not excepting little Boys."[24]

Now, why did Bosman include a young boy imitating having sexual intercourse with the initiated public prostitute? Emmanuel Akyeampong has explained Bosman's deviation from the other two accounts about public prostitutes in West Africa with the fact that social institutions never replicate themselves exactly, and that therefore "public prostitution" would also never be quite the same in two different places.[25] Adam Jones has not specifically addressed the differences between Bosman's account and the others, but he has mentioned elsewhere that Bosman did at times employ "*poetische Freiheit*" (poetic license) to entertain his readers.[26] However, a broader look at Bosman's account suggests not only that he probably had personal reasons for including a young boy as an active sexual agent in the initiation rite but also that his descriptions of West African women's sexual behavior were shaped by a male sexual fantasy in which all women are willing and easily available, and sexual intercourse has few social consequences for men or women.

Bosman was sixteen when he left Holland for West Africa. His account consists of a series of letters to his uncle back in Amsterdam, and in several places the text functioned as pornography in the male-to-male communication between Bosman and his uncle. The connection between the two men is particularly clear when Bosman lapses into personal and direct communication with his uncle, as when he describes how prostitutes in Fida (Ouidah) receive many customers during one day in their small huts and therefore must be very tired in the evening, and adds, "If Livia was alive, I should ask her whether this is not sufficient to satisfie her."[27] Bosman does not mention who Livia was, but she was probably a European woman that his uncle also knew. For our present purpose the content of the question Bosman would have asked Livia is of greater importance. In his porno-tropic fantasy Bosman assumed that slave prostitutes in small huts on the side of the road were seeking and gaining pleasure from customers, who pay them very little and whom they have not chosen to have sex with. And with this knowing reference to a shared pool of sexual knowledge, Bosman drew his uncle into his fantasy.

On the Gold Coast, Bosman recounted, both men and women marry late, and single women outnumber single men. Men marry as soon as they can afford the bride price, but women wait as long as possible, because they can live more "free and pleasant" lives when unmarried, "being now at perfect liberty to admit the embraces of any or several men if they please." Women are not disregarded or "rudely accounted whores" if they have sex before marriage, and even after they are married they seldom content themselves with only one man.[28] In general, according to Bosman, women on the Gold Coast had an extraordinary sexual appetite, which was partly due to their "hotter" nature, and partly to the institution of polygamy, which forced many women to share a man. Even with strict punishment, it was almost impossible to keep the women from adultery: "They are continually contriving how to gain a Lover, and would rather suffer Death than forbear the delicious Sin." The men, however, were afraid of being punished for adulterous relations, and would therefore try to refuse the women, but the women would throw themselves at the men and tear off their clothes or seduce them in secret during the night.[29]

In Bosman's account, the distinction between prostitutes and other African women is quickly erased. In some places, Bosman wrote, they have no public whores, but this is no problem for the young men, "for there is no want of Unmarried Women, and they without any distinction, than that of being too young, are a'most all Whores, tho' they indeed don't bear that name."[30] When a European man wanted to have sex with a West African woman, age was the only limiting factor; class or marriage status was no hindrance. Bosman related a boastful story of visiting the king of Fida (Ouidah), who had given his daughter in marriage to an English trader. Jokingly Bosman told the king that he should have offered him the princess first, to which the king supposedly replied that "though his Daughter was married, she was yet at my service, if I desired her, since one word was sufficient to call her home." In a direct remark to his uncle, Bosman thereafter replies, "What think you, Sir, are not this King's Daughters very cheap?"[31]

Inside the textual male-to-male communication between Bosman and his uncle it is not surprising to find that a young man is specifically chosen to imitate a sexual act with a prostituted woman in a public marketplace. Just as prostitutes are satisfied by their customers and young women want to stay unmarried to have sex with whomever approaches them, I suggest that Bosman's little boy in the initiation rite was a figment of a sixteen-year-old boy's imagination, coherent with the pornographic theme and undertone of his text.

A second example of European pornography exported to the tropics is found in William Smith's English account *A New Voyage to Guinea* from 1744.[32] After mentioning African women only a few times in the first several hundred pages, Smith added an appendix to his account in which he compared courting and sexual behaviors in England and on the Gold Coast. Possibly because he was uncertain whether the subject would offend readers in Europe, he presented his opinions as an interview with a Mr. Charles Wheeler, with whom he claimed to have conversed on board a ship returning to Europe.[33] Mr. Wheeler had been a factor for the Royal African Company on the Gold Coast for ten years, and William Smith had decided to write his story, since it could not be "displeasing to the reader." The conversations with Mr. Wheeler depict the Gold Coast as a male sexual fantasy world like Bosman's, where African women are readily available, sexual relations have few social consequences, and where, in going beyond Bosman's version, women and men benefit equally from sexual liberation. As in much modern interracial pornography, women's bodies are easily available for men's sexual pleasure.

Smith's Mr. Wheeler told the story of how he visited an unnamed king on the Gold Coast who in addition to his wives had many concubines. According to Mr. Wheeler, it was customary for kings and other "grandees" to offer a visiting European one of his concubines to sleep with for the duration of his visit. The first time this happened to Mr. Wheeler, he politely asked for the reasoning behind such a practice, and the king answered that it was to keep him chaste and regular. When Mr. Wheeler then suggested that fornication was not the way to make a man chaste, the king asked, "Why . . . is it a sin to lie with a woman?" Mr. Wheeler confirmed that if you were not married to the woman, it was considered a sin, which compelled the king to ask if Mr. Wheeler had never slept with a woman. Mr. Wheeler declined to answer that question, and the king then insisted, "Take her, take her, he said, you seem to know what use to make of her." The king presented with a "young lady in her prime," and Mr. Wheeler and the king's concubine then retired to a private room. Mr. Wheeler described how beautiful the concubine was, how easily and naturally they had sex, and, he went on to say, "in that situation I soon forgot the complexion of my bedfellow. . . . Greater pleasure I never found, and during my stay, if paradise is to be found in the enjoyment of a woman, I was then in the possession of it."[34] In addition to being beautiful, the king's concubine was also sexually liberated, well mannered, and intelligent (she had been educated by a French doctor who had stayed with her while visiting the king).

The concubine in Mr. Wheeler's story is remarkably similar to a stereotype in contemporary eighteenth-century European pornography that Kathryn Norberg has called the "libertine whore."[35] In her study of French pornography, Norberg found "whore" biographies or confessions to be increasingly common in the genre during the eighteenth century. The libertine prostitute was usually presented as the narrator of her own story—which is different from Mr. Wheeler's story, in which he speaks on the concubine's behalf—but otherwise she fit the stereotype perfectly: she was well-read and sophisticated, and, like Norberg's prostitutes, her sexual appetite was "moderated by a healthy dose of philosophy."[36] She was woman of "a good natural judgement," and had she been white, Mr. Wheeler would have asked the king for permission to marry her.

As Lynn Hunt has argued, until the mid- or late eighteenth century, European pornography was almost always an adjunct to something else. Most often early modern pornography employed explicit descriptions of sex or sexual organs in order to criticize religious and political authorities, the shock of references to sexual organs or acts serving as provocation, satire, and cultural criticism.[37] Similarly, the story of Mr. Wheeler and the king's concubine is a direct criticism of English sexual, marriage, and courting practices, which connects Smith's ethnographic description of West African women directly to the genre of contemporary eighteenth-century pornography in Europe. After they had sex, Mr. Wheeler and the concubine had several conversations in which they compared English and Gold Coast practices, and focusing in particular on the faults of the former.

Mr. Wheeler's first concern was to argue for the practice of polygamy. Not only was polygamy in accordance with the bible, where the patriarchs of the Old Testament all had many wives, there were also practical reasons to import the practice to Europe. Polygamy made women strive harder to please their husbands but never forced men to have more wives than they wanted. Most men had only two to four wives, which was enough to make it unnecessary to seek "variety" outside the home.[38] Also, Wheeler continued in more general terms, men in Africa were much less sexually repressed than European men. The long, painful waiting and courting period that European men had to go through before they could marry and have sex with a woman did not exist in Africa, and the king's concubine agreed with Mr. Wheeler's criticism of English courtship, in which the young men based their decisions about whom to marry on the woman's wealth and family and not on "nature." She suggested that the European courtship routine would cause young men to "court away" their love for a woman before they got married.[39]

On the Gold Coast, Mr. Wheeler recounted, young men were free to gain sexual experience before they settled in a marriage. An unmarried man could either visit a prostitute or buy a slave woman in the market, "co-habit with her as long as he pleases, and then sell her again," and, unlike in Europe, prostitutes on the Gold Coast were modest and chaste. They slept with only one man at a time, and only in private, unlike European whores, who will "admit as many to be present at the act as please" and lie with men in the fields and in the streets.[40] A young man on the Gold Coast could also simply approach any one of the young women around him, since "the women of this country make no scruple, if they have the opportunity to meet the embraces of a man." Young women on the Gold Coast were not brought up to believe that sex was a sin, as European women were, and therefore they never turned down a suitor, which meant that rape was un-heard of. Imagine, Mr. Wheeler continued, if only young men in Europe could purchase a concubine and live with her as long as he wanted and then sell her again. This would be much better than men's common prac-tice to "cuckold their neighbours, debauch their daughters, and get with child with their own maid-servants."[41]

In Bosman's and Smith's accounts, West African women were not just available to European men but were hypersexual and willing. Unlike in the earlier accounts, these West African women were physically similar to European women, and it was not the ethnic "otherness" of the women that gave the texts their pornographic potential but the extreme availability and willingness of West African women. Bosman and Smith's porno-tropics were worlds in which marriage was not a prerequisite to getting access to women's bodies. In the encounter between European men and African women, European male expectations of cultural supremacy connected powerfully to colonialism, and there was no question ideologically: Afri-can women were available to European men not always because they were culturally inferior but because they were both Africans and women. Surely the "exotic," porno-tropic scenery of the descriptions shaped the extreme willingness of the depicted West African women, but in these two accounts West African women's bodies are (in hindsight) surprisingly similar to Eu-ropean women's bodies: had the concubine only been white, Mr. Wheeler would have begged her from the king. He probably would have gotten her too, in a porno-tropic utopia where even a sixteen-year-old sailor such as Bosman could get to marry a king's daughter "cheap."

White male fantasies—such as Bosman's and Smith's—of easy access to black women's bodies did not begin in the modern era. From the very beginning of early modern European expansion, European colonialism carried and employed masculine connotations and symbols: a virgin America was conquered; a mysterious Orient was unveiled; and a dark Africa was penetrated.[42] In travel accounts the outcome of the European Expansion was discursively given for centuries as upright and dressed men encountered naked and virgin lands and peoples. European colonialism always came with expectations of sexually available indigenous women. White male fantasies did not stop with Bosman and Smith, either. In the next historical phase, ethnopornographic depictions of West African women's sexual behavior would be shaped by centuries of modern scientific-biological racism that would take the sexualized descriptions of "other" women to a whole new level before the genre of modern American interracial pornography appeared on the scene.

Degrading Black Women's Bodies

As Sander Gilman has shown in his work on sexual and racial stereotypes, the sexualization of prostitutes, Africans, and children achieved its modern meaning in the specific historical context of nineteenth-century Europe.[43] As Lynn Hunt has argued, this was not only the time when the genre of European pornography lost its political connotations and changed to a commercial "hard-core" business, but also the time when racial differences were studied intensely by scientists, and modern racism related racial difference to pathology. In Europe this process of defining race in its modern scientific form was in important ways linked to specific studies of African women's bodies, defining the sexualized African women as deviant and degraded, at the very bottom of any social hierarchy.[44]

In this same historical period some descriptions of easily available West African women display a racial degradation that, I suggest, speaks more directly to the modern genre of interracial pornography. One example of this modern ethnopornography is a watercolor by the French prince of Joinville, François d'Orléans, who visited the last Danish governor, Edward Carstensen, for lunch at Fort Christiansborg in present-day Accra

FIGURE 7.1 The prince of Joinville's watercolor of a lunch at Christiansborg in January 1843. Copy at the Danish Maritime Museum at Kronborg Castle in Helsingør, Denmark.

in January 1843 (see figure 7.1). The prince was on a Grand Tour of the Atlantic world—after Africa, he went on to Brazil. He represented the French state seeking to expand its colonial territories, and he depicted relations between white men and black women embedded in a clear colonial order informed by a modern concept of race.

The prince of Joinville painted himself centrally seated with his back to the sea, watching one of Governor Carstensen's men making a toast to the king of France. The watercolor represents a familiar colonial order with powerful white upper-class men in control of themselves and their subaltern subjects. Unbent and proper, Joinville has his eyes focused on the toasting man while a naked woman is bending over to serve him. Unlike the bearded lunch guest at the end of the table, Joinville apparently resisted a closer look at the serving women. At some point, however, he must have turned to inspect the women. Indeed, the women seem to have been the most memorable attraction of his visit to Christiansborg. In his diary of his travels in Africa he described their hair, skin, and smell in a way that echoes nineteenth-century ideas of biological race. Remarking how the women's skin was particularly soft—did he touch them anyway?—he leaped from the particular women who served him at Christiansborg to all Africans and "negroes" in general and described their peculiar and ir-reducible smell:

> I have never been able myself to endure the odour of negroes of either sex; but I have known people whom it quite intoxicated, and who were always trying to get reappointed to Senegal, so as to get back to it, in spite of having their health shattered by African fevers. All these young ladies' coquetry had gone to the dressing of their wooly hair, which was clipped, like garden shrubs, into the most fanciful shapes, and to the fineness of their skins, which were as soft and shiny as satin. This re-sulted from the daily baths they were in the habit of taking, rubbing themselves also with fine sand. But, unluckily the rubbing could not get rid of the negro scent.[45]

In Joinville's description African women are passive servants with whom European men could become intoxicated, and all Africans are grouped to-gether by sharing the same odor. Their difference from Europeans is not merely cultural, in the sense that it can be transformed or removed. Bath-ing and rubbing can transform their skin to satin, but nothing can erase a smell of difference, and when white men and black women stand close, as in the watercolor, the colonial order is shown as fixed and irreversible.

The women in the watercolor are stereotypes; they are almost identi-cal, and they should not be considered realistic renderings of Gold Coast women but rather an ethnopornographic French male fantasy. In fact, the image is ethnopornographic in the modern sense of the concept; it refers not only to an inherent racial hierarchy that would prevail between the races in the modern period but also to the degradation of African women's bodies: their hair is like garden shrubs, their smell is appalling. The eth-nopornographic intentions of the image are obvious. The man at the end of the table invites the viewer to participate in his undisguised gaze at one of the African women, and the women's exotic underwear that shows both hips and buttocks would have been considered provocative in both Gold Coast and European society. Unlike the completely naked French woman in Éd-ouard Manet's more famous lunch setting *Le Déjeuner sur l'herbe* twenty years later (1863), the West African women in Joinville's lunch image do not return the viewer's glance.[46]

The only similarity between Manet's and Joinville's images is the scene—dressed European men having lunch with naked women—the differences are more striking. Manet's naked woman participates in the lunch, and, like the men, she is in a relaxed posture on the grass. Her complete naked whiteness, though placing her in a vulnerable and subordinate position to the properly dressed men (one still with his hat on), connotes cleanliness and purity. In contrast, in Joinville's setting the exotic hair and underwear sexualizes the women in an ethnopornographic sense, referring to the exotic and "other" bodies of the African women. The barriers between black and white are in place on all fronts. The black are women, subservient, naked, and sexually available. The men are not just white but most are also dressed in shining white (and pure) clothes in contrast to the black women. When the serving woman bends over and is—inappropriately?—close to the French prince, as he turns his head away, the image plays specifically on the breaching of the modern (in)transgressable racial barriers that the image is structured around. According to Joinville, European men were especially attracted to the unique smell of African women, and he employed a perceived biological and bodily difference in West African women specifically to arouse sexual desire.

This nineteenth-century sexualizing depiction of West African women speaks to broader developments in the perception of black women in the modern era. As McClintock and Gilman have noted in different contexts, Africa had become the "quintessential zone of sexual aberration and anomaly," and Africans—women and men—were "icons for deviant sexuality."[47] The social categories falling into place by the nineteenth century, controlling and reconfirming imperial and colonial control, produced an image of the native, African, woman as "needing control," and in that process, the European man became her polar opposite.[48] "Miscegenation" became an integrated word in late nineteenth-century vocabulary on sexuality, and the racial dividing lines between white and black on which modern interracial pornography plays were solidified by a pathologizing of black women's bodies.

Conclusion

At least some early modern European travel accounts from West Africa have much in common with the modern genre of interracial pornography as Linda Williams has defined it: they play specifically on fantasies of white men's easy and uninhibited access to hypersexualized black women's bodies. Yet when we read travel accounts such as those of William Bosman and

William Smith as ethnopornography, we not only need to consider them as examples of a particular genre of ethnopornographic writing but also, simultaneously, as "typical" eighteenth-century European pornography. Their sexualized depictions of West African women are strikingly similar to other early modern European pornography in their focus on prostitutes and in the ways that the sexualized depictions of West African women are used as political and social criticism. In short, early modern ethnopornography has connections to both modern interracial pornography and to eighteenth-century European pornography.[49]

However, as I have suggested in this chapter, modern American interracial pornography plays on fantasies of much more than white men's simple access to black women's bodies. In my comparison of the eighteenth-century ethnopornographic descriptions with an example from the nineteenth-century Gold Coast—the watercolor by the prince of Joinville—I argue that modern ethnopornography refers to an "othering" of West African women of a whole different caliber: color was no longer something that could disappear in the dark (as in Jean Barbot's account from 1670); race had been essentialized and pathologized. If we then add a century and a half of racial degradation and segregation, and a specific lived historical practice of race relations in the United States, then it is not surprising that the racial hierarchies transgressed in modern American interracial pornography are loaded with powerful collective pools of meaning.

Notes

1   English translation in Albert van Dantzig and Adam Jones, eds. and trans., *Pieter de Marees: Description and Historical Account of the Gold Kingdom of Guinea (1602)* (Oxford: Oxford University Press, 1987), 258. The translators and editors of de Marees's account give the following explanation to the last part of the sentence: "the verb *di* (Fante: *dzi*) means 'to eat,' but also 'to have sexual intercourse.'"

2   English translation in Adam Jones, ed., *German Sources for West African History, 1599–1669* (Wiesbaden, Germany: Coronet Books, 1983), 157.

3   Irvin Cemil Schick, *The Erotic Margin: Sexuality and Spatiality in Alterist Discourse* (London: Verso, 1999), 79, 77.

4   Linda Williams, "Skin Flicks on the Racial Border: Pornography, Exploitation, and Interracial Lust," in *Porn Studies*, ed. Linda Williams (Durham, NC: Duke University Press, 2004), 302.

5   Williams, "Skin Flicks," 271.

6   Schick, *Erotic Margin*; Anne McClintock, *Imperial Leather: Race, Gender and Sexuality in the Colonial Contest* (New York: Routledge, 1995); Felicity Nussbaum, "The Other Woman: Polygamy, *Pamela*, and the Prerogative of Empire," in *Women, "Race," and Writing in the Early Modern Period*, ed. Margo Hendricks and Patricia Parker (London: Routledge, 1994).

7   On the concept of "porno-tropics," see McClintock, *Imperial Leather*, 21–24.

8   See Andrea Dworkin, *Pornography: Men Possessing Women* (1979; repr. with new intro., New York: Dutton, 1989); Catharine MacKinnon, *Only Words* (Cambridge, MA: Harvard University Press, 1993); or Linda Williams's response to MacKinnon in Williams, "Skin Flicks," 11.

9   Williams, "Skin Flicks," 12.

10   Nussbaum, "Other Woman," 140.

11   For an introduction to the field of historical travel writing, see, e.g., Peter C. Mancall's introduction to *Travel Narratives from the Age of Discovery: An Anthology* (Oxford: Oxford University Press, 2006); and Peter Hulme and Tim Youngs, *The Cambridge Companion to Travel Writing* (Cambridge: Cambridge University Press, 2002).

12   English translation of quote by Andreas Josua Ulsheimer in Jones, *German Sources*, 33. Ulsheimer's account also contains both cannibals and devils. In Hans Jacob Zur Eich's account, women are dancing around *"the evil one"*; see Jones, *German Sources*, 266.

13   Samuel Brun cited in Jones, *German Sources*, 72. See also Johann von Lübelfing (1599–1600) in Jones, *German Sources*, 16.

14   See Jennifer L. Morgan's work on monstrous African women in early modern travel accounts in *Laboring Women: Reproduction and Gender in New World Slavery* (Philadelphia: University of Pennsylvania Press, 2004), 12–49.

15   McClintock, *Imperial Leather*, 22–24.

16   See, for example, "pornography" in *Britannica Concise Encyclopædia* (Chicago: Encyclopædia Britannica Inc., 2008).

17   Jean Barbot originally wrote in French, but he later settled in England, where his travel account from West Africa was published in English. Quote from P. E. H. Hair, Adam Jones, and Robin Law, eds., *Barbot on Guinea: The Writings of Jean Barbot on West Africa, 1678–1712*, Vol. 2 (London: Hakluyt Society, 1992), 496.

18   Johannes Rask, *En kort og sandferdig rejsebeskrivelse til og fra Guinea* (Trondheim, Norway: Jens Christensen Winding, 1754), 130; translation mine. Rask stayed in West Africa from 1709 to 1712.

19   See, for example, Jean Barbot in Hair, Jones, and Law, *Barbot on Guinea*, 85.

20   Lynn Hunt has noted that the word "pornography" was first used specifically to describe writing about prostitution; see Lynn Hunt, "Pornography and the French Revolution," in Lynn Hunt, ed., *The Invention of Pornography: Obscenity and the Origins of Modernity, 1500–1800* (New York: Zone Books, 1993), 303. In Kathryn Norberg's chapter in the same volume, "The Libertine Whore: Prostitution in French Pornography from Margot to Juliette," she concurrently noted, "The prostitute plays

a particularly important role in the history of pornography; she was present at its birth"; Norberg, "Libertine Whore," 225. Walter Kendrick, *The Secret Museum: Pornography in Modern Culture* (Berkeley: University of California Press, 1987), also has a history of the word.

21 William Bosman, *A New and Accurate Description of the Coast of Guinea* (London: J. Knapton et al., 1967); original published in Dutch in 1704; first English edition published in 1705.

22 Within thirty years of the first Dutch edition, Bosman's account was printed three more times in Dutch, two times in English, once in French, and once in German. See John Ralph Willis's introduction in Bosman, *New and Accurate Description,* xix.

23 Emmanuel Akyeampong, "Sexuality and Prostitution among the Akan of the Gold Coast c. 1650–1950," *Past and Present* 156 (August 1997): 144–73. Adam Jones, "Prostitution, Polyandrie oder Vergewaltigung? Zur Mehrdeutigkeit europäischer Quellen über die Küste Westafrikas zwischen 1660 und 1860," in *Außereuropäische Frauengeschichte: Probleme der Forschung,* ed. Adam Jones (Pfaffenweiler, Germany: Centaurus Verlag, 1990), 128.

24 Bosman, *New and Accurate Description,* 212.

25 Akyeampong, "Sexuality and Prostitution," 155.

26 Jones, "Sexuality and Prostitution," 130, 141.

27 Bosman, *New and Accurate Description,* 214.

28 Both quotes from Bosman, *New and Accurate Description,* 211.

29 Bosman, *New and Accurate Description,* 206.

30 Bosman, *New and Accurate Description,* 206–4.

31 Bosman, *New and Accurate Description,* 346.

32 William Smith, *A New Voyage to Guinea* (London: Frank Cass & Co., 1967). Smith was in Africa twenty-five years after Bosman, and he might have adopted some of his pornographic tone from Bosman, since he also borrowed about half of his account of West Africa from him. See Adam Jones, "Semper Aliquid Veteris: Printed Sources for the History of the Ivory and Gold Coasts, 1500–1750," *Journal of African History* 27 (1986): 217.

33 The language and tone of the appendixed story is very similar to the rest of William Smith's account, which, combined with the fact that he speaks warmly of the practice of polygamy both in the main text and in the appendix, suggest that he was not just reporting Mr. Wheeler's views but probably also shared them. See also Jennifer Morgan's reading of this part of Smith's account in Morgan, *Laboring Women,* 45–46.

34 Smith, *New Voyage,* 251–54.

35 Norberg, "Libertine Whore," 225–52.

36 Norberg, "Libertine Whore," 235.

37 Hunt, "Pornography and the French Revolution," 10. See also 30 and 35.

38 Smith, *New Voyage,* 244.

39 Smith, *New Voyage,* 255–60.

40 Smith, *New Voyage*, 250.

41 Smith, *New Voyage*, 246–48.

42 McClintock, *Imperial Leather*, and Ann Laura Stoler, *Carnal Knowledge and Imperial Power: Race and the Intimate in Colonial Rule* (Berkeley: University of California Press, 2002), both contain good introductions to works on gender and the European expansion.

43 Sander L. Gilman, *Difference and Pathology: Stereotypes of Sexuality, Race, and Madness* (Ithaca, NY: Cornell University Press, 1985), 37; and Yvette Abrahams, "Images of Sara Bartman: Sexuality, Race, and Gender in Early Nineteenth-Century Britain," in *Nation, Empire, Colony: Historicizing Gender and Race*, ed. Ruth Roach Pierson and Nupur Chaudhuri (Bloomington: Indiana University Press, 1998).

44 Hunt, "Pornography and the French Revolution," 42; and Gilman, *Difference and Pathology*, 38.

45 Translated from the French by Lady Mary Loyd in *Memoirs (Vieux Souvenirs) of the Prince de Joinville* (New York: Macmillan, 1895), 276–77.

46 Several copies of Manet's painting are accessible on the net; see, for instance, Wikimedia, accessed April 7, 2019, http://upload.wikimedia.org/wikipedia/commons/f/fc/Édouard_Manet_-_Le_Déjeuner_sur_l'herbe.jpg.

47 McClintock, *Imperial Leather*, 22; and Gilman, *Difference and Pathology*, 83.

48 Gilman, *Difference and Pathology*, 107.

49 In a further study of ethnopornography in early modern travel accounts, it would be interesting to do a more systematic comparison of pornography in Europe (perhaps set both in metropoles and in the country?) and in the porno-tropics.

"Men Like Us"

The Invention of Ethnopornography

The subject of this chapter is the invention of the term "ethnopornography." The term, in the form "Ethno-pornography," was first used by Walter Roth as the title of the final chapter and of a plate of illustrations in his work *Ethnological Studies among the North-West-Central Queensland Aborigines* (1897).[1] Roth was a doctor in the Boulia area in colonial Australia when he collected the materials for the book, and was appointed as the Northern Protector of Aborigines in the state of Queensland in 1898, and as the Chief Protector in 1904.[2] Roth provided no explanation for his choice of the term in his work, and the topics covered in the final chapter of *Ethnological Studies* do not all fall within conventional understandings, then or now, of "pornography." The topics covered in this chapter include initiation rites of men and women, marriage, betrothal, love charms, venery, pregnancy and labor, abortion, babyhood, menstruation, micturition and defecation, and, finally, foul language. Roth begins the chapter with a consideration of social rank, and ends the chapter (and the book) with the sentence, "I have no evidence as to any practice of masturbation or sodomy anywhere among the North-West-Central Queensland aboriginals."[3]

However, Roth noted that he considered the final chapter to be "far from suitable for the general lay reader," and added an apologia for its inclusion in the book's preface: "The subject matter, however, being essential to a scientific account of these aboriginals, I have decided upon its publication, at the same time placing it at the very last, in the hope that those who do not wish to peruse its pages need not unwittingly find themselves doing so."[4] Moreover, an "Author's Note" opens the final chapter: "The following chapter is not suitable for perusal by the general lay reader."[5] Roth's sense of the chapter's "unsuitability" in this way was echoed by his contemporaries. The Queensland Government Printer, for example, sent a memo to the Under Secretary of the Home Department, Sir Horace Tozer, asking, "You are doubtless aware that the last chapter—ch: xiii and the last plate (pl. xxlv)[—]deal with indelicate subjects, is it likely they may be in violation of the Indecent Advertisements Acts, and, if they are, is the author's note, at the head of the chapter, a sufficient protection?"[6] Roth later commented on the Government Printer's caution to his fellow anthropologist Baldwin Spencer,

> The government originally intended omitting the last chapter with accompanying plate, and publishing it separately for special distribution to certain people only; mainly for the purpose of drawing public attention to the present condition of certain of the aborigines in view of the legislation proposed [the *Aboriginals Protection and Restriction of the Sale of Opium Act 1897*] to be enforced. The ordinary reading public had in a sense to be protected by being told that such and such a chapter was obscene, and that they could please themselves if they chose to read it. And after all, scientific and interesting as these particulars are to men like us, they are certainly not so to the general lay reader.[8]

Roth's choice of the term "ethno-pornography," in other words, was to act both as a warning to "the ordinary reading public" or "the general lay reader," and as a password to "men like us," who would understand the work in terms of scientific inquiry and practices.

In order to understand fully the invention of the term "ethnopornography," I think it is crucial to explore its provenance in Roth's conception of what scientific inquiry among the "savages" involves. Throughout this chapter, I use the term "savages" (and "natives") as used by Roth and others, in part because to shy away from using it here would be misleading as to how such terms were then considered entirely consonant with a scientific perspective in anthropological work. My explorations around ethnopornography concern what is the character of Roth's conception of (anthropological) science, and my argument is that his conception is one that incorporates a voyeuristic interest in "exotic" sexual practices and bodies. The scientific gaze in this context is a form of knowing that shadows the shattering sexual violence of colonialism. And the report of what that gaze saw, and the circulation of its representation among "men like us," and more widely, is complicit in the impact of colonialism. A scientific ethnopornography, then, is not merely a procedure for the collection of certain materials about the "natives"; it is also a practice of representation through which to make a spectacle of them. The circulated report of what the anthropological gaze saw is an exertion of mastery through which the "native" is subordinated, and it is on and through such reports that the character and solidarity of "men like us" is constituted.

This chapter first places Roth within the context of colonialist practices of display and spectacle involving Australian "natives." I argue that anthropological work in Roth's time was connected both empirically and conceptually with more popular "entertainment" such as traveling shows and circuses. This connection was exploited for mutual advantage by scientific men and showmen such as P. T. Barnum. In this complex of practices, the nakedness of "savages" was essential as a sign of authenticity, such that sexual violation of Aborigines, for example, was a necessary aspect of scientific study. Secondly, I explore more informal or impromptu sexual "performances," stage-managed by anthropologists themselves, in order to collect materials in and for the scientific study of "wild" Australians. These "performances" were often requested to provide evidence around the practice of subincision, and of its significance, a topic of much anthropological fascination in Walter Roth's time. I conclude by reflecting on my own position in regard to the troubling questions that this research raises for ethnography now.

The "Greatest Show on Earth": Anthropology as Popular Pedagogy

In *Tristes Tropiques*, an account of his fieldwork, Claude Lévi-Strauss writes about European travelers who come face to face with what they believe to be wild or untouched territory. Lévi-Strauss cautions us that the seemingly wildest or most virgin nature is rather a "battlefield" on which are inscribed the efforts and achievements of men, even though vegetation may have regrown in the battle's aftermath, "re-emerging in a confusion which is all the more deceptive since it preserves, beneath a falsely innocent exterior, memories and patterns of past conflicts."[9] This section is concerned not with vegetation but with what was plotted on the battlefield of colonial Australia in the late nineteenth century, that is, with how "wild Australia" was created and authenticated.

The armed battles and conflicts on colonial Australian territory have been well analyzed by historians in the last thirty years or so, being the subject of considerable controversy. Striking examples of the clearance of territory through killing and massacre in Roth's northwestern Queensland are the efforts of Frederic Urquhart.[10] In March 1884, Urquhart left the Gregory River in Queensland, where he had been in charge of the Native Police, in order to restore law and order in Cloncurry, after white settlers had complained that Aborigines in the area placed (white) men and women in fear of their lives.[11] After James White Powell, a partner of the settler Alexander Kennedy, was attacked in the Calton Hills, Urquhart accompanied Kennedy on a mission of revenge. Urquhart celebrated his massacre of the Kalkadoon (Kalkatungu) by writing a poem titled "Powell's Revenge," the finale to which announced that the field was now clear.[12] Hudson Fysh pictured Urquhart on patrol in the aftermath of the massacre, seated at a campfire, "with nothing but naked savages and the wild and lonely bush around, reading the latest poetical work of a recent copy of the Spectator. This was the proof of the man, and it is so of every man; Urquhart chose to conquer environment and look ahead to progressive steps to come, not to sink to the level of inferior surroundings as so very many others did in the solitude of early pioneering life."[13]

This plaintive "solitude" of the Australian landscape was created by the very murderous clearances Urquhart initiated, creating a "wild and lonely bush around" that was haunted only by spectral figures of "naked savages." The landscape was enduringly marked as wild by the circulation of such representations through the publication of poetry, prose, and sketches. Those "savages" who survived the clearances could find a place in colonial representations as memories of what once was, and as mementos of conquest.

The life and efforts of Archibald Meston are illustrative of such a representational dynamic. A contemporary of Roth, like Urquhart, Meston was at various times a property manager, member of Parliament, newspaper editor, and the head of a government expedition to far north Queensland.[14] He was appointed the Southern Protector of Aborigines in 1898 (when Roth was the Northern Protector), and became Chief Protector on Roth's resignation from the position. A particular interest of Meston was the arrangement of "displays" of indigenous life, in the form of tableaux vivants of Aborigines titled "Wild Queensland" or "Wild Australia." These exhibitions were accompanied by a lecture and commentary from Meston.[15]

A typical event at the Brisbane Theatre Royal in 1892, for example, involved Meston lecturing on the tribes of Australia, "a subject he has made peculiarly his own," as a local newspaper reported.[16] The report of the event noted that for several evenings the theater "was literally packed with audiences who not only listened with pleasure to the remarks of the lecturer but also gained more knowledge of the customs of the native races than they could have done through reading the works of the many writers who have essayed the task of describing the ways and customs of a fast disappearing people."[17] An expanded version of Meston's lecture at the Brisbane Opera House around the same time was illustrated by the curtain rising on a performance of "a typical wild Australian scene, of which the kangaroo, the emu, gunyahs, and aboriginals formed a part," played out against a panorama of north Queensland mountain ranges (where Meston had done his "fieldwork"). All was accomplished with an apparently meticulous fidelity to savage life, in line with Meston's insistence that he had no use for domesticated or "tame" Aborigines. The newspaper report on the event noted,

> Several of the men [onstage] have lately been brought into contact with civilisation for the first time, and they enter into the corrobborees, combats, &c., with a zest which could not have been displayed had the troupe been composed of "tame" blacks such as those with whom the dwellers of Brisbane and the cities and townships of the colony are familiar. The highest point of realism is attained; and the audience witness on the stage scenes which have in the past only been looked on by explorers who have penetrated far into the interior in these later days, or by old settlers who in the early portion of the colony's history had the unpleasant privilege to look upon a tribal fight, a war corrobboree, or it may be some mysterious rite practised by the tribes.[18]

The troupe of theatrical warriors, in war paint, performed a war dance "accompanied with their weird and savage cries," after which they squatted in front of the gunyah and rubbed sticks together to make fire. This "entertainment" was followed by a Werrmugga (cockatoo) corroboree, performed by warriors with weapons, then by another "realistic combat with shields and nullas." The item earned calls for an encore from the audience, but the "artistes" appeared not to know the convention of encores. Meston then introduced to the audience three of the troupe: the chief of the Prince of Wales Island tribe, his wife, and a little boy, who performed a Rengwinna (iguana) corroboree and woomera spear throwing.[19] The second part of the program went along roughly similar lines, wrapped up by a series of tableaux vivants "illustrative of the massacre of a bushman [settler], the tracking of the [Aboriginal] murderer, and the doom which overtakes him and the members of his tribe, as also civilisation's results in the case of aborigines."[20]

The reenactment on stage of their own disappearance by its victims produced the look of "authenticity" to the audience, allowing the spectators to consume in safety that "unpleasant privilege" of looking upon wildness, and allowing them the pleasure of seeing the conquest of wildness by men like themselves. What enabled this privilege to be attained in the theater was the guidance of Meston as impresario, who produced and "voiced" the action on stage, and could subdue the "weird and savage cries" of the wild warriors in his interpretative commentary. Meston made a spectacle of the Aborigines at the same time as putting his "knowledge" of Aborigines and of Aboriginal life on display. Indeed, it is tempting to see the lecture not so much as interpretative of the tableaux but rather as itself the "main game," for which the "artistes" were so many illustrations.

Meston's lecture in turn acted as the guarantor of the authenticity of the warriors he had mustered. Meston was a keen detective of authenticity, and seems to have been very concerned to educate his audiences as to the difference between his "real" Aborigines and the rest. In his efforts, he was assisted by Mr. B. Purcell, whom Meston persuaded to join him in expanding the "Wild Australia" entertainment, with a view to taking the troupe on a long world tour to England, the United States, and other colonies. For this project, Purcell was allocated the task of amassing "specimens of a doomed race": "Mr. Purcell was dispatched to the uttermost parts of the colony to get together representatives of different tribes, and he has been very fortunate in collecting some of the finest specimens of a doomed race that could be secured for the purposes of illustrating an ethnological lecture." Meston explained to his theater audiences that some Aborigines had visited England in the past, but they had been semi-civilized blacks from urban areas, and therefore in his view had conveyed an erroneous impression of Aborigines and their life to English audiences. In contrast, Meston explained that the thirty-two "specimens" that "he had succeeded in collecting were such as were seen by the pioneers of Australia a hundred years ago."[21]

Meston's exhibitions of Aboriginal life that toured Australian towns echoed in miniature the great traveling spectaculars of P. T. Barnum and other showmen in the United States and Europe. In August 1882, for example, Barnum had written to hundreds of American consulates and agencies around the world to ask for their help in collecting human "specimens." Barnum noted that he had long harbored the idea of "forming a collection, in pairs or otherwise[,] of all the uncivilized races in existance [sic]," his aim being "to *exhibit* to the American public, not only *human beings of different races*, but also where practicable, those who possess extraordinary peculiarities such as giants, dwarfs, singular disfigurements of the person, dexterity in the use of weapons, dancing, singing, juggling, unusual feats of strength or agility etc."[22]

One of those who answered Barnum's call to contribute exhibits in an "Ethnological Congress of Savage Tribes" was Robert A. Cunningham, who periodically visited Australia as manager or agent for ventriloquists and circus companies. Cunningham "captured" a collection of "specimens" from north Queensland in 1883, and exhibited them in the role of boomerang-throwing cannibals in Barnum's "Greatest Show on Earth."[23] When the circus season of 1883 wound up, Cunningham's collection toured dime museums with other "specimens" from Barnum's "Ethnological Congress," before he took them as an ethnological exhibition for a grand tour of Europe.

The story of Cunningham's "specimens" is told in Roslyn Poignant's wrenching *Professional Savages: Captive Lives and Western Spectacle.* One of the most striking things in Poignant's account is how closely (professional) anthropologists worked with showmen like Barnum, in something like an entertainment-ethnological complex. A crucial interest of the showmen in such a relationship lay in having their exhibits scientifically "authenticated." In most of the European cities visited by Cunningham, for instance, the members of the troupe were taken to be examined by anthropologists, with a view to Cunningham's obtaining a testimonial or certificate of authenticity for them. For example, members of Cunningham's troupe were examined in Paris in November 1885 by the anthropologist Paul Topinard,

231

who provided Cunningham with a testimonial that the Aborigines in the troupe were authentic, while also noting that they were dying fast so that it was prudent to take the opportunity to see them straightaway.[24]

The gaining of such a scientific imprimatur of authentic wildness usually involved requiring the human "specimens" to take off their clothes in front of the anthropologist, who by the late nineteenth century was almost always accompanied by a photographer. In part, of course, the reason for this requirement is simple: wearing fancy European clothes would not support a claim of being "wild" or "untamed." The report to the Société d'anthropologie de Bruxelles of the Belgian anthropologists Emile Houzé and Victor Jacques on their "minute study" of Cunningham's boomerang throwers noted the resistance of the troupe to their request: "[W]e had asked them to remove as much as possible of their rags; but our savages, who had already admired themselves in their dress, in the photographs executed in London, didn't intend at all to allow themselves be photographed again without posing with all their finery."[25] Again, when Houzé and Jacques attempted to use their instruments and measuring devices on the "savage" bodies, the Aborigines only reluctantly allowed themselves to be touched, and consented to be photographed on condition that only their upper garments were removed.[26] Nevertheless, the anthropologists claimed that "one of them" had, undetected, briefly observed the external genitals of one woman.[27] Such examinations accrued to the benefit of the anthropologists as much as to the showmen. It should go without saying that the Aborigines subjected to these practices received no benefit from them, and the accounts of the examinations frequently register their resistance to such practices, as in this account by Houzé and Jacques. They were rarely "untouched."

A similar encounter of Cunningham's troupe came during their exhibition at Castan's Panoptikum in Berlin in 1884, when they were examined by Professor Rudolf Virchow, a physician by training, who, with Adolf Bastian, had in 1869 founded the Deutsche Gesellschaft für Anthropologie, Ethnologie und Urgeschichte (German Society for Anthropology, Ethnology, and Prehistory).[28] When Virchow asked the women to undress, they refused to do so, although they did take off their clothes for the photographer.[29] That some Europeans seem also to have voiced complaints against exotic exhibitions as prurient curiosity is suggested by Virchow's defense of the practice of exhibiting exotic specimens in presenting his "results." He noted, "The persistence of members of the public who make daily pilgrimage to see the Australians is a visible sign of appreciation. It proves that those who condemn exhibitions are not right when they state that these only serve curiosity. It surely will further the understanding of nature and history of the people and will become the duty of science to have more understanding and for deeper questions to be asked concerning the Australian Aborigines in order to inform a wider public."[30] That is, Virchow's response here was that the exhibition of human specimens was not simply vulgar entertainment but a popular pedagogy—a pedagogy that served to link scientific inquiry with the pleasure of the public in a relationship of mutual benefit.

From the side of the showmen also, Barnum's advertising for the "Ethnological Congress" stressed the seriousness of his own aspirations to scientific significance: "The public can form no adequate idea of the enormous costs and difficulties involved; or the dangers braved, the privations endured, the obstacles overcome, the disappointments sustained, and the disheartening losses incurred, in collecting this greatest and best of *Object Teaching Schools* from the desert-environed wilds of Africa, the remote and pathless jungles of Asia, the dreadful and unexplored solitudes of Australia, the interior of Brazil and Central America, and the mysterious islands of the southern seas."[31] Barnum conceived his exhibitions as not primarily a pleasure palace, in other words, but a teaching school. The pedagogy here consisted in part in stripping the natives, to make them more "real," the semblance of which would in turn render a higher scientific or intellectual pleasure to the pupils.

The exhibitions organized by Barnum and those by Cunningham, like Meston's "ethnological lectures," usually included a running commentary by a "non-savage." That commentary emphasized the authenticity of those in the exhibition, often with aspersions on the dubious wildness of competing groups of "savages." Stephen Orgel has emphasized in his discussion of the Elizabethan masque that the identity of characters on stage is rarely self-evident, and that, for instance, allegories must step forward in introducing themselves as, for example, "I am a Spring . . ."[32] But unlike Spring, the Aborigines of the traveling exhibitions could not announce themselves in words understood by their audience, could not speak of their lives, without compromising their wildness. Their status as "wild" permitted them to make "weird and savage cries." Their nakedness was a fundamental token of wildness, permitting both to the anthropologist and to the general lay "reader" a voyeuristic pleasure in the bodies of exotic others, a pleasure validated by the stamp of scientific curiosity. Aborigines were known as (authentic) Aborigines in and by their nakedness. Their nakedness spoke for them. At the same time as abusing their bodies, the brutality of colonial sexual violation maimed their voices, such that the story they told in their spectacle was in a very radical sense not "their own."

Walter Roth and Anthropological *Brüderschaft*

I have sketched here only an outline of the complex of scientific and popular practices of violation that produced at once the pleasure of knowledge and the pleasure of spectacle. The complex of practices included more informal performances than those of Barnum and Meston, however. In Queensland, and in other parts of Australia, white men had been staging impromptu educational soirées of their own throughout the nineteenth century. One of these stagings led to the resignation of Walter Roth as Protector of Aborigines in 1905.[33] In 1900 or 1901, Roth arranged for an Indigenous couple to have sex with each other, on the understanding that he would photograph their act (the photographs were not published). When questions about these photographs were first raised in the Queensland parliament in 1904, Roth responded in his defense that the photographs were identical to figure 433, a sketch in *Ethnological Studies among the North-West-Central Queensland Aborigines*.[34] Similar sketches, and in some cases photographs, can be found throughout ethnological and anthropological literature of the time.

Roth understood himself to be involved in scientific activity in taking the photographs at issue. He claimed to have commissioned the photographs to support his conjecture that the genital cutting (subincision or introcision) of Aboriginal men was intended as mimicry of the vulva, rather than for prophylactic purposes, as many of his contemporaries had hypothesized. In reply to a request for an explanation from his friend the Bishop of Carpentaria, Roth wrote, "The description and illustration of the posture assumed in the sexual act was of the highest anthropological interest in that it in large measure defended my thesis that the mutilation known as Sturt's terrible rite, or sub-incision (by Professor Stirling) or intro-cision (by myself) did *not* act as had hitherto been supposed as a preventive to procreation."[35] The purpose of Roth's photographs was to provide evidence that insemination by an introcized man was possible. Roth concluded to White, "The photograph was taken for purely scientific purposes only and is one of a series (defecation, micturition, tree climbing, sitting, standing) of natural postures which every anthropologist makes inquiry about, with a view to ascertaining the connections (if any) between the highest apes and the lowest types of man."[36]

Roth noted that when *Ethnological Studies* was published, he had received written and verbal communications doubting the physical possibility of such a "posture" of copulation as he insisted was used by Aborigines. In the meantime, Roth said, he had found the same posture everywhere: "I thereupon informed my scientific friends of the very interesting corollary that the sexual mutilation now met with [in certain parts of Australia] was probably traditionally practised throughout the entire Continent."[37] That is, for Roth, the incidence of the "posture" in certain areas was a sign that the subincision of men had originally been practiced there despite its contemporary absence. According to Roth, an opportunity for scientific vindication of his hypothesis came in 1900 or 1901, when an aged married couple on a rural station "agreed to posture for me," in exchange for money, tobacco and flour. Roth concluded of his conduct in this matter, "I have been guilty of no conduct unworthy of a gentleman and a man of honour."

The scandal around Roth's photographs of "the peculiar method of copulation" adopted by Aborigines was related to the very core of his scientific speculations as an anthropologist, designed to uphold his conjectures about introcision in the Boulia area—and in turn, about ritual and customs across the Australian continent. However, I am skeptical that a straightforward scientific curiosity about all facets of Aboriginal life can explain the significance of Roth's conduct. Roth's anthropological curiosity can be better analyzed if placed in the context of other informal practices of constructing Aboriginal subjects as sexual spectacle (and as related to the formal practices sketched above in this chapter).

The ubiquity of such practices of spectacle was remarked upon in the 1920s by the anthropologist Herbert Basedow,[38] who was, like Roth, one of the more sympathetic observers of Aboriginal life and mourners of its destruction. In *Knights of the Boomerang*, Basedow lamented that "no other will have a chance of seeing again what I have here described," given the "harvest of sorrow, disease and death" that brought the decay and demoralisation of Aboriginal life, mores and religion.[39] For Basedow, one disturbing part of this decay was the practice of showing Aborigines as spectacle, a practice in which anthropologists themselves were complicit: "It is an open secret that natives living near certain railways are bribed, and even forced, to show themselves at stations for the fulfilment of the promise set forth in tour-programmes that tourists will see wild blacks along the route. Modern scientific investigators, too, as method of study, send agents in advance to 'round up' as many of the nomadic subjects as possible at a convenient depôt for the purpose of facilitating the work of a dozen or more experts who overhaul them *en masse*."[40] Basedow exempted himself from such criticisms: he was a scientific investigator, as indicated, for example, by his declaration of authorship in his work: "by Herbert Basedow M.A., M.D., Ph.D., B.Sc." He held the office of Chief Medical Officer and Protector of Aborigines in the Northern Territory, and later Special Aborigines Commissioner, but he saw his role differently, as an "avowed chief, magician and tribal father."[41]

In spite of his scruples about the conduct of other anthropologists, Basedow was, like Roth, fascinated by the sexual and erotic life of Aborigines, in particular by circumcision and initiation ceremonies. In "Subincision and Kindred Rites of the Australian Aboriginal" (1927),[42] Basedow discussed the theory that subincision was adopted as a Malthusian measure, noting, like Roth, that its ineffectiveness could be demonstrated by observation of Aboriginal sexual practices: "Admitting this is an established fact, which can be verified any day among the tribes still living, it becomes a matter of scientific importance to know whether the aboriginal adopts a regular and peculiar method of conception." It was in the context of this question that Basedow noted the more informal practices of sexual voyeurism and exploitation among "men of low moral character" in colonial Australia:

> Observations upon this subject are scarce, and some of the earlier accounts are misleading. I do not mean to dispute the accuracy of early investigation, but it is a well-known fact that men of low moral character used to make a habit of giving quantities of rum, gin, and other spirituous liquors to the natives who would then, in a semi-intoxicated condition, be persuaded or forced to perform in a way which may have satisfied the lustful humour of the white villain, but was opposed entirely to the sense of decency and modesty of a primitive people. But an inspiration emanating from the mind of a drunken white man, under conditions such as these[,] could never be admitted scientifically as a custom of the colored man, even though the latter had to carry it into effect practically.[43]

I have puzzled over whether Basedow means here that white men were persuading or forcing Aboriginal women to have sex with them in certain positions. But I think the phrase "the colored man, even though the latter had to carry it into effect practically" leaves little doubt that what Basedow has in view here is not the prostitution of Aboriginal women by white men, although this was certainly also a widespread practice. Rather, he is referring to white men taking the position of voyeur of a staged spectacle of Aborigines having sexual intercourse with each other.

After reading this passage, I looked for evidence of this "well-known fact" about "men of low moral character" in memoirs of Australian bushmen and other sources. For example, the *wünderkammer* work *Woman: An Historical Gynaecological and Anthropological Compendium*, in a section titled "Position in Coitus" in the chapter "Woman in the Sexual Act," sets out the sexual positions adopted in different parts of Australia, and continues, "[Nicholas] Miklucho-Maclay collected more exact information, for the aborigines were not shy of undertaking copulation before onlookers in broad daylight if they were promised a glass of gin. They adopt one of the squatting positions depicted by Miklucho-Maclay."[44] The account then describes the position in more detail,[45] before noting a form of curiosity taken by white men in the Australian bush:

> A. Morton, a reliable young man, further reported as eye-witness, that, one evening, finding himself near a camp of aborigines, it occurred to him to ask a native who begged him for a glass of gin, to perform the sexual act. The native went off willingly to call a woman, who appeared at once. Without any sign of embarrassment, with only the thought of earning his glass of gin quickly, the man went near the woman, whereupon the couple assumed the above-mentioned position. . . . *In consequence of what had been told him by other experienced white people,* Morton's attention was drawn to the woman after the coitus. He noticed then that after the man had got up and reached for the glass of gin the woman also rose, stood with legs apart, and with a sinuous movement of the middle part of her body she threw, by a jerk towards the front, a bubble of whitish slimy substance (sperm?) on the ground, after which she went away. This way of getting rid of the sperm, which is indicated by a word in the native dialect, is, according to the statements of white settlers in North Australia, usually employed by native women after coitus, with the intentions of having no further consequences from being with a white man.[46]

The side-comment on Morton's familiarity with accounts of "other experienced white people" points to the wider occurrence of this and similar practices.

Basedow also makes reference to the "reliable young" informant "A. Morton" in another discussion of subincision in which he sets out a similarly detailed description of an act of sexual intercourse and its aftermath, quoting (in German) the passage from *Woman: An Historical Gynaecological and Anthropological Compendium* (1935), and adding a reference to the work of Anderson Stuart, a professor of physiology at the University of Sydney.[47] Piecing together these various references enables an identification of the informant as Alexander Morton, who visited Port Darwin in 1878 as a curator's assistant for the Australian Museum in Sydney, and later became, inter alia, an eminent museum director in Tasmania and general secretary of the Australasian Association of Science.[48] Morton's reports of "experienced white people" and his own "eye-witness" account seem to have initially circulated in a report by Nicholas Miklucho-Maclay.[49]

Basedow, however, expressed doubt as to the existence of such a "knack" by Aboriginal women as was noted in these reports to be a conclusion of their sexual intercourse with white men:

> I remember discussing this point some years ago with my friend the late F. J. Gillen, who declared that he had never heard of the custom, and was inclined to doubt that it existed, at any rate so far as the tribes he was familiar with were concerned. I have not recorded it from any part of Australia; and indeed, in view of what has already been said about the aboriginal's idea of conception, one would not expect to find so cute a knack in vogue among these simple people. Experienced prostitutes in other parts of the world are said to have developed this method to some degree of perfection.[50]

The reference to the "cute . . . knack" of "experienced prostitutes in other parts of the world" here is telling, suggesting that the anthropologist in pursuit of sexual knowledge was more than a scientific (disinterested) observer. And indeed, Basedow himself participated in most of the practices about which he had scruples.

In the opening chapter of *Knights of the Boomerang*, titled "Tales out of School," Basedow noted that most of the tribes with whom he had dealings, under normal and unrestrained conditions, moved about in a state of utter, and apparently unconscious, nudity: "At any time, the sexes may be seen to mix with absolute frankness and walk about *en déshabille* without attracting the slightest attention or giving the least offence to anyone among themselves. On the other hand, in accordance with a firmly established and generally accepted decorum among all classes, all persons, particularly females, endeavour to avoid exposing themselves unduly."[51] Basedow also documented the mayhem that ensued when he attempted to take explicit photographs, and recounted an incident in which "it so happened that for scientific purposes it was necessary for me to photograph a semi-civilised lubra of the Daly River district in an attitude that under other conditions would have been considered most unbecoming." Basedow wrote that although the woman "submitted to the ordeal, she later complained to the district magistrate that Basedow 'been take 'em wrong picture longa me,'" and asked for him to be officially reported.[52] Another incident involved an Aboriginal man, Tommy, of whom Basedow said, "He was dressed in European garments; but the pathological trouble I wished to show demanded that he should pose for my camera in the nude. He acquiesced with apparent complacence." Tommy then took out his anger at the incident by battering his wife.[53]

The clearest examples of Basedow's implication in practices such as that noted by Alexander Morton, however, is given where Basedow sets out the process by which a young Aboriginal man ("Romeo") courted a woman: "I watched the woman from the seclusion of my camp—in the interest of science playing the objectionable rôle of Peeping Tom. She walked towards the man as he reappeared to resume his seat on the ground. With a demonstrative movement she took her place beside him. The man remained stolidly indifferent; but the woman seemed excited. Although they were some distance away, I could, with the aid of my glasses, perceive that her fingers and toes were moving spasmodically; and I believe her eyes were closed."[54] Basedow's account of the fascination of white men with the bodies and sexual conduct of Aboriginal men and women conveys his own implication in the practices by which this fascination led them to force or otherwise coerce Aborigines to perform sexual acts for science-entertainment. My argument is that ethnologists and anthropologists such as Walter Roth and others were complicit in this form of sexual violation, even though they sought to distinguish the scientific "glasses" of the work of "men like us" from the prurient voyeurism of the "ordinary reading public."

Conclusion

In this chapter I have explored the provenance of the term "ethnopornography" in a complex of practices of collection and representation, in which distinctions between science and entertainment, and between scientific and ordinary people, were blurred. These practices are forms of sexual violation, and our recognition of this fact is sharpened by our knowledge of the resistance to them that was registered even in the writings that served to contain the gestures of refusal, as in the report of the encounter of Cunningham's troupe with the Belgian anthropologists Houzé and Jacques. For the white men involved, both such formal and informal encounters turned on the freedom of entitlement. The refusal of the "natives" to play the subordinate part, the part of unfreedom, in such staged spectacles, was contained as a form of resistance to the progress of scientific understanding, that is, as itself a violation of "the duty of science to have more understanding and for deeper questions to be asked." Even such resistance by the "savages" to "science," as is occasionally glimpsed in the writings of anthropologists themselves, forms part of the way in which the "wildness" of the subjects was constructed as a spectacle of entertainment and as an object teaching school by and for "men like us."

A final note. In writing this chapter, I have reflected on the question of what my own position could be in relation to the practices about which I have written. I have tried in some cases not to rehearse in my own account what the anthropologist saw and represented. For example, I have tried to avoid reciting the detail in which sexual acts are described (or depicted) by those labouring under the "duty of science." Although I can to an extent "disown" some practices as masculine and therefore not mine, I know only too well how white women were complicit in, and benefited from, practices of masculinity and of domination and violation on the colonial frontier. I know only too well how the disciplines of the humanities are built on their history, and on the "science" of our predecessors. There remains mourning, for lives violated and disappeared. It is not, however, enough.

Notes

1   W. E. Roth, *Ethnological Studies among the North-West-Central Queensland Aborigines* (Brisbane, Aus.: Edmund Gregory, 1897).

2   The *Australian Dictionary of Biography* (ADB) provides outlines of the life of the major figures in this chapter. For Roth, see Barrie Reynolds, "Roth, Walter Edmund (1861–1933)," ADB, http://adb.anu.edu.au/biography/roth-walter-edmund -8280. See also John Whitehall, "Dr WE Roth: Flawed Force of the Frontier," *Journal of Australian Studies* 26, no. 75 (2002): 59–69. A recent collection of studies on

Roth is Russell McDougall and Iain Davidson, eds., *The Roth Family, Anthropology, and Colonial Administration* (Walnut Creek, CA: Left Coast Press / Institute of Archaeology, University College London, 2008).

3 Roth, *Ethnological Studies*, 184.

4 Roth, *Ethnological Studies*, v–vi.

5 Roth, *Ethnological Studies*, 169.

6 Memo from Government Printing Office to Undersecretary of the Home Department, October 13, 1897, and reply by Sir Horace Tozer, October 16, 1897, Queensland State Archives (QSA) A/58550.

7 Available at Museum of Australian Democracy, "Anno Sexagesimo Primo: Victoriae Regiae, No. [17]," accessed April 7, 2019, http://www.foundingdocs.gov.au /resources/transcripts/qld5_doc_1897.pdf. See also Regina Ganter and Ros Kidd, "The Powers of Protectors: Conflicts Surrounding Queensland's 1897 Aboriginal Legislation," *Australian Historical Studies* 25 (1993): 536–54; and William Thorpe, "Archibald Meston and Aboriginal Legislation in Colonial Queensland," *Historical Studies* 21 (1984): 52–67.

8 Roth to Baldwin Spencer, letter dated January 19, 1898, quoted in John Mulvaney, "From Oxford to the Bush: WE Roth, WB Spencer and Australian Anthropology," in McDougall and Davidson, *Roth Family*, 113.

9 Claude Lévi-Strauss, *Tristes Tropiques*, trans. John Weightman and Doreen Weightman (1955; repr., London: Penguin Books, 1976), 117.

10 See W. Ross Johnston, "Urquhart, Frederic Charles (1858–1935)," *ADB*, http://adb .anu.edu.au/biography/urquhart-frederic-charles-8901; Hudson Fysh, "Kennedy, Alexander (1837–1936)," *ADB*, http://adb.anu.edu.au/biography/kennedy-alexander -3942; and J. Percival, "Fysh, Sir Wilmot Hudson (1895–1974)," *ADB*, http://adb.anu .edu.au/biography/fysh-sir-wilmot-hudson-6263. A more comprehensive picture of Urquhart is set out in Helen Pringle, "Reading the Spectator with Frederic Urquhart," unpublished paper.

11 W. H. Fysh, *Taming the North* (1933), 2nd ed. (Sydney: Angus & Robertson, 1950), 142.

12 Fysh, *Taming the North*, 147.

13 Fysh, *Taming the North*, 150–51.

14 See S. E. Stephens, "Meston, Archibald (1851–1924)," *ADB*, http://adb.anu.edu.au /biography/meston-archibald-4191. Other useful studies include Faith Walker, "The Reinvention of the 'Noble Savage': Archibald Meston and 'Wild Australia,'" *Bulletin (Olive Pink Society)* 9, no. 1–2 (1997): 130–38; Cheryl Taylor, "Constructing Aboriginality: Archibald Meston's Literary Journalism, 1870–1924," *Journal of the Association for the Study of Australian Literature* 2 (2003): 121–39; and Judith McKay and Paul Memmott, "Staged Savagery: Archibald Meston and His Indigenous Exhibits," *Aboriginal History* 40 (2016): 181–203.

15 A fuller picture of Meston's activities is provided in Helen Pringle, "An Illustrated Ethnological Lecture: Archibald Meston's 'Wild Australia,'" unpublished paper.

16 "The Opera House: Wild Australia," *The Queenslander*, December 10, 1892, 1149–1150.

17 "Opera House," 1149.

18 "Opera House," 1149.

19 "Opera House," 1150.

20 "Opera House," 1150.

21 "Opera House," 1149. Meston added that they were all Queenslanders, and hence would serve to advertise Queensland for settlement throughout "the civilised world," a point that was reported to be enthusiastically applauded by the audience.

22 P. T. Barnum, letter dated August 9, 1882, in Permanent Administrative Files, Smithsonian Institution Archives, reproduced in Roslyn Poignant, *Professional Savages: Captive Lives and Western Spectacle* (New Haven, CT: Yale University Press, 2004), 58.

23 See "Queensland Blacks for Barnum's Museum," *The Queenslander*, March 3, 1883, 348.

24 Poignant, *Professional Savages*, 164–67.

25 Emile Houzé and Victor Jacques, "Communication de MM. Houzé et Jacques sur les Australiens du Nord," *Bulletin de la Société d'Anthropologie de Bruxelles* 3 (1884): 53–155, quoted in Poignant, *Professional Savages*, 16.

26 Poignant, *Professional Savages*, 126–27.

27 Poignant, *Professional Savages*, 197.

28 Robert Proctor, "From *Anthropologie* to *Rassenkunde* in the German Anthropological Tradition," in *Bones, Bodies, Behavior: Essays on Biological Anthropology*, ed. George W. Stocking Jr., History of Anthropology vol. 5 (Madison: University of Wisconsin Press, 1988), 140–42.

29 Poignant, *Professional Savages*, 131–32.

30 Rudolf Virchow, "Australier von Queensland," *Zeitschrift für Ethnologie* 16 (1884), 417, quoted in Poignant, *Professional Savages*, 133.

31 Barnum's Advance Courier, 1884, cited in Poignant, *Professional Savages*, 66; emphasis mine.

32 Stephen Orgel, *The Jonsonian Masque* (New York: Columbia University Press, 1981).

33 Roth faced a litany of complaints, and there is no doubt that some of these complaints were well-founded, as, for example, his disposition of the artifacts he had collected in his official capacity; see "Revelations Regarding Roth—The Ethnological Specimens Sold to Sydney Museum—Complete Official List—Giving Dates and Localities," *Truth Sunday*, April 15, 1906, 9, http://trove.nla.gov.au/newspaper/article/198983693/. A fuller account of this incident and its background is given in Helen Pringle, "Walter Roth and Ethno-Pornography," in McDougall and Davidson, *Roth Family*.

34 On questions raised, see "Question to Home Secretary re 'Photographing of Gins,'" *Queensland Parliamentary Debates* (QPD) xc (1902), 904; see also question of William Hamilton, October 28, 1902, QPD, xc, 958. On the defense, see William Hamilton to Minister for Lands, June 13, 1904, QPD, xcII (1904), 578–89. This was

a book that, moreover, Roth had sent to the Prince of Wales. See also Vincent. Lesina, QPD, November 24, 1905, 1810.

35 Walter Roth to Bishop White, June 19, 1904, QSA A/58850, tabled in QPD, XCII, July 13, 1904, 585. Bishop White wrote to Roth on June 3, 1904, and he telegrammed that he was satisfied with Roth's explanation in a letter of July 8, 1904.

36 Roth to White, June 19, 1904.

37 Roth to White, June 19, 1904.

38 See Ian Harmstorf, "Basedow, Herbert (1881–1933)," ADB, http://adb.anu.edu.au/biography/basedow-herbert-5151; and, more broadly, Heidi Zogbaum, Changing Skin Colour in Australia: Herbert Basedow and the Black Caucasian (Melbourne: Australian Scholarly Publishing, 2010).

39 Herbert Basedow, Knights of the Boomerang: Episodes from a Life Spent among the Native Tribes of Australia (1935) (Victoria Park, Aus.: Hesperian Press, 2004), xiii, xi.

40 Basedow, Knights of the Boomerang, xi.

41 Basedow, Knights of the Boomerang, xii.

42 Herbert Basedow, "Subincision and Kindred Rites of the Australian Aboriginal," Journal of the Royal Anthropological Institute of Great Britain and Ireland 57 (January–June 1927): 123–56, reprinted as "The Strange Erotic Ritual of Australian Aboriginals," in Venus Oceanica: Anthropological Studies in the Sex Life of the South Sea Natives, ed. R. Burton, privately printed for subscribers (New York: Oceanica Research Press, 1935).

43 Basedow, "Subincision," 151.

44 See R. W. de M. Maclay, "Mikluho-Maklai, Nicholai Nicholaievich (1846–1888)," ADB, http://adb.anu.edu.au/biography/mikluho-maklai-nicholai-nicholaievich-4198; and Elsie May Webster, The Moon Man: A Biography of Nikolai Miklouho-Maclay (Berkeley: University of California Press, 1984). Note that the spelling of his surname differs depending on context.

45 Hermann Heinrich Ploss, Max Bartels, and Paul Bartels, Woman: An Historical Gynaecological and Anthropological Compendium, ed. Eric John Dingwall, 3 vols. (London: William Heinemann, 1935), 2:61–62. The reference is unclear, but it seems to be "Verh, Berl. Ges. F. Anthrop., etc., 1880, 12, 88": 3:499.

46 Ploss, Bartels, and Bartels, Woman, 2:63; emphasis mine.

47 Basedow, "Subincision," 154. The reference to Stuart is to T. P. Anderson Stuart, "The 'Mika' or 'Kulpi' Operation of the Australian Aboriginals," Journal and Proceedings of the Royal Society of New South Wales 30 (1896): 122.

48 Morton acted as a collector for the museum; the human remains he collected at that time were returned to the Larrakia community in 2002: see Vu Tuan Nguyen, Case Study: Larrakia 1996/2002, updated November 20, 2018, Australian Museum, http://australianmuseum.net.au/Case-Study-Larrakia-1996-2002. On Morton's life and career more generally, see Peter Mercer, "Morton, Alexander (1854–1907)," ADB, http://adb.anu.edu.au/biography/morton-alexander-7666.

49 Nicholas Miklucho-Maclay, report "Uber die Mika-Operation in Central-Australien,"
    "Sitzung vom 17. April 1880," *Verhandl. Berliner Gesellschaft für Anthropologie* 12
    (1880): 83–124.

50 Basedow, "Subincision," 154.

51 Basedow, *Knights of the Boomerang*, 1–2.

52 Basedow, *Knights of the Boomerang*, 2.

53 Basedow, *Knights of the Boomerang*, 2.

54 Basedow, *Knights of the Boomerang*, 7.

HELEN PRINGLE

Ethnopornography Coda

Although studies of ethnopornography are not new, several previous analytical approaches have tended to separate readings of colonial sexuality from the violence of colonialism more generally, emphasizing instead
the emergence of gender categories and modes of sexuality as forms of
symbolic and ideological violence. Certainly, the gender categories and
sexual modalities fostered in colonial contexts are still with us and, on-
tologically speaking, the postcolonial will never actually arise since it is a
temporal and not a historical construct. So, if there is no final escape from
the legacies of colonialism, only a reworking of colonial legacy—in itself
a highly contingent and variant set of circumstances when viewed cross-
culturally—then the roles of the sexual and the violent in cross-cultural
relationships are ever present and always connected with each other—a
concern about today no less than about yesterday.

Anne McClintock, in *Imperial Leather: Race, Gender, and Sexuality
in the Colonial Contest*, proposes that such legacies might be dealt with
through a distinction between textual and material violence, with the idea
that material violence was used to resolve the indecisiveness of colonial
text and representation.[1] However, violence, like, sex, is a way of knowing—a
social relationship, not the absence of interactional meaning. For this reason,
the focus here is on the synergy of sexuality and violence in the colonial

process, and on how that history becomes a legacy in the ethnological (or archival) gaze, as practiced both by professional anthropology (and history), and also by cultural commentators more widely. Such an epistemological regime is pornographic not because of the fact that other bodies are being represented but rather for the way in which such representations circulated and informed their own usage. However, the notion of "ethno-pornography" defies simple definition, as the term is the attempt to call attention to the multiple histories and positionalities present in the history of colonial relationships while at the same time suggesting a regularity to the modes and purpose of certain forms of representation and cultural practice that share an ethnological aesthetic and style.

As a result of historical conditions, the ethnological gaze is always potentially pornographic, but at the same time sexuality is not simply comprised of desire for others' bodies but also of their possession in other modes of interaction, such as violence. Likewise, visual and textual representations may be differently inflected with these modalities of sexuality and violence, and so it becomes possible to appreciate the layers of meaning and signification in such "ethnopornographic" representation as being capable of performing the cultural work of colonialism at multiple levels. Subject bodies are thus disciplined and controlled through an interlaced regime of violence and sexuality that is at one and the same time possessive, destructive, and transformative.

However, the enactment of colonialism brings with it consequences for the colonizer no less than the colonized. As José Esteban Muñoz points out in *Disidentifications: Queers of Color and the Performance of Politics*, it is the self-consciousness of the colonizer under the native gaze that drives the need for a mimetic representation of the native.[2] Native potential for both violence and sexuality thus threatens to destabilize the project of colonial control, the paradox being that the violent sexuality of the colonizer is no less in need of control, lest the political and economic potential of the colonial relationship be undermined by an excess of killing, rape, and miscegenation.

Following the writings of Ann Laura Stoler in *Race and the Education of Desire: Foucault's History of Sexuality and the Colonial Order of Things*, we note that stabilized structures of colonial power and hierarchy become the means through which this potential excess of native and colonial lust and violent desire is domesticated.[3] The failure of the indigenes to "live up" to this imagining is thus always met with a colonial response that is not just instrumentally violent in terms of economic and political repression but also sexually inflected and patterned by the categories of ethnological representation.

Is the anthropological project inherently pornographic? In one sense the answer is clearly "yes," especially if "pornography" is understood as the production and circulation of representations that invite sexual response. The cultural meaning of anthropology itself is in this way part of the epistemological heritage of colonialism. However, in a historical sense, such an epistemology of others is also the inevitable outcome, in all cultures, of the human potential to form relationships through violence and sex. So, the "ethnopornographic" need not be thought of as a unique aspect of Western sociocultural knowing, and decisions to "fuck or fight" are implicit in a wide array of non-Western theories of social interaction, as the anthropological literature from Amazonia to New Guinea amply illustrates.

As an idea, ethnopornography points to the analysis of the sexualities of others and how they might be engaged, understood, and entailed in our own processes of sexual understanding. The intellectual project this implies is therefore both historical and anthropological, self-reflective and perhaps ultimately redemptive of the possibility for forms of sexual engagement that do not endlessly reproduce the oppressive and repressive categories of colonial sexualities.

What, then, is this object we have termed "ethnopornography"? We see that ethnographic imaginations and practices, colonial appropriations, and even the postcolonial use of images in the anti-imperial project are related to pornography. The reader understands that such pornography has appropriated a sense of indigenous eroticism, a notion of native truth, to reflect upon European desires. We witness amateur and professional ethnographers alike using their perceptions of indigenous sexualities as a foil against Victorian repression. And we note particularly the figure of the sexually seductive "native" woman as a supposed signifier of truth; it is through her penetration that the European or Western man attempts to fulfill his desire for complete knowledge and control.

Here I wish to offer a few concluding observations related to the concepts of the native, the gaze, and the importance of the ethnopornographic relationship. For here we have thought seriously about ethnopornography, but we can imagine ethnographers (or historians of sexuality) saying, "Yes, we know about this relationship. So what do we do about it?" We would answer that recognition of the problem is key but not sufficient. Instead, we must work to disrupt ethnopornography by developing an alternative reading practice.

We must recognize that, in the work we are doing here, we face a series of problems. First, we must avoid the tendency to assume any transhistorical, transcultural unity in pornographic formulations. While it appears to us that, in a wide variety of times and places, colonizers, explorers, and ethnographers have sought to eroticize the populations with which they came into contact, each group did so in vitally different ways. Hence, my own work participates in ethnopornography when I discuss and analyze the kanaimà—dark shamans in the upper Amazon River basin in Guyana and Brazil—who violently mutilate the mouth and anus of their victims, and then suck the juices of putrefaction. As I have written, part of the ritual is as follows: "A stick is inserted through the ground directly into the cadaver, then the stick is extracted and the maba (honey-like) juices sucked off.... If the corpse is indeed sufficiently 'sweet,' it will be partially disinterred in order to recover bone material and, ideally, a section of the anal tract."[4] Such an ethnopornographic representation is significantly different from the ways in which colonial French officials portrayed, for example, African men and women.

Second, we must note that commodification is a key component of pornography. Modern pornographers (minimally) frame narratives in such a way as to sell an audience on the power of sex. In this, they attempt to directly show the "truth" of the sex act. Linda Williams argues that this truth is envisioned as experiencing the pleasure of the other: "Hard-core pornography is a speculation about pleasure that begins ... from a phallic perspective, journeys to the unseen world of the sexual other, and returns to tell the story."[5] This sounds so much like early ethnography—like the final chapter, "Ethno-pornography," of Walter Roth's *Ethnological Studies among the North-West-Central Queensland Aborigines* (1897)—that we cannot ignore the parallels. As we expand the framework for understanding pornography into other contexts, we must continually keep in mind the relationship between pornography and the direct portrayal of the sexual "truth" of the other for the express purpose of selling a commodity to somebody willing to purchase it.

Finally, we must consider the ways in which pornographers and ethnographers use "racialized sexuality" to maintain particular discourses of power that often are different from bourgeois sexual discourses. Here we must understand that studies of pornography have shown that racialized sexuality alternates between a massive attempt at silencing the discussion of race in the nonpornographic sexual realm and an erotic exoticism that foregrounds race in the pornographic sexual realm. We must acknowledge the knowledge practices involved in the ethnographic relationship. At the outset of the professionalization of ethnography in the nineteenth century, anthropologists configured the practice as a search for the truth of the Other; hence its object became the native informant. In this regime of knowledge, the ethnographer must always seek to get "under the skin" of the informant in order to get the necessary information to write the ethnography.

Of course, much recent work in anthropology has critiqued the concept of ethnographic truth, but the other model that they have proposed involves self-reflexivity, acknowledging the presence of the ethnographer in the ethnographic space. And they have not answered the key question: what is the goal of anthropology, ethnohistory, and ethnography, at least in their early disciplinary iterations, if not to seek out the truth of the Other? In our critique of ethnopornography, we have attempted to show that anthropologists and historians, much like the hard-core pornographers that Linda Williams describes in *Hard Core: Power, Pleasure, and the "Frenzy of the Visible,"* have used the body of the Other as a particular kind of sign and, in particular, how indigenous bodies are rendered as signifiers of "true" uninhibited sexual desire. For early anthropologists, ethnographers, and cultural commentators repeatedly envisioned them as unlocking the desires of their audience, repressed by centuries of civilization.

Some readers might rightly critique the decision to use images—either visual or textual—in *Ethnopornography*. Rey Chow, for one, in "Where Have All the Natives Gone?," asks how scholars can engage in such a project while not reinvesting in ethnopornography, and we answer that we cannot.[6] But still she asks vital questions of us: Can we struggle against such representations without reifying the position of the native woman as Other, without promoting the very symbolic violence to her person that here we seek to discuss? How can we rerepresent the imagery, yet at the same time disrupt its symbolic power? Chow reminds us that we cannot simply seek to get behind the image of the native, get to the reality beneath it, to the true native, as if such a subject can exist in our society. The preference for no images, however, runs the risk of producing an ignorance related to the production of ethnopornography. Thus, when the image is read about without being presented, the reader cannot see the ethnopornographic representation. Still, if the reader does see the representation, then a certain amount of symbolic violence is destined to occur. And, even with a careful reading of the materiality of ethnopornographic images, we always will partly fail in our attempts at resignification. While such a failed reading will produce violence, it also will create a greater understanding of the symbolic presence of ethnopornographic violence and its circulation throughout society.

To the extent that relations of power are implied by the knowledge project in its entirety—not just in an ethnographic sense but also, for example, in history, sociology, and psychology more widely—then it may be that neither abstinence from ethnopornographic imaging, nor trying to disrupt its reading, is sufficient. In other words, as ethnography has itself become a postmodernist answer to the collapse of enlightenment structures of knowledge by replacing such "knowledge" with "experience" and its literary or media expression (paper and print culture, photography, sound recordings, moving images, etc.), then this may also reveal a way out of this otherwise impossible dilemma. If we are desiring subjects, then the open acknowledgment of that and its incorporation into the practice of ethnography and ethnohistory does not end the potential and possibility for the production of ethnopornography within academic frameworks, but it does change the purpose of ethnographic engagement and writing.

It may not be possible to "save" ethnography as we know it, but we can reinvent it to serve other purposes than those of normative, modernist social science. Just as we have repositioned our relations with animals, distancing ourselves from ideas of other animals as merely "zoological objects" and attempting rather to find a route to see ourselves and other animal as potent subjectivities, so too "other humans" are no longer to be simply understood as culturally distorted versions of ourselves. Incorporating emerging ideas from cyberanthropology, we identify the possibility for a truly posthuman anthropology in which the ethnographic object becomes visible only through the overt and explicit engagement of our own subjectivity. Sexualized and violent engagements thus become explicit, and the ethics of such engagements visible.

NEIL L. WHITEHEAD

Notes

This coda has been compiled and edited by Zeb Tortorici and Pete Sigal. Before he passed away, Neil, in consultation with Pete, wrote an introduction to what would eventually become this volume. While the volume has changed far too much to include that introduction, we have incorporated many of Neil's ideas into the final introduction. We decided then to compile some remaining ideas from Neil as a sort of final word and provocation on ethnopornography.

1   Anne McClintock, *Imperial Leather: Race, Gender, and Sexuality in the Colonial Contest* (New York: Routledge, 1995).

2   José Esteban Muñoz, *Disidentifications: Queers of Color and the Performance of Politics* (Minneapolis: University of Minnesota Press, 1999).

3   Ann Laura Stoler, *Race and the Education of Desire: Foucault's History of Sexuality and the Colonial Order of Things* (Durham, NC: Duke University Press, 1995).

4   Neil L. Whitehead, *Dark Shamans: Kanaimà and the Poetics of Violent Death* (Durham, NC: Duke University Press, 2002), 15.

5   Linda Williams, *Hard Core: Power, Pleasure, and the "Frenzy of the Visible"* (Berkeley: University of California Press, 1999), 279.

6   Rey Chow, "Where Have All the Natives Gone?," in *Displacements: Cultural Identities in Question*, ed. Angelika Bammer (Bloomington: Indiana University Press, 1994), 125–51.

Contributors

JOSEPH ALLEN BOONE is the Gender Studies Endowed Professor of Gender and Media in the Department of English at the University of Southern California. The recipient of Guggenheim, ACLS, National Humanities Center, Stanford Humanities Center, Huntington Library, and other fellowships, he is the author of *Tradition Counter Tradition: Love and the Form of Fiction* (1987); *Libidinal Currents: Sexuality and the Shaping of Modernism* (1998); and *The Homoerotics of Orientalism* (2014).

PERNILLE IPSEN, associate professor in gender and women's studies and history at University of Wisconsin–Madison, specializes in gender, race, colonialism, and slavery in the early modern Atlantic world. Her first book, *Daughters of the Trade: Atlantic Slavers and Interracial Marriage on the Gold Coast* (2015) is a history of five generations of marriages between African and European slave traders on the Gold Coast and how these marriages and the children who followed contributed to the production of race as a category of difference in the Atlantic world.

SIDRA LAWRENCE is associate professor of ethnomusicology at Bowling Green State University. The focus of much of her research has been on women's musical practices in Africa—and, more recently, has been expanding toward explorations of gender and sexuality in Africa and the African diaspora as viewed through the field of sound studies. She is particularly interested in the ways in which sound and movement are productive of shared intimacy and erotic experience between women. Her first book, *this animal called culture: Performing Feminism and the Politics of Everyday Solidarities*, is an investigation of sonic performativity as one of the strategies with which the Dagara women of Ghana and Burkina Faso articulate an indigenous politics of feminist solidarity.

BEATRIX MCBRIDE is an independent scholar, consultant, and tarot reader in Chicago. She holds a master's in information from the University of Michigan and is involved in HIV activist and queer archival spaces and practices. Her current project, *Deep Faggotry*, brings together gay/trans culture, queer nostalgia, and the metaphysical in a multimedia collection of recordings, performances, and essays.

MIREILLE MILLER-YOUNG is associate professor of feminist studies at the University of California, Santa Barbara working at the intersection of black feminist theory and sexual archives. She the author of *A Taste for Brown Sugar: Black Women in Pornography* (2014), which was awarded the Sara A. Whaley Prize by the National Women's Studies Association, and the John Hope Franklin Prize by the American Studies Association. Miller-Young is also an editor of *The Feminist Porn Book: The Politics of Producing Pleasure* (2013) and of the anthology *Black Sexual Economies: Race and Sex in a Culture of Capital* (2019).

BRYAN PITTS is associate director of the Center for Latin American and Caribbean Studies at Indiana University Bloomington. In addition to his research on race, sexuality, and the nation in Brazil, he is completing a book manuscript on the shifting relationship of the Brazilian political class to the military and civil society during the country's 1964–85 military dictatorship. His work has appeared in journals such as the *Hispanic American Historical Review* and *Revista Brasileira de História*, and he writes regularly on contemporary Brazilian politics for media outlets in both the United States and Brazil.

HELEN PRINGLE is a senior lecturer at the School of Social Sciences, Faculty of Arts and Social Sciences, at the University of New South Wales in Australia. Her research interests are in human rights and justice (with a focus on questions of sex and gender), and in political theory (with a focus on the seventeenth and nineteenth centuries). She is working on a research project concerning the place of pornography within considerations of free speech, titled *Practising Pornography*. Parts of this project concern discrimination in the workplace, child pornography, and "ethnopornography" in Australia. A second ongoing project involves a revisioning of the regulation of religious speech in Western secular contexts through laws against blasphemy and blasphemous libel, and the antivilification provisions of discrimination laws.

PETE SIGAL is professor of the history of sexuality and Latin American history at Duke University. He is author of *The Flower and the Scorpion: Sexuality and Ritual in Early Nahua Culture* (2011), a study on the interaction of writing and sexual representation in sixteenth- and seventeenth-century indigenous Nahua societies of Mexico that won the Erminie Wheeler Voegelin Award from the American Society of Ethnohistory for the best book published in 2011. He is completing a study of colonialism and sexuality, "Sustaining Sexual Pleasure: A History of Colonial and Postcolonial Voyeurism," that takes four objects: the naked native in the colonial circum-Caribbean; Saartjie Baartman, the so-called the Hottentot Venus; black leather, black skin, and black men in Robert Mapplethorpe's photographs; and black and Latino men in hard core pornography in the United States to relate modern sexual pleasure to the colonial gaze. Sigal has moved from studying sexual desires in indigenous communities to examining the colonial cultural processes that create global concepts of modern sexuality, gender, masculinity, and femininity. Sigal also is author of *From Moon Goddesses to Virgins: The Colonization of Yucatecan Maya Sexual Desire* (2000), and editor of *Infamous Desire: Male Homosexuality in Colonial Latin America* (2003).

ZEB TORTORICI is associate professor of Spanish and Portuguese Languages and Literatures at New York University. He is the author of *Sins against Nature: Sex and Archives in Colonial New Spain* (2018), which was co-awarded the 2019 John Boswell Prize on lesbian, gay, bisexual, transgendered, transsexual, and/or queer history, and he is the editor of *Sexuality and the Unnatural in Colonial Latin America* (2016). He has coedited *Centering Animals in Latin American History* (2013) with Martha Few, two special issues of *Radical History Review* on the topic of "Queering Archives" (2014 and 2015) with Daniel Marshall and Kevin P. Murphy, and an issue of *TSQ: Transgender Studies*

Quarterly on the topic of "Trans*historicities" (2018) with Leah DeVun. He also recently co-edited the three-volume *Global Encyclopedia of Lesbian, Gay, Bisexual, Transgender, and Queer (LGBTQ) History* (2019). His current research project is on "archiving the obscene" in Latin America, from the eighteenth to the mid-twentieth century, for which he is receiving formal methodological training in the fields of information studies and archival science with the support of a Mellon New Directions Fellowship.

NEIL L. WHITEHEAD was professor and chair of Anthropology at the University of Wisconsin–Madison. His scholarship on dark shamanism, ritualized violence, and post-human anthropology have profoundly influenced the fields of anthropology and ethnography. Among his many publications are his monograph, *Dark Shamans: Kanaimà and the Poetics of Violent Death* (2001), and numerous edited or co-edited volumes including *Anthropologies of Guayana: Cultural Spaces in Northeastern Amazonia* (2016); *Virtual War and Magical Death: Technologies and Imaginaries for Terror and Killing* (2013); *Human No More: Digital Subjectivities, Unhuman Subjects, and the End of Anthropology* (2012); *Of Cannibals and Kings: Primal Anthropology in the Americas* (2011); *Hans Staden's True History: An Account of Cannibal Captivity in Brazil* (2008); *Terror and Violence: Imagination and the Unimaginable* (2006); *In Darkness and Secrecy: The Anthropology of Assault Sorcery and Witchcraft in Amazonia* (2004); and *Histories and Historicities in Amazonia* (2003). In the decade before his death, Neil branched out of his traditional areas of Latin American anthropology and ethnohistory to focus globally on the war on terror, goth music and culture, digital subjectivities, posthumanism, and sexuality. Neil has provided incisive critiques of the discipline of anthropology, provocatively examining the tensions and connections between ethnographic methods, modes of torture, and pornography.

Index

Note: *Italic* page numbers indicate illustrations.

native gaze, 246

nature, sins against, 28, 173–74, 179

Needham, Catherine, "Skin Flicks," 6–7

negaçã do Brasil, A (Zito de Araújo), 69–70

Négresse, meaning of term, 65n36

negros, in Brazilian racial system, 91n3

Nelson, Diane, 25

New and Accurate Description of the Coast of Guinea, A (Bosman), 211–14, 216–17, 220–21, 223n22

New Spain: indigenous languages in, 143, 144, 151; observation in colonialization of, 141. *See also* Franciscans

New Voyage to Guinea, A (Smith), 211, 214–17, 221, 223nn32–33

Nguyen, Tan Hoang, *A View from the Bottom*, 12

Nichols, Bill, "Skin Flicks," 6–7

Nizami, 201n14

Noble, Billy, 15

nobles, Maya, blood sacrifice by, 147–50, *148, 149*

Norberg, Kathryn, 215, 222n20

nudity: of Aborigines, 232, 233–34, 238–39; African views on, 58; in *G Magazine*, 73, 74, 76; in paintings, 218–20; in photos of slaves, 43–49; in postcards, 52–54; white European views on, 49, 58

Nussbaum, Felicity, 208

obscenity, in archives, 28

observation: in anthropology, 130–31; by Franciscans, 140–41. *See also* participant observation

odor, of Africans, 219, 220

one-drop rule, 91n3

Orgel, Stephen, 233

Orientalism (Said), 173

Orientalist stereotypes, 105–6, 108

Orkut, 78, 90n2

Osman Aga, Temesvarli, 202n20

Ottoman Empire: expansion of, 200n10; Greece in, 170

Ottoman male homoeroticism, 21, 169–98; in *Account of the Present State of the Ottoman Empire* (Hill), 190–93; in *The Book That Repels Sorrows* (Gazali), 188; in coffeehouses, 181–82, *183*, 184–86, 202n26;

European projections of, 171–72; in *Heft han* ('Atayi), 173, 175–81; in *Histoire generalle du Serrail* (Baudier), 188–90; participant observers of, 193–98; at sohbets, 177, 191–93, 201n17; in *Tables of Delicacies* (Âli), 182–84, 186, 187–88, 190; in *The Totall Discourse* (Lithgow), 186–87; in *Travels* (Southgate), 197–98; in *Travels in Assyria* (Buckingham), 193–97; tropes of excess describing, 186–93; in *The True Narrative of a Wonderful Accident*, 173–75; in *A Voyage into the Levant* (Blount), 197; voyeurism regarding, 180–81, 186–91; in wine taverns, 182–84, *185*

Paasonen, Susanna, 105

pain: in Franciscan self-flagellation, 141–43; in Maya penis-piercing rite, 140, 145

paintings, nudity in, 218–20

Paper (magazine), 17

pardos, 91n3, 94n40

Parker, Richard, 70

Parreñas Shimizu, Celine, 10; *Hypersexuality of Race*, 22–23

participant observation: by academics, 27, 30; by European travelers, 193–98

Patai, Raphael, *The Arab Mind*, 18

patlache, 153, 155, *156*

pecado nefando, 151–53

Peçevi, İbrāhīm, *Tarih-i Peçevi*, 182

penis: Aborigine, subincision of, 234–38; black, in photos and stories of *G Magazine*, 77–80; as focus of gay pornography, 77; Maya, piercing of, 139–40, 144–51; nomenclature of size of, 80

performative engagement, 27, 29

Perlongher, Nestor, 70

personal ads, in *G Magazine*, 82

perversion, sexual, Franciscans on, 140

phallic images: in Maya iconography, 147–48, 166n51; in Nahua iconography, 159, 168n79

Philip (king of Spain), 141

photography: of Aborigines, 232, 234–35, 239; of African women (*See* African women); of Afro-Brazilians (*See* G Magazine); early history of, 42–43; expansion of, 51–52; of female slaves, 12–13, 43–49, *46, 47*; of

photography (continued)
Guantanamo Bay prisoners, 104; of racial types, 44, 54
Pinho, Osmundo, 70
Pitts, Bryan: chapter by, 67–90; comments on, 14
Playboy (magazine), in Brazil, 73, 81–82
pleasure: black, in archives, 10; female, invisibility of, 101–2; in Franciscan self-flagellation, 143, 146; in Maya penis-piercing rite, 140, 146; through violence, Franciscans on, 142
Poignant, Roslyn, *Professional Savages*, 231–32
politics: in early modern pornography, 215, 221; in porn studies, 113–14; racial, in *G Magazine*, 68–69, 81–90
polygamy: in Ottoman Empire, 181; in West Africa, 213, 215–16
polygenesis, theory of, 44, 49
Porn Archives, 114
pornography: anthropology as type of, 247; commodification in, 248; definitions of, 209, 247; differences between ethnography and, 1–2; empire as type of, 43; vs. the erotic, 125–26; ethnography as type of, 2, 6–7; etymology of term, 6, 211; genealogy of, 6; maximum visibility principle of, 98, 101; political and social criticism in, 215, 221; prostitution as subject of, 211, 222n20; Rule 34 of, 97; as sexual abuse, 207. *See also specific forms*
pornotopia, 14
porno-tropics, 207, 209, 211–17
porn studies: absence in, 114; invisibility in, 99, 101–2; multiculturalism in, 116n38; politics in, 113–14; the visible as focus of, 9, 98–99, 101–2; Williams's influence on, 101–2, 113
postcards: censorship of, 52, 65n25; messages written on, 54–55; photos of African women on, 51–56, 55, 56; photos of white women on, 54–55; rise in use of, 52, 65n25
postcolonialism, 245
posters, film, Latinas in, 11, *11*
Poulson-Bryant, Scott, 80
Povinelli, Elizabeth, *Empire of Love*, 25

Powell, James White, 228
power relations: in field research, 123–24; in interracial heterosexual porn, 9, 206–7, 221
Pratt, Mary Louise, 44, 62
pretos, 91n3
Primeros memoriales (Sahagún), 152, *152*, 157
Pringle, Helen: chapter by, 225–40; comments on, 7, 21, 187
Professional Savages (Poignant), 231–32
projection: by European travel writers, 171–72; by Franciscans, 141, 162–63
prostitutes: libertine, 215; Nahua, in images of *Historia general*, 155–57, *156*; as subject of pornography, 211, 222n20; West African, European travel writing on, 211–14, 216
Puar, Jasbir, 105, 108, 109, 111
Pugini, Klifit, 69
Purcell, B., 230

queens, Maya, blood sacrifice by, 147–50, *148*, *149*
Queensland (Australia). *See* Aborigines; *Ethnological Studies among the North-West-Central Queensland Aborigines* (Roth)
Queensland Government Printer, 226
queering: of Maya men, by Landa, 146; meaning and use of term, 165n41
queerness: and disorientation, 116n6; and terrorism, 109–10
Queerty (blog), 98
quilombos, 76, 94n27

Rabinowitz, Paula, 24
race(s): ethnography and ethnology as study of, 6; and fantasy in porn, 105–7; polygenesis theory of evolution of, 44; review of literature on, 9–12; and sexuality, in field research, 16, 122–33; and social class, in Brazil, 70–71, 92n8; summary of chapters on, 12–16. *See also specific groups*
Race and the Education of Desire (Stoler), 246
racial democracy, in Brazil, 68, 71, 81, 83–84
racial hierarchies, in interracial heterosexual porn, 9, 206–7, 221

www.ingramcontent.com/pod-product-compliance
Lightning Source LLC
Chambersburg PA
CBHW020843270326
41928CB00006B/527